Further credits and acknowledgments appear on pages 398–400, which constitute an extension of this copyright page.

Copyright © 2014 by Scholastic Inc. All rights reserved.

Published by Scholastic Inc.   Printed in the U.S.A.

ISBN-13: 978-0-545-62353-7

ISBN-10: 0-545-62353-7

(meets NASTA specifications)

1 2 3 4 5 6 7 8 9 10   123   22 21 20 19 18 17 16 15 14 13

COMMON CORE
CODE X™

STUDENT EDITION
[COURSE III]

W9-CMV-067

[Welcome!]

Dear Reader,

Do you ever ask yourself big questions like, "What inspires the will to survive in an extreme environment?" or "How does art influence everyday life?" These are some of the questions you will explore together as you read Code X.

The first codex was created almost 2,000 years ago, when ancient Romans stacked sheets of paper on top of each other and bound them together to form the first bound book. The codex soon replaced long, bulky scrolls, revolutionizing the way that people wrote and read.

Just as the ancient Romans built up sheets of paper to form the codex, we have created our Code X to allow you to build on what you know. The more you learn, the deeper you can dig into the texts you read. The Common Core Code X gives you a whole new way to access texts. You'll ask questions to analyze and understand different kinds of texts from *Wired* magazine and *The New Yorker*. You will write about the qualities of a good team and create a work of historical fiction.

There's a lot to learn and investigate in Code X, so it's time to get started. Let us know what you think! Email us at CodeX@scholastic.com.

Sincerely,

The Editors

The Editors

UNIT 6

CHILDREN OF WAR

WRITING PERFORMANCE TASK

Analyze in detail how Ung's and Boyd's early experiences impacted their adult lives.

CONTENT AREAS

TEXT 1   TEXT 2

TEXT 3

UNIT 7

DO THE RIGHT THING

WRITING PERFORMANCE TASK

Many events of the Little Rock Nine tested the strength of people to be brave, heal, and forgive. Write a narrative to describe one such event.

CONTENT AREAS

TEXT 1   TEXT 2

TEXT 3   TEXT 4

NOVEL STUDIES

Throughout the course of the year you will read two novels. You will read some sections with your teacher and peers and some sections on your own.

- In **Make Lemonade**, Virginia Euwer Wolff describes the unlikely friendship between college-bound, fourteen-year-old LaVaughn and Jolly, a teenage mother of two.

- In **Endangered**, Eliot Schrefer tells the story of fourteen-year-old Sophie, who must save a group of bonobos—and herself—from a violent rebellion in the Congo.

Make Lemonade
by Virginia Euwer Wolff

Endangered
by Eliot Schrefer

CONTENT AREA ICON KEY

As you read the texts, you will learn about science, economics, history and the arts. The more you read the more you will learn about the world around you.

 US History

 Science

 Individual and Society

 World History and Geography

 Economics

 Math and Statistics

 Fine Art

 Earth and Weather

 Civics and Government

 Technology

 Environment

 Literature

COLLEGE 101

What does it take to achieve success in today's world of higher education?

WRITING PERFORMANCE TASK

Analyze which college applicant (Mendoza, Gregory, or Gallagher) would be the best candidate to take open online courses. Discuss what traits of this applicant make him or her well-suited for the online environment Pappano describes in her article.

Unit Introduction

In the essays and news article featured in this Unit, examine how teens distinguish themselves to get into college, and question whether such steps will be needed as higher education evolves to meet the future.

In "Essays That Make a Difference," two teens highlight their individual qualities in college-admission essays, while a third teen uses his essay to mock the process.

In the second reading, Laura Pappano spells out the complex future of higher education in "The Year of the MOOC."

Academic Vocabulary

"Essays That Make a Difference"

Rate your understanding of each Target Word. Then read its meaning and write a sample sentence.

Word	Meaning	Example
admission (n.) p. 11 ① ② ③ ④	the right or permission to enter	
unique (adj.) p. 11 ① ② ③ ④	one of a kind; unlike any other	
empathize (v.) p. 12 ① ② ③ ④	to understand and share someone else's feelings; to give understanding	
product (n.) p. 12 ① ② ③ ④	a person whose identity and qualities are the result of certain influences and experiences	
attribute (n.) p. 14 ① ② ③ ④	trait, quality, or characteristic	
dynamic (adj.) p. 16 ① ② ③ ④	exciting	

Rating Scale | ① I don't know the word. | ② I've seen it or heard it.
| ③ I know its meaning. | ④ I know it and use it.

Word Study

Context Clues

Context Clues are words in a text that help you figure out the meaning of an unfamiliar word.

Find the context clues to determine the meaning of the bold words in the sentences below.

1. I didn't just wake up one morning and think, "I'm proud to be Hispanic," but as I have matured, I have learned not to be ashamed of my **ethnicity**. Instead of hiding who I really am, I have embraced my Mexican heritage . . ."

2. I refuse to give up before I attain this dream; I have the **persistence** of the little glob of peanut butter that sticks to the roof of your mouth. No matter how many times you smack your mouth, I will not go away.

Essays That Make a Difference

¶1 Writing an **admissions** essay for college can be a scary process. The goal of this kind of essay is to show a college admissions committee that you're an individual—that you're more than just grades, test scores, sports, and activities.

¶2 What does a successful college essay really look like? Two of the essays that follow are real examples of exactly what a great college admissions essay should be. The writers present themselves in a positive way and find something **unique** about themselves or their lives to write about. The third essay is a **parody** of an admissions essay that portrays its author in a **superhuman** way.

I absolutely love being different

I refuse to give up

The laws of physics do not apply to me

Words to Know

parody: (n.) a humorous piece of writing that imitates and makes fun of a serious piece of writing.

superhuman: (adj.) having greater powers than ordinary humans

Close Reading

Text Structure

1. What rhetorical question does the author ask in **paragraph 2**? What does this question suggest about the reading?

Rhetorical Question

A **rhetorical question** is one that the author asks to emphasize a point but does not expect the reader to answer.

Key Ideas and Details

2. In **paragraph 2**, the author describes "successful" college essays. What would be an example of an unsuccessful college essay?

Close Reading

Key Ideas and Details

3. In **paragraph 1**, why does Mendoza state that she did not "look or act like everyone else" in her community? Provide details to support your answer.

Academic Vocabulary

4. In **paragraph 2**, Mendoza writes that her mother couldn't *empathize* with her. What kind of person might have been able to empathize with Mendoza?

Key Ideas and Details

5. In **paragraph 3**, why would Mendoza's other family members not have "any trouble fitting in"?

I Couldn't Imagine Wanting to Dye My Hair Blond
by Christina Mendoza

¶1 Growing up in a small, conservative community, it's easy to be shoved into your own category if you don't look or act like everyone else. My hair and eyes, instead of being blond and blue like all of my Czech classmates', were chocolate and espresso. My last name had a "z" in it, and my grandmother called me "mija." By the time I was in grade school, the teasing began, and I was hurt and confused. Didn't all grandmothers call their grandchildren "mija"? Why did everyone except me have blue eyes?

¶2 After an afternoon of teasing and tormenting from my classmates, I asked these questions to my mother, between sobs. By this time, she had become extremely good at giving me the "you're unique and beautiful" speech, but it was hard for her to truly **empathize** with me because neither she nor my father knew how I felt. She was a Caucasian who grew up in California; he was a Mexican American who grew up as the majority in San Antonio. I was the **product** of the two — the "half-breed" daughter who was raised in the small town of Seymour, population 2,800.

¶3 My other family members didn't seem to have any trouble fitting in. My father's ethnicity is well respected. He is the only doctor within a fifty-mile radius who can speak Spanish. My sister was the beauty queen of our town — her sleek, glossy hair and olive complexion were the envy of every girl. My little brother received the recessive genes (fair skin, blue eyes), so he looks like everyone else in Seymour. I felt I was stuck somewhere in the middle of my siblings, stuck in the middle of two cultures, and not accepted by either.

Words to Know

"**mija**": *(n.)* Spanish slang for "my daughter" or "my girl"

"**half-breed**": *(n.)* an offensive term for someone whose parents are of different races

recessive: *(adj.)* relating only to genes that are passed to a child by both parents

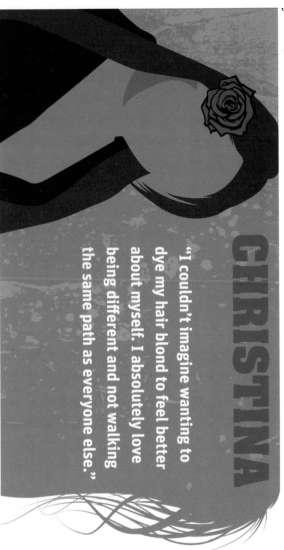

¶4 Time does have a way of healing things. I didn't just wake up one morning and think, "I'm proud to be Hispanic," but as I have matured, I have learned not to be ashamed of my ethnicity. Instead of hiding who I really am, I have embraced my Mexican heritage and have become proud of it. Finding out about the many opportunities that are available to students of Hispanic descent has motivated me even more to delve deeper into my culture.

¶5 Looking back, I couldn't imagine wanting to dye my hair blond to feel better about myself. The blond girls are unique in their own way, but diversity makes the world go round. I absolutely love being different and not walking the same path as everyone else. The last racist comment I received was after I was named a National Hispanic Scholar. My assailant said in a mocking tone, "I wish I could be a smart Mexican." Feeling sorry for his cultural ignorance, I smiled and replied, "Yeah, I bet you do."

CHRISTINA

"I couldn't imagine wanting to dye my hair blond to feel better about myself. I absolutely love being different and not walking the same path as everyone else."

Words to Know

<u>assailant:</u> (n.) attacker

<u>diversity:</u> (n.) variety; the state of including many kinds of people or things

<u>descent:</u> (n.) family origins

Close Reading

Text Structure

6. How does Mendoza's attitude change in **paragraph 4**? What sentence signals this shift in Mendoza's attitude?

Words and Phrases in Context

7. What is the meaning of embraced in **paragraph 4**? Find context clues that help you determine its meaning.

Writing

8. What does Mendoza mean when she states that she loves "not walking the same path as everyone else" in **paragraph 5**? Which words and phrases help you infer the meaning of her statement?

When Mendoza states that she loves "not walking the same path as everyone else," she means ___.

Some words and phrases that help me infer the meaning of this statement are ___.

Close Reading

Words and Phrases in Context

9. In **Line 7**, what is Gregory trying to say with the following metaphor: "the world is very much like one large PB&J, filled with many different ingredients"? What is he saying about his role in **Lines 9–12**?

Metaphor

A **metaphor** is a figure of speech that compares two unlike things by stating that one *is* (or is *like*) the other.

Text Structure

10. Gregory uses the word "however" to connect two different ideas in **Lines 14–15**. What are these ideas?

Writing

11. In **Lines 22–23**, Gregory states that his most important attribute is his "willingness to sacrifice to help others." What are some of his other attributes?

In addition to his willingness to help others, Gregory's attributes include

---

Chunky Peanut Butter
by James Gregory

1   To really understand who I am, remember your childhood. Remember the pleasure that eating a great big peanut butter and jelly sandwich delivered? How it seemed to just slide down your throat and ease into your stomach? That sandwich is the result of the perfect combination of ingredients, all working together to create a satisfying experience. If any one ingredient were

5   missing, the whole sandwich would fall apart. In fact, I would argue that the world is very much like one large PB&J, filled with many different ingredients. People can be <u>classified</u> according to their personality and similarity to these ingredients. I am like the chunky peanut butter. Although I may not be as showy as the jelly or as visible as the bread, I am the heart of the sandwich. I

10   am essential to the sandwich's success. I work behind the scenes, holding it all together, keeping all the ingredients organized and focused on their task. I lead through example, but I am flexible. I am able to work with any kind of jelly. I am slightly shy, so I do not need to be at the center of attention; I am content in leading without recognition. However, you always know I am there. You

15   taste all my chunks, all the little <u>quirks</u> that set me apart from the rest. Whether it is my dry sense of humor, my volunteer work at a summer day camp for kids, or my <u>fervent</u> school spirit, each unique piece guarantees that your experience will not be mundane or bland. With every bite you take, you taste more of me: my excellent grades, my size 15 feet, and my dedication to Student Council. I

20   am more fun than creamy peanut butter; you never know what to expect, but you know that it is going to be good. However, my most important **attribute** is

---

Words to Know

<u>classified</u>: *(adj.)* put into groups with other similar people or things

<u>quirks</u>: *(n.)* variety; the state of including many kinds of people or things

<u>fervent</u> *(adj.)* believing or feeling something strongly or sincerely

my willingness to sacrifice to help others. I have unselfishly stepped aside on
the basketball court to let the team as a whole shine, and I enthusiastically

25 devote time to service projects through Junior Civitans that help the
community. This desire to help is ingrained in my personality, and drives my
plan to become a physician and continue my service to others. I refuse to give
up before I attain this dream; I have the persistence of the little glob of peanut
butter that sticks to the roof of your mouth. No matter how many times you

30 smack your mouth, I will not go away. This drive has enabled me to achieve
academic success, success that I will continue into my higher education, and
into my life. I am fun, I am good for you, and I am more than the sum of my
pieces. I am the chunky peanut butter.

JAMES

"I have the persistence
of the little glob of
peanut butter that
sticks to the roof of
your mouth. This drive
has enabled me to
achieve academic
success."

Close Reading

Words and Phrases in Context

12. What does *drives* mean in **Line 26**?
How is it different from the meaning
of the word *drive* in **Line 30**?

Writing

13. What is Gregory's goal? What
qualities and experiences described
in **Lines 25–27** will help him achieve
this goal?

Gregory's goal is _____.

Some qualities and experiences that
might help Gregory achieve his goal

are _____.

Close Reading

Academic Vocabulary

14. In **paragraph 1**, Gallagher states that he is "a dynamic figure." What details does he give to support his claim? How do these details create humor?

Key Ideas and Details

15. On page 11, you read that this essay is a parody, or "a humorous piece of writing that imitates and makes fun of a serious piece of writing." Cite one example from **paragraph 3** that demonstrates this. Explain your answer.

Text Structure

16. In **paragraph 4**, Gallagher uses the word *yet* to connect two different ideas. What are these ideas?

Words and Phrases in Context

17. In **paragraph 5**, Gallagher states that he "read *Paradise Lost*, *Moby Dick*, and *David Copperfield* in one day." What can you infer from Gallagher's essay about the lengths of these books?

Essay 3A

by Hugh Gallagher

¶1 I am a **dynamic** figure, often seen scaling walls and crushing ice. I have been known to remodel train stations on my lunch breaks, making them more efficient in the area of <u>heat retention</u>. I write award-winning operas. I manage time efficiently. Occasionally, I tread water for three days in a row.

¶2 I woo women with my <u>sensuous</u> and godlike trombone playing. I can pilot bicycles up severe inclines with unflagging speed. And I cook Thirty-Minute Brownies in twenty minutes. I am an expert in stucco, a veteran in love, and an outlaw in Peru.

¶3 Using only a hoe and a large glass of water, I once single-handedly defended a small village in the Amazon Basin from a horde of ferocious army ants. I play bluegrass cello. I was scouted by the Mets. I am the subject of numerous documentaries. When I'm bored, I build large suspension bridges in my yard. I enjoy urban hang gliding. On Wednesdays, after school, I repair electrical appliances free of charge.

¶4 I am an abstract artist, a concrete analyst, and a <u>ruthless</u> bookie. Critics worldwide swoon over my original line of corduroy eveningwear. I don't perspire. I am a private citizen, yet I receive fan mail. I have been caller number nine and have won the weekend passes. I bat 400. My <u>deft</u> floral arrangements have earned me fame in international <u>botany</u> circles. Children trust me.

Words to Know

<u>**heat retention:**</u> *(n.)* the ability to trap heat

<u>**sensuous:**</u> *(adj.)* pleasing to the senses

<u>**ruthless:**</u> *(adj.)* having or showing no pity or compassion for others

<u>**deft:**</u> *(adj.)* skillful

<u>**botany:**</u> *(n.)* the study of plants

¶5 I can hurl tennis rackets at small moving objects with deadly accuracy. I once read *Paradise Lost*, *Moby Dick*, and *David Copperfield* in one day and still had time to refurbish an entire dining room that evening. I know the exact location of every food item in the supermarket. I have performed several <u>covert</u> operations for the CIA. I sleep once a week; when I do sleep, I sleep in a chair. While on vacation in Canada, I successfully negotiated with a group of terrorists who had seized a small bakery. The laws of physics do not apply to me.

¶6 I balance, I weave, I dodge, I frolic, and my bills are all paid. On weekends, to let off steam, I participate in full-contact origami. Years ago I discovered the meaning of life but forgot to write it down. I have made extraordinary four-course meals using only a mouli [food grater] and a toaster oven. I breed prizewinning clams. I have won bullfights in San Juan, cliff-diving competitions in Sri Lanka, and spelling bees at the Kremlin. I have played Hamlet. I have performed open-heart surgery. And I have spoken with Elvis.

¶7 But I have not yet gone to college.

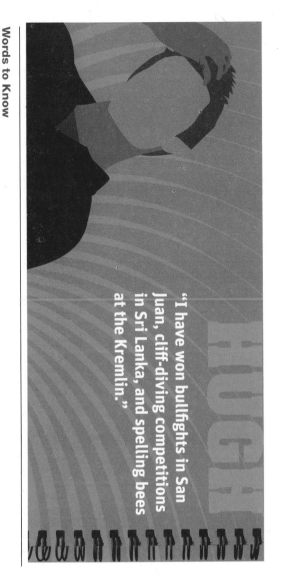

HUGH

"I have won bullfights in San Juan, cliff-diving competitions in Sri Lanka, and spelling bees at the Kremlin."

Words to Know

<u>covert</u>: *(adj.)* secret or hidden

Close Reading

Key Ideas and Details

18. What does the sentence in **paragraph 7** suggest about Gallagher's opinion of college? Explain.

Writing

19. How does Gallagher's essay differ from Mendoza's essay? What can you infer about Gallagher's personality from his essay? Explain your answer.

Gallagher's essay is ____ (descriptive detail) in contrast to Mendoza's essay, which is ____ (descriptive detail). Gallagher's essay suggests that he is ____ (adjective).

Identify Evidence | Analyze Individuals and Experiences

Reread "Essays That Make a Difference", highlighting the examples the writers use to describe their individual traits and experiences. What do these traits and experiences reveal about the writers?

- As you read, use the Evidence column to record examples from the text that describe each writer's traits and experiences.

- In the Explanation column, analyze how the evidence introduces, illustrates, or elaborates upon the individual or his/her experiences.

Evidence	Source	Page	Explanation
1. "Growing up in a small, conservative community, it's easy to be shoved into your own category if you don't look or act like everyone else . . . By the time I was in grade school, the teasing began."	Mendoza	12	
2. "It was hard for her to truly empathize with me because neither she nor my father knew how I felt. She was a Caucasian who grew up in California; he was a Mexican American who grew up as the majority in San Antonio."	Mendoza	12	
3. "The blond girls are unique in their own way, but diversity makes the world go round. I absolutely love being different and not walking the same path as everyone else."	Mendoza	13	
4. "I am like the chunky peanut butter. Although I may not be as showy as the jelly or as visible as the bread, I am the heart of the sandwich . . . I work behind the scenes, holding it all together."	Gregory	14	

Evidence	Source	Page	Explanation
5. "Whether it is my dry sense of humor, my volunteer work at a summer day camp for kids, or my fervent school spirit, each unique piece guarantees that your experience will not be mundane or bland."	Gregory	14	
6. "However, my most important attribute is my willingness to sacrifice to help others. I have unselfishly stepped aside on the basketball court to let the team as a whole shine, and I enthusiastically devote time to service projects through Junior Civitans that help the community."	Gregory	14–15	
7. "I am a dynamic figure, often seen scaling walls and crushing ice. I have been known to remodel train stations on my lunch breaks, making them more efficient in the area of heat retention."	Gallagher	16	

Key Ideas and Details

Determining the Central Idea

1. What is the central idea of the first essay in this reading? Using evidence from the essay, summarize the key idea that Mendoza conveys about herself and the details she uses to support her idea.

2. What metaphor does Gregory use to describe himself throughout his essay? What key idea does he convey about himself, and what details does he use to support this key idea?

3. Hugh Gallagher's "Essay 3A" is a parody of a college essay. Summarize the message Gallagher conveys in his parody. What elements of serious college essays does he mock?

Craft and Structure

Structure of the Essay

1. To engage their reader, the writers of these college essays use descriptive paragraphs. Descriptive paragraphs contain sensory details to describe a person, place, experience, emotion, or a situation. On the chart, note at least one sensory detail used by each writer.

Christina Mendoza	James Gregory	Hugh Gallagher

2. What does Mendoza's response to her "assailant" convey about her perspective on her culture?

3. What is Gregory's perspective on his ability to achieve success in "higher education"?

4. Choose one action described in Gallagher's essay that suggests he disagrees with the process of writing a college admission essay. Explain.

Sensory Detail

A **sensory detail** is a word or phrase that helps the reader see, hear, taste, feel, or smell what the author is describing.

Perspective

An **author's perspective** is the way an author thinks or feels about something.

Academic Vocabulary

from "The Year of the MOOC"
by Laura Pappano from *The New York Times*

Rate your understanding of each Target Word. Then read its meaning and write a sample sentence.

Word	Meaning	Example
lecture (n.) p. 23 ① ② ③ ④	a speech given to a class or audience, usually for the purpose of teaching something	*My history teacher gave a lecture about the causes of the Civil War.*
disruption (n.) p. 24 ① ② ③ ④	an interruption; a forceful break or change in the way something is done	
traditional (adj.) p. 24 ① ② ③ ④	following ideas and methods that have existed for a long time, rather than doing anything new	
enrollment (n.) p. 24 ① ② ③ ④	the act of signing up for a class or activity	
monitor (v.) p. 25 ① ② ③ ④	to supervise; to check for issues needing attention	
participant (n.) p. 30 ① ② ③ ④	a person who becomes involved in something	

Rating Scale | ① I don't know the word. ② I've seen it or heard it. ③ I know its meaning. ④ I know it and use it.

Word Study

Base Words and Suffixes

A base word is a word to which prefixes, suffixes, and endings may be added.

A suffix is a letter or letters added to the end of a base word to form a new word, such as *-less* in *careless* or *-ly* in *suddenly*.

You can use these word parts to determine the meaning of a word.

- The base word *enroll* means "to sign up for."
- The suffix *-ment* means "the act of" or "the state of."
- Therefore, the word *enrollment* means "the act of signing up for."

Identify the base words and suffixes in the words below.

1. excitement
2. finally
3. engagement
4. ultimately
5. endless

The Year of the MOOC

by Laura Pappano

November 2, 2012

¶1 In late September, as workers applied joint compound to new office walls, hoodie-clad colleagues who had just met were working together on deadline. Film editors, code-writing interns and "edX fellows"—grad students and postdocs versed in online education—were translating videotaped **lectures** into MOOCs, or massive open online courses. As if anyone needed reminding, a row of aqua Post-its gave the dates the courses would "go live."

¶2 The paint is barely dry, yet edX, the nonprofit start-up from Harvard and the Massachusetts Institute of Technology, has 370,000 students this fall in its first official courses. That's nothing. Coursera, founded just last January, has reached more than 1.7 million—growing "faster than Facebook," boasts Andrew Ng, on leave from Stanford to run his for-profit MOOC provider.

¶3 "This has caught all of us by surprise," says David Stavens, who formed a company called Udacity with Sebastian Thrun and Michael Sokolsky after more than 150,000 signed up for Dr. Thrun's "Introduction to Artificial Intelligence" last fall, starting the revolution that has higher education gasping. A year ago, he marvels, "we were three guys in Sebastian's living room and now we have 40 employees full time."

Words to Know

colleagues: *(n.)* people who work together

courses: *(n.)* classes; courses of study

nonprofit: *(adj.)* not set up for the purpose of making money

revolution: *(n.)* a complete change in ways of thinking or working

Text Structure

1. What is Pappano's tone in **paragraph 2**?

Tone

Tone is the writer's attitude toward the topic. Tone is set through word choices, descriptive details, dialogue, and setting.

Key Ideas and Details

2. What evidence does Pappano provide in **paragraphs 2 and 3** that suggests MOOCs are becoming popular?

Close Reading

Academic Vocabulary

3. What is the *disruption* that Agarwal refers to in **paragraph 4**? What can you infer from Agarwal's job title about the way he feels about the *disruption*? Explain.

Key Ideas and Details

4. What details in **paragraph 5** support the writer's claim that "this is the year everyone wants in" to the MOOCs?

Text Structure

5. "What Is a MOOC Anyway?" is a subheading for this section of the article. What will the writer describe in this section? How do you know?

Subheading

A **subheading** is a heading given to a subsection of a piece of writing. A subheading describes the section that follows, much like the title of an article.

¶4 "I like to call this the year of **disruption**," says Anant Agarwal, president of edX, "and the year is not over yet."

¶5 MOOCs have been around for a few years as **collaborative** techie learning events, but this is the year everyone wants in. Elite universities are partnering with Coursera at a furious pace. It now offers courses from 33 of the biggest names in postsecondary education, including Princeton, Brown, Columbia and Duke. In September, Google unleashed a MOOC-building online tool, and Stanford unveiled Class2Go with two courses.

¶6 Nick McKeown is teaching one of them, on computer networking, with Philip Levis. Dr. McKeown sums up the energy of this grand experiment when he gushes, "We're both very excited." Casually draped over auditorium seats, the professors also acknowledge that they are not exactly sure how this MOOC stuff works.

¶7 "We are just going to see how this goes over the next few weeks," says Dr. McKeown.

What is a MOOC Anyway?

¶8 **Traditional** online courses charge **tuition**, carry credit and limit **enrollment** to a few dozen to ensure interaction with instructors. The MOOC, on the other hand, is usually free, credit-less and, well, massive.

¶9 Because anyone with an Internet connection can enroll, faculty can't possibly respond to students individually. So the course design — how material is presented and the interactivity — counts for a lot. As do fellow students. Classmates may lean on one another in study groups organized in their towns, in online forums or, the prickly part, for grading work.

Words to Know

collaborative: *(adj.)* involving two or more people working together to achieve something

tuition: *(n.)* a fee paid to take a class or go to a school

¶10 The evolving form knits together education, entertainment (think gaming) and social networking. Unlike its <u>antecedent</u>, open courseware—usually written materials or videotapes of lectures that make you feel as if you're spying on a class from the back of the room—the MOOC is a full course made with you in mind.

¶11 The medium is still the lecture. Thanks to **Khan Academy's** free archive of snappy instructional videos, MOOC makers have gotten the memo on the benefit of <u>brevity</u>: 8 to 12 minutes is typical. Then—this is key—videos pause perhaps twice for a quiz to make sure you understand the material or, in computer programming, to let you write code. Feedback is electronic. Teaching assistants may **monitor** discussion boards. There may be homework and a final exam.

Students who take MOOCs do not have to sit in a classroom.

Words to Know

<u>antecedent</u>: (*n.*) a thing or event that came before another similar thing

<u>brevity</u>: (*n.*) shortness or quickness; the quality of being brief

Close Reading

Text Structure

6. Words that appear inside parentheses are sometimes used to help clarify an idea. What is the author trying to clarify in **paragraph 10**? Why would the author need to clarify this?

Words and Phrases in Context

7. How is the meaning of *medium* in **paragraph 11** different from the usual meaning of the word?

Writing

8. According to the information Pappano provides in **paragraph 11**, what feature is a key part of MOOC videos? What type of students would this feature benefit?

   According to Pappano, a key part of MOOC videos is _____.

   This feature would likely benefit students who _____ because _____.

Close Reading

Words and Phrases in Context

9. What does the word *proctored* mean in **paragraph 12**? Use context clues to help determine the meaning.

Writing

10. Find details in **paragraph 13** that explain why few students complete a MOOC. What can you infer from this about the expectations of most students who sign up for MOOCs?

The article states that few students complete a MOOC because _____.

I can infer from this that most students _____.

Key Ideas and Details

11. Find details in **paragraph 14** that convey the sense of excitement MOOC creators feel about the future of MOOCs. Explain how Pappano's word choice creates this feeling of excitement.

¶12 The MOOC certainly presents challenges. Can learning be <u>scaled up</u> this much? Grading is imperfect, especially for nontechnical subjects. Cheating is a reality. "We found groups of 20 people in a course submitting identical homework," says David Patterson, a professor at the University of California, Berkeley, who teaches software engineering, in a tone of disbelief at such <u>blatant</u> copying; Udacity and edX now offer proctored exams.

¶13 Some students are also ill prepared for the university-level work. And few stick with it. "Signing up for a class is a lightweight process," says Dr. Ng. It might take just five minutes, assuming you spend two devising a stylish user name. Only 46,000 attempted the first assignment in Dr. Ng's course on machine learning last fall. In the end, he says, 13,000 completed the class and earned a certificate—from him, not Stanford.

¶14 That's still a lot of students. The shimmery hope is that free courses can bring the best education in the world to the most remote corners of the planet, help people in their careers, and expand intellectual and personal networks. Three-quarters of those who took Dr. Patterson's "Software as a Service" last winter on Coursera (it's now on edX) were from outside the United States, though the opposite was true of a course on circuits and electronics piloted last spring by Dr. Agarwal. But both attracted highly educated students and both reported that over 70 percent had degrees (more than a third had graduate degrees). And in a vote of confidence in the form, students in both overwhelmingly endorsed the quality of the course: 63 percent who completed Dr. Agarwal's course as well as a similar one on campus found the MOOC better; 36 percent found it comparable; 1 percent, worse.

¶15 Ray Schroeder, director of the Center for Online Learning, Research and Service at the University of Illinois, Springfield, says three things matter most in online learning: quality of material covered, engagement of the teacher and

---

Words to Know

<u>scaled up</u>: *(v.)* adjusted to fit a larger number or amount of something; e.g., students in a class

<u>blatant</u>: *(adj.)* done openly and unashamedly

interaction among students. The first doesn't seem to be an issue—most professors come from elite campuses, and so far most MOOCs are in technical subjects like computer science and math, with straightforward content. But providing instructor connection and feedback, including student interactions, is trickier.

¶16 "What's frustrating in a MOOC is the instructor is not as available because there are tens of thousands of others in the class," Dr. Schroeder says. How do you make the massive feel intimate?

¶17 That's what everyone is trying to figure out.

¶18 Many places offer MOOCs, and more will. But Coursera, Udacity and edX are defining the form as they develop their brands.

The Flavor of the MOOC

¶19 Coursera casts itself as a "hub"—Dr. Ng's word—for learning and networking. The learning comes gratis from an impressive roster of elites offering a wide range of courses, from computer science to philosophy to medicine. Not all are highbrow or technical; "Listening to World Music" from the University of Pennsylvania aims to broaden your iPod playlist.

¶20 While Coursera will make suggestions, Dr. Ng says, "ultimately all pedagogical decisions are made by the universities." Most offerings are adapted from existing courses: a Princeton Coursera course is a Princeton course. But the vibe is decidedly Facebook—build a profile, upload your photo—with tools for students to plan "meetups" with Courserians in about 1,400 cities worldwide. These gatherings may be bona fide study groups or social sessions. Membership may be many or sparse.

Words to Know

elite: (adj.) the best of their kind or group

gratis: (adv.) without charge; free

highbrow: (adj.) intellectual

pedagogical: (adj.) relating to teaching methods or the practice of teaching

Close Reading

Writing

12. What is one advantage and one disadvantage of MOOCs described in **paragraphs 15 and 16**?

The author states that one

advantage is ___.

One disadvantage is ___.

Words and Phrases in Context

13. What does *flavor* mean in the subhead "The Flavor of the MOOC"? Find context clues in the following paragraphs that indicate how *flavor* is used.

Key Ideas and Details

14. How does a Coursera course differ from a traditional college course? Use details in **paragraph 20** to support your answer.

¶21 No one showed at the meet-up that Stacey Brown, an information technology manager at a Hartford insurance company, scheduled for a 14th-floor conference room on a Thursday after work, despite R.S.V.P.'s from a few classmates in the area. He's taking three Coursera MOOCs, including "Gamification" from the University of Pennsylvania Wharton School. In addition to the learning—and dropping to bosses that he's taking a Wharton course—Mr. Brown says, "I hope to get a network."

¶22 Others like the discipline a group offers. Kimberly Spillman, a software engineer, started taking seven MOOCs and completed three. "The ones I have study groups with people, those are the ones I finish," Ms. Spillman says. She first joined a group for Dr. Thrun's artificial intelligence course, and then ran one for a Udacity course on building a search engine, organizing Thursday-evening discussions of the week's material followed by a social hour. Fifteen people met each week at the Ansir Innovation Center, a community space with big tables and comfortable chairs, in the Kearny Mesa neighborhood of San Diego.

¶23 Udacity has stuck close to its math and computer science roots and emphasizes applied learning, like "How to Build a Blog" or "Building a Web Browser." Job placement is part of the Udacity package. "The type of skills taught in computer science, even at elite universities, can be very theoretical," Dr. Stavens explains.

¶24 Udacity courses are designed and produced in-house or with companies like Google and Microsoft. In a poke at its university-based competition, Dr. Stavens says they pick instructors not because of their academic research, as universities do, but because of how they teach. "We reject about 98 percent of faculty who want to

Words to Know

applied learning: (n.) classes and instruction that teach job skills, or how to do a specific thing

in-house: (n.) on-site; a product made "in-house" is made at or by the same company that will sell the product

---

Close Reading

Writing

15. What are the benefits of working with classmates described in **paragraphs 21 and 22**? Why are MOOCs an unreliable way of connecting with classmates?

The benefits of working with classmates include_____.

Key Ideas and Details

16. In **paragraphs 21 and 22**, the author describes the experiences two different students have had with MOOCs. How are Kimberly Spillman's experiences different from those of Stacey Brown?

Key Ideas and Details

17. In **paragraph 23**, why would classes like "How to Build a Blog" and "Building a Web Browser" be examples of applied learning?

teach with us," he says. "Just because a person is the world's most famous economist doesn't mean they are the best person to teach the subject." Dr. Stavens sees a day when MOOCs will disrupt how faculty are attracted, trained and paid, with the most popular "compensated like a TV actor or a movie actor." He adds that "students will want to learn from whoever is the best teacher."

¶25 That means you don't need a Ph.D. While there are traditional academics like David Evans of the University of Virginia, "Landmarks in Physics," a first-year college-level course, is taught by Andy Brown, a 2009 M.I.T. graduate with a B.S. in physics. "We think the future of education is guys like Andy Brown who produce the most fun," Dr. Stavens says. Mr. Brown's course is an indie version of "Bill Nye the Science Guy"—filmed in Italy, the Netherlands and England, with opening credits for "director of photography" and "second camera and editor."

¶26 Whether explaining what the ancients believed about the shape of the earth or, in Dr. Thrun's statistics course, why you are unpopular, statistically speaking, voice-overs are as nonthreatening as a grade school teacher.

¶27 "You feel like you are sitting next to someone and they are tutoring you," says Jacqueline Spiegel, a mother of three from New Rochelle, N.Y., with a master's in computer science from Columbia who has enrolled in MOOCs from Udacity and Coursera. While taking "Artificial Intelligence," she discovered she liked puzzling through assignments in online study groups.

Words to Know
academics: (n.) college professors and others who research academic subjects as a career
ancients: (n.) people who lived long ago

Close Reading

Key Ideas and Details
18. Based on the information in **paragraph 24**, what type of teachers does Udacity hire?

Academic Vocabulary
19. How is Andy Brown not a traditional academic, as noted in **paragraph 25**?

Key Ideas and Details
20. What details does the author provide about Brown's course in **paragraph 25**? What can you conclude about why people like his course?

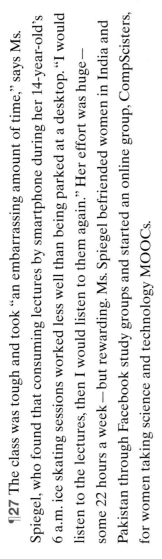

Close Reading

Words and Phrases in Context

21. What does *consuming* mean in **paragraph 27**? Find context clues that help you determine its meaning.

Key Ideas and Details

22. How can an online learning environment be challenging for a student? Use evidence from **paragraph 27** to support your answer.

Words and Phrases in Context

23. What is the meaning of *intentionality* in **paragraph 30**? Find clues that help you determine its meaning.

¶27 The class was tough and took "an embarrassing amount of time," says Ms. Spiegel, who found that consuming lectures by smartphone during her 14-year-old's 6 a.m. ice skating sessions worked less well than being parked at a desktop. "I would listen to the lectures, then I would listen to them again." Her effort was huge—some 22 hours a week—but rewarding. Ms. Spiegel befriended women in India and Pakistan through Facebook study groups and started an online group, CompScisters, for women taking science and technology MOOCs.

¶28 If Udacity favors stylish hands-on instruction, edX aims to be elite, smart and rigorous; don't expect a gloss of calculus if you need it but never took it. Some 120 institutions have been in touch; only Berkeley and the University of Texas system have been admitted to the club.

¶29 EdX's M.I.T. roots show in its staff's geeky passion for building and testing online tools. They collect your clicks. Feedback from the MOOC taught last spring by Dr. Agarwal (who, students learn, is obsessed with chain saws) revealed that **participants** would rather watch a hand writing an equation or sentence on paper than stare at the same paper with writing already on it.

¶30 The focus is on making education logical. "Someone who is consuming the course should know it is not <u>serendipity</u> that the course is chunked in a certain way, but that there is intentionality to sequencing video," says Howard A. Lurie, vice president for content development.

Words to Know

<u>serendipity:</u> *(n.)* luck; things that work out well by accident, rather than as a result of planning

Close Reading

Key Ideas and Details

24. How has Dr. Agarwal's course changed over time? Use details from **paragraph 31** to support your answer.

Writing

25. What do the "tool sets" Mr. Lurie describes in **paragraph 32** allow students to do? What kind of student might benefit from this?

The "tool sets" allow students to _____.

A student who _____ would benefit from these tool sets.

¶31 With mini-notebook in hand, he has been leading the "daily stand-up" meeting (so called because attendees lean against walls) to keep course development on schedule. After one meeting, Lyla Fischer, a 2011 M.I.T. graduate and edX fellow, sat at her computer, a tag still dangling from the chair, and edited the answers for problem sets in Dr. Agarwal's course. Last spring, students could download PDFs with brief answers. Now, she says, "there is a full explanation of how to do it, here are the steps," right on the site.

¶32 "We are trying to use the magic of all the tool sets we have," Mr. Lurie says. Students control how fast they watch lectures. Some like to go at nearly double the speed; others want to slow down and replay. Coming: If you get a wrong answer, the software figures out where you went wrong and offers a correction.

A MOOC professor is videotaped for his lecture.

Identify Evidence | Analyze Experiences

Reread "The Year of the MOOC," highlighting the examples the writer uses to describe what students experience when they are enrolled in a MOOC.

- As you read, use the Evidence column to record examples from the text that describe the experience of participating in a MOOC, and that allow you to infer who will—or won't—thrive in this environment.
- In the Explanation column, explain how the evidence introduces, illustrates, or elaborates on MOOC experience and the individuals who succeed in it, or find it frustrating.

Evidence	Source	Page	Explanation
1. "The MOOC, on the other hand, is usually free, credit-less and, well, massive. Because anyone with an Internet connection can enroll."	*Pappano*		
2. "Classmates may lean on one another in study groups organized in their towns, in online forums"	*Pappano*		
3. "The evolving form knits together education, entertainment (think gaming) and social networking."	*Pappano*		
4. "We found groups of 20 people in a course submitting identical homework."	*Pappano*		
5. "Some students are also ill prepared for the university-level work. And few stick with it."	*Pappano*		
6. "What's frustrating in a MOOC is the instructor is not as available because there are tens of thousands of others in the class," Dr. Schroeder says.	*Dr. Schroeder*		

Evidence	Source	Page	Explanation
7. "No one showed at the meet-up that Stacey Brown, an information technology manager at a Hartford insurance company, scheduled. 'The ones I have study groups with people, those are the ones I finish,' Ms. Spillman says."			
8. "Dr. Stavens says they pick instructors not because of their academic research, as universities do, but because of how they teach."	Dr. Stavens		
9. "'We are trying to use the magic of all the tool sets we have,' Mr. Lurie says. Students control how fast they watch lectures. Some like to go at nearly double the speed; others want to slow down and replay."	Mr. Lurie		
10. "Coursera uses peer grading: submit an assignment and five people grade it; in turn, you grade five assignments. But what if someone is a horrible grader?"	Pappano		

Key Ideas and Details

Determining the Central Idea

1. What is the central idea of "The Year of the MOOC"? Review details from Pappano's article to help summarize the key idea.

Collaborate and Present

Plan and Deliver a Presentation

Assignment: Work with a group to discuss whether you would prefer to take MOOCs or attend classes in person at a traditional brick-and-mortar college or university. Collect evidence from the text to support your responses. Follow the steps below to conduct your discussion and present your results to the class.

Analyze the Content

1. Consider the following questions:

- According to Pappano, what are the advantages of taking a MOOC over a traditional college class? What are the disadvantages?

- In what ways would a MOOC suit you? Consider factors such as your personality, learning style, study habits, and the subjects you plan to study.

- How might a brick-and-mortar college be more—or less—suitable for you than a MOOC?

2. Go back to the text and gather evidence that supports your responses. Create a chart of reasons and text evidence that supports and justifies your position.

I would prefer to attend	My reasons	Evidence that supports my reasons

Organize Your Presentation

3. Use the items on your reasons and evidence chart as talking points for your presentation.

- Draft an outline of the information to present to the class.

Present

4. Present the results of your group's discussion to the class.

Seeking Clarification

- Are you saying that . . .
- Do you mean . . .
- Can you give an example of . . .

Reporting Ideas

- _____ suggests that
- _____ seems to be implying
- _____ argues that

Presentation

- Be still and use good posture.
- Speak loudly and clearly.
- Make eye contact with your audience.

Presentation Checklist

Use the checklist below to evaluate your collaboration skills, reasoning, and final presentation.
Think carefully about your work. If you completed an item thoroughly, give yourself a check (✓).

COLLABORATE AND PRESENT CHECKLIST

Comprehension & Collaboration

☐ Engage in group discussions with diverse partners on topics and issues that you read about.

☐ Come to discussions prepared, having read and researched the material.

☐ Refer to evidence to probe and reflect on and contribute to the discussion.

☐ Follow rules for discussions and decision-making.

☐ Ask and respond to specific questions.

☐ Make informed comments about topics that are being discussed.

☐ Demonstrate understanding of the key ideas presented by classmates by reflection and paraphrasing.

Number of ✓s in this category: __

Evidence & Reasoning

☐ Explain the purpose of the presentation.

☐ State the type of learning institution I would prefer to enroll in.

☐ Explain why I would prefer one type of learning institution over the other.

☐ Explain my opinion with evidence from the text.

Number of ✓s in this category: __

Presentation of Knowledge & Ideas

☐ Adapt my language to a variety of contexts and tasks to demonstrate knowledge of formal English.

☐ Use quotes from the text as evidence to strengthen my claims and add interest.

☐ Express my opinion clearly.

☐ Use appropriate volume/tone (clear, not too fast, too slow, or too loud) and avoid using *like* or *ummm*.

☐ Have strong posture, a confident stance, and make frequent eye contact.

☐ Occasionally move from one spot to another, without fidgeting.

☐ Smile and act relaxed.

Number of ✓s in this category: __

Total # of ✓s: __

Add up the total number of checks (✓) in each category. Then use the scoring guide below to calculate your final score.

Scoring Guide

16 to 18 ✓s	13 to 15 ✓s	11 to 12 ✓s	10 or less ✓s
④ Exemplary	③ Meets Standards	② Needs Work	① Does Not Meet Standards

Step 1 | Gather Evidence

Analyze which college applicant (Mendoza, Gregory, or Gallagher) would be the best candidate to take open online courses. Discuss what traits of this applicant make him or her well-suited for the online learning environment Pappano describes in her article.

What You Need to Know | Examine the evidence you have collected about the traits of the college applicants and details about the "MOOCs". (See pages 18 and 34.)

What You Need to Write | Note the evidence that supports your claim about which college applicant is the best candidate.

"Essays That Make a Difference"

Applicant:

Traits:

Page # _____

Applicant:

Traits:

Page # _____

Applicant:

Traits:

Page # _____

"The Year of the MOOC"

Evidence for or against the applicant:

Page # _____

Evidence for or against the applicant:

Page # _____

Evidence for or against the applicant:

Page # _____

Step 2 | Organize Ideas

Use the outline below to record your thesis statement and organize your claims or counterclaims, as well as supporting evidence into paragraphs.

Introduction
Thesis Statement:

Body:	
Claim/Counterclaim:	Relevant Evidence:
Claim/Counterclaim:	Relevant Evidence:
Claim/Counterclaim:	Relevant Evidence:

Conclusion
Restate and why it matters

Step 3 | Draft

Write a draft of your essay on the computer or on paper.

Language Study | Constructing a Thesis Statement

See It | A thesis statement has two parts: (a) a statement of opinion and (b) supporting evidence.

Example: In his novel *The Graveyard Book*, Neil Gaiman flexes his creative writing muscles when he takes the plot of a classic novel and turns it on its head, stretches the imagination and disbelief of his readers, and artfully ties everything together in a satisfying conclusion.

Statement of opinion: *In his novel, The Graveyard Book, Neil Gaiman flexes his creative writing muscles.*

Supporting evidence: *He takes the plot of a classic novel and turns it on its head, stretches the imagination and disbelief of his readers, and artfully ties everything together in a satisfying conclusion.*

Try It | Find the two parts of a thesis statement in each passage below.

1. Everyone should read the novel *The Chosen*, by Chaim Potok, because it beautifully portrays the relationships between fathers and sons, and teaches what it means to be a friend.

   Statement of opinion: _____

   _____

   Supporting evidence: _____

   _____

2. Through her description of the dangers people faced before the Revolutionary War, and the drama and intrigue in the government at the time, author Esther Forbes makes the novel *Johnny Tremain* one of the best historical novels.

   Statement of opinion: _____

   _____

   Supporting evidence: _____

   _____

3. By writing about the protagonist's vision, courage, and sensitivity, author Theodore Taylor creates one of the most authentic characters in young adult literature in his novel *The Cay*.

   Statement of opinion: _____

   _____

   Supporting evidence: _____

Apply It | Think about the thesis statement you wrote about in your essay. Use the sentence frames for ideas on how to improve your thesis statement.

1. After analyzing the evidence in _____'s essay, _____, it is my opinion that
   (applicant's name)   (title)

   (he/she) is the best candidate for an online learning environment because (he/she) is

   _____.
   (supporting evidence)

2. Because _____ proves (himself/herself) to be _____, and _____, and
              (applicant's name)   (evidence 1)   (evidence 2)

   _____ in (his/her) essay, _____, I contend that (he/she) is the best candidate
   (evidence 3)   (title)

   for the online learning environment.

3. _____'s essay, _____, provides ample evidence of (his/her) _____,
   (applicant's name)   (title)   (evidence)

   which supports (his/her) suitability to attend the online "reinvented college."

   Now, **go back to your draft** and select the thesis statement you wrote. Rewrite your
   sentence to make it clearer and less repetitive.

   _____

   _____

   _____

   _____

Conventions Study | Understanding Verbals

See It | Verbals are verbs that function as different parts of speech.

- Gerunds function as nouns: **Skating** is fun.
- Participles function as adjectives: The **freezing** wind stung my eyes, OR the **frozen** water was melting.
- Infinitives function as adjectives, adverbs, or nouns.
  - Adjective: This is a good movie **to watch.**
  - Adverb: **To cook**, you need the right ingredients. OR You need the right ingredients **to cook.**
  - Noun: **To star in the play** is my goal. OR My goal is **to star in the play.**

Try It | Find the verbal in the sentence below from the model. How does the verbal function?

[Khadijah's growing awareness of what she wants to do with her degree is another reason I contend that she would only thrive in a brick-and-mortar school.]

Apply It | Now look for nouns, adjectives, and adverbs in a few sentences in your draft. Rewrite each sentence to include a verbal.

Step 4 | Revise and Edit

Revise your draft with a partner.

Organization and Clarity					
State titles and authors of the texts in the introductory paragraph.	Self	1	2	3	4
	Partner	1	2	3	4
Provide a thesis statement in the introduction that clearly declares the position.	Self	1	2	3	4
	Partner	1	2	3	4
Include topic sentences in the body paragraphs that present the general reasons that support the claim.	Self	1	2	3	4
	Partner	1	2	3	4

Evidence and Reasoning					
Analyze a news article about MOOCs and essays written by college applicants to determine which applicants are suited for online learning.	Self	1	2	3	4
	Partner	1	2	3	4
Include in the thesis statement the evidence to be presented in each body paragraph.	Self	1	2	3	4
	Partner	1	2	3	4
Provide specific claims in each body paragraph and relevant evidence from the texts to support each claim.	Self	1	2	3	4
	Partner	1	2	3	4

Language and Conventions					
Explain the function of verbals.	Self	1	2	3	4
	Partner	1	2	3	4
Demonstrate a command of English grammar and punctuation.	Self	1	2	3	4
	Partner	1	2	3	4
Use domain-specific vocabulary from the texts as appropriate.	Self	1	2	3	4
	Partner	1	2	3	4
Establish and maintain a formal style and reasonable tone throughout the essay.	Self	1	2	3	4
	Partner	1	2	3	4

Scoring Guide | ① needs improvement ② average ③ good ④ excellent

Step 5 | Publish

Publish your essay either in print or digital form.

Publish

Publish your essay either in print or digital form. Use the rubric below to assess your final performance task.

PERFORMANCE TASK RUBRIC

Score Point	Organization and Clarity	Evidence and Reasoning	Language and Conventions
Exemplary (4)	• introductory paragraph includes an **assertive thesis statement that takes a position** and **previews** the argument and supporting evidence • body paragraphs are **effectively organized** and **present logical reasons and evidence** to support the position and refute any counterclaims • includes **well-chosen** text evidence, precise language, and effective use of verbals • concluding statement **restates the thesis statement**	• **accurately explains and convincingly argues** which applicant is the best candidate for online learning • includes **relevant** factual evidence from the essay and news article to support each logical reason • ends by **effectively restating** the thesis statement and leaving readers with **something to think about**	• demonstrates a **strong command** of the conventions of standard English grammar and usage, as well as of standard English capitalization, punctuation, and spelling • vocabulary is **appropriate** to the topic (vocabulary about MOOCs and personality traits; accurate vocabulary for an assertive thesis statement and convincing argument; vocabulary for making a claim supported with logical reasons)
Meets Standards (3)	• introductory paragraph includes **an adequate thesis statement** that **previews** the argument and supporting evidence • body paragraphs are **logically organized** and **present reasons and evidence** to support the position and refute any counterclaims • includes **some** text evidence, precise language, and verbals • concluding statement **restates the thesis statement**	• **adequately explains and argues** which applicant is the best candidate for online learning • includes **some relevant** factual evidence from the essay and news article to support each logical reason • ends by **restating** the thesis statement and **attempting** to leave readers with something to think about	• demonstrates **a near command** of the conventions of standard English grammar and usage, as well as of standard English capitalization, punctuation, and spelling **with some errors** • vocabulary is **appropriate** to the topic (vocabulary about MOOCs and personality traits; accurate vocabulary for an assertive thesis statement and convincing argument; vocabulary for making a claim supported with logical reasons)

PERFORMANCE TASK RUBRIC

Score Point	Organization and Clarity	Evidence and Reasoning	Language and Conventions
Needs Work ②	• introductory paragraph includes **a weak thesis statement that attempts to preview** the argument and some supporting evidence • body paragraphs are **somewhat logically organized** and **partially present reasons and evidence** to support the position • any counterclaim is **partially refuted with evidence** • includes **a limited amount** of text evidence, precise language and effective use of verbals • concluding statement **restates the thesis statement**	• **partially explains and minimally argues** which applicant is the best candidate for online learning • includes **one or two examples of relevant** factual evidence from the essay and news article to support each logical reason • ends by **restating** the thesis statement	• demonstrates a **marginal command** of the conventions of English grammar and usage, as well as of standard English capitalization, punctuation, and spelling • there **are many errors; however, the text is still understandable** • includes only **one or two examples** of vocabulary that is appropriate to the topic (vocabulary about MOOCs and personality traits; accurate vocabulary for an assertive thesis statement and convincing argument; vocabulary for making a claim supported with logical reasons)
Does Not Meet Standards ①	• introductory paragraph is **unclear** and does not include a thesis statement that states a position or previews the argument and supporting evidence • body paragraphs are **not organized logically** and/or **do not present reasons and evidence** • any counterclaim is **not refuted with evidence** • essay includes **little text evidence** and minimal use of verbals • concluding statement is **unclear**	• response is a **partial or inaccurate argument** about which applicant is the best candidate for online learning • includes **no factual textual evidence** from the essay and news article • there **are many errors that disrupt** the reader's understanding of the text • **does not include** vocabulary that is appropriate to the topic (vocabulary about MOOCs and personality traits; accurate vocabulary for an assertive thesis statement and convincing argument; vocabulary for making a claim supported with logical reasons)	• demonstrates **almost no command** of the conventions of standard English grammar and usage, as well as of standard English capitalization, punctuation, and spelling

Questions

Key Ideas and Details

1. What can you infer about the author's impression of Khadijah in **paragraph 1**? Explain your answer using details from the text.

Words and Phrases in Context

2. What is the meaning of the word *transient* in **paragraph 3**? What context clues help you determine the meaning?

from "A Homeless Girl's Dream"

by Jeannine Amber from Essence

¶1 She could be any college freshman, walking across her quiet, tree-lined campus with a book bag slung across her shoulder. "It's so great to meet you," Khadijah Williams exclaims cheerfully as she arrives for breakfast at a quaint Cambridge, Massachusetts, restaurant, where she orders a smoked salmon omelet on a croissant. Outside it is a bleak and rainy February morning, yet Khadijah's enthusiasm seems boundless as she speaks about her school, her friends and the debate team. But ask her about her childhood, and she stops short. Khadijah, 19, looks off in the distance, then apologizes. "There's so much of it I've blocked out," she says. "I've had to push a lot of my past away."

¶2 For most of her life, Khadijah has been homeless. Currently 1.5 million children in the country are without a permanent place to live, a number that experts predict will grow under the weight of the recession, which is affecting African-Americans more than any other group. Khadijah knows all too well the rootlessness of this particular American story. "We lived in an apartment at first," she remembers. "I was about 4. But then my mother couldn't afford the rent, so we moved into a shelter."

¶3 For years, the family shuttled from one facility to another, in and around Los Angeles. "I've lived in San Diego, Orange County, San Bernardino, Santa Ana, Ventura County, San Pedro," she rattles off. "Sometimes we got money from welfare. When we didn't, my mother would redeem cans and bottles or stand in line for the dollar man"—a clergyman who would give one or two dollars to homeless people at the shelter each week. Other times Khadijah's mother would do temporary manual labor. Money was always scarce and housing transient. Often, on a moment's notice, Khadijah's mother would announce to her and her younger sister, now 12, that

Words to Know

quaint: *(adj.)* unusual and attractive, especially in an old-fashioned way

recession: *(n.)* a period of time when there is less trade and business activity in a country than usual

the family had to pack up and move. Maybe their time had run out at a temporary shelter, or maybe she sensed the conditions were becoming unsafe. The girls would hurriedly stuff their belongings into plastic trash bags and board a city bus in search of a new facility, often in a different school district.

¶4 Despite such upheavals, Khadijah has accomplished a goal many girls her age can only dream of reaching: In May she completed her freshman year at top-ranked Harvard University. Khadijah, who receives financial aid, just shrugs when you ask her how she did it. She says that going to Harvard was the plan all along.

¶5 A 2009 report by the Campaign to End Child Homelessness notes that the nation's one in 50 children without a home will likely endure a multitude of impediments to education—a lack of structure, lost school records, poor physical and mental health and high absenteeism. Many of these students will lack even the most basic of requirements—from school supplies that are stolen in the night to clean clothes to put on in the morning. For homeless children, getting through high school is a feat in and of itself. Three out of four never graduate.

¶6 But for Khadijah, school was a refuge, a reminder that outside the shelter was a world filled with possibility. "People focus on the material things you don't have when you're homeless," she says now. "But a lot of the challenge for homeless children is psychological. No matter how nice a shelter is, you never feel safe, and all you see around you are people who are down on their luck. It's not the kind of atmosphere that makes you think big. Books helped me escape all of that." And so Khadijah read—the backs of cereal boxes, old copies of *Reader's Digest* that she would find at the shelters and any books she could get her hands on. *Black Beauty*, the story of a horse that is shunted from one owner to another, was one of her favorites.

Words to Know

multitude (*n.*) a large number

impediments (*n.*) situations or events that make it difficult or impossible for someone or something to succeed or make progress

feat (*n.*) an achievement that requires great courage, strength, or skill

Questions

Text Structure

3. What events in Khadijah's life does the author contrast in **paragraphs 3 and 4**? What word or phrase does the author use to signal that she is making a contrast?

Key Ideas and Details

4. Why does the author describe getting through high school "a feat in and of itself" for homeless children in **paragraph 5**? What does this suggest about Khadijah?

Questions

Key Ideas and Details

5. What is the purpose of the story that Khadijah "recalls" in **paragraph 8**?

Key Ideas and Details

6. What do Khadijah's efforts in **paragraphs 9 and 10** reveal about her character?

¶7 "There's been a lot of discussion recently about the newly homeless," she reflects, "but what people don't talk about is that once you get inside this cycle, it's very hard to see a way out. I think that's what happened to my mom." But Khadijah grasped early on that education meant opportunity. "There were times that I couldn't go to classes because we were moving around so much," says Khadijah, who missed her entire first grade year. "Sometimes I would cry about it. But the first thing that my mom did when we were in a new place was enroll me. She saw that school was really important to me. She would use her last money to do laundry to make sure I had clean clothes to wear, so I didn't feel self-conscious. She always had my back."

¶8 Khadijah recalls the time in third grade when she tested in the 99th percentile on a standardized test: "The school was like. 'Oh, this is probably a mistake.' They didn't really think it was possible for me to get that high a score. But my mom went in and put them straight. By standing up to the teachers, she was telling me, *I know you're smart, don't listen to them.* She said as long as I did my best she would be proud of me. My mom didn't always know how to navigate the school system, but she knew her daughter. She always had high expectations of me. If she hadn't, I don't know where I'd be today."

¶9 By the time Khadijah reached high school she'd been to more than half a dozen schools. She was granted gifted status while at one school, then lost it when she moved and her records were misplaced. She was absent so often, sometimes for months at a time, that she was marked as <u>truant</u>, and fell two grades behind.

¶10 "In eighth grade, I realized I was two years older than everybody else," she remembers. "I stayed in that class for less than a month, then we moved to another county. When we got there my mother took me to the high school. We spoke to the <u>administrators</u> and they agreed to put me in the tenth grade. But I had to make up the subjects I'd missed at a community college, so for a while I was doing that along with high school. By eleventh grade I was taking honors and AP classes."

Words to Know

<u>truant:</u> (*adj.*) away from school without permission

<u>administrators:</u> (*n.*) people responsible for running a business

¶11 In her junior year Khadijah was living in a shelter so faraway from the school that she had to wake up at 4:30 a.m. and take three different buses to make it to her first class. The commute home during rush hour was even longer. But she <u>soldiered on</u>. She'd balance her books on her lap and do her homework on the bus. And sometimes, after lights out at the shelter, she would slip into the hallway or bathroom to study.

¶12 Among the residents of the shelters Khadijah became known as the girl who was trying to make something of herself. Not everyone was supportive. "Some people would say, 'What makes you think you're so special?'" she remembers.

¶13 At school she was "very friendly," but she never got so close that someone might expect an invitation to her house. "I told them my mom didn't like visitors," she says. "For me it was like, if I told anyone at school I was homeless, then I would have to admit to myself what was really going on. I had to disconnect from that reality in order to focus on my goal."

¶14 Even today Khadijah's discomfort with her past is evident. She pauses frequently as she speaks about her childhood. "I can feel myself getting tense and emotional just thinking about it," she admits. She credits her mother, who she notes is still struggling with homelessness, for setting the foundation for her achievements. Khadijah also availed herself of every program she could find that offered academic assistance, guidance and support to low-income students. There was School on Wheels, which provided supplies and tutors, and Upward Bound and Higher Edge Scholars, which focused on preparation for college. In her junior year she linked up with South Central Scholars, a privately funded program aimed at highly motivated but financially disadvantaged students. Randy Winston, president of student services at South Central Scholars, says he was immediately struck by Khadijah's ability to maintain her focus.

Words to Know

<u>soldiered on:</u> (v.) continued working in spite of difficulties

Questions

Key Ideas and Details

7. Why does Khadijah state that she had to "disconnect from that reality in order to focus on [her] goal" in **paragraph 13**? Use evidence you've learned about Khadijah throughout the article.

Words and Phrases in Context

8. What is the meaning of the phrase *availed herself of* in **paragraph 14**? Use context clues to determine the meaning.

"She created her own protective world that revolved around the pursuit of knowledge," he says. Winston adds that Khadijah only admitted to him she was homeless after he'd arranged for her to go to a semiformal function with some African-American alumni from Dartmouth, and she didn't have appropriate clothing. "She kept telling me her clothes were in storage. It was only after I pressed her that she finally told me the truth. She was truly embarrassed."

¶15 Winston, who picked up Khadijah at the shelter on occasion, describes the living arrangement as deplorable. "It was a situation that no one would want to be in," he says. "Her mother did her best to protect Khadijah and her younger sister, but there wasn't a whole lot of privacy. It was like a gymnasium after a disaster—just a room with a whole lot of cots lined up."

¶16 But Khadijah refused to let her concentration waver. "From the moment I met her she talked about going to an Ivy League institution, where she could be challenged," recalls Winston. "Her desire has always been to go to the top." The founders of South Central Scholars, Dr. James and Patricia London, also noticed Khadijah's extraordinary ambition. They bought her a laptop and invited her to live with them during her last few months of high school.

¶17 Khadijah says she "went crazy," applying to 26 colleges in all, including Princeton, Yale, Stanford, and Columbia. Instead of hiding her homelessness during college interviews she did as her advisers had encouraged—she pointed to her life circumstances as a measure of her determination. "I told the interviewers my life was proof that I could succeed, no matter what," says Khadijah. She was accepted into 22 of the 26 colleges to which she applied.

¶18 Months later, on a warm spring day, Khadijah is dressed in crimson-colored Harvard sweats and a white T-shirt with her braids pulled up in a ponytail. With

Words to Know

waver: (v.) become weaker or less certain

crimson: (adj.) deep red

Questions

Words and Phrases in Context

9. What is the meaning of the word *deplorable* in **paragraph 15**? Use context words to determine the meaning.

Key Ideas and Details

10. What is the author's purpose for including Winston's quote in **paragraph 15**?

freshman year just completed, she is packing up her dorm room for the summer, folding eight loads of laundry and filing away a year's worth of class notes.

¶19 "It's not just the academics that I've appreciated here," says Khadijah, who intends to pursue a Ph.D. and perhaps a career in education policy. "I've never spent so much time just thinking about everything: class, race, diversity. Now I realize we aren't just fighting poverty, but also the assumptions others have about Black people. At the same time, I've met so many strong, professional Black women, and they've become my role models. In just one year, college has made me realize there is so much I can do to help myself and to be more useful to society."

¶20 Ironically, Khadijah's past may have helped ease her adjustment to the Ivy League. "A lot of her peers have never faced any kind of disagreeable situation," says Rita Poussaint Nethersole, who is Khadijah's "host mother" at Harvard. "But Khadijah knows a bad situation is not the end of it all. You pick yourself up, you figure out what to do, and you keep moving. She's doggedly determined to succeed."

¶21 For the summer Khadijah is headed to New York for an internship at a company that focuses on education and technology. "If it wasn't for Harvard I probably wouldn't have this opportunity," she says. "Harvard really helps get your foot in the door. Actually," she adds with a laugh, "you can basically just walk right through the door. That's what Harvard does for you. It says, 'This person is smart and driven.' It really adds to your confidence when people already believe in you. This year hasn't been without its bumps, but I definitely wouldn't want to be anywhere else."

Words to Know

doggedly: *(adv.)* strongly or persistently

Questions

Key Ideas and Details

11. In **paragraph 21** Khadijah describes people's opinion of her today. How has attending Harvard University changed people's perception of Khadijah? Use information you've learned about Khadijah throughout the story to support your answer.

Literature Circle Leveled Novels

The Tequila Worm by Viola Canales
When Sofia is offered a scholarship to an exclusive boarding school, she jumps at the chance to build a better future for herself, but she soon realizes how much she learned in her old neighborhood. **Lexile®** measure: 830L

We Beat the Street by Dr. Sampson Davis, et al.
Three high school students from a tough neighborhood form a pact with one another to attend medical school and serve their community as doctors. **Lexile®** measure: 860L

Yes We Can!: A Biography of Barack Obama by Garen Thomas
Despite early obstacles, Barack Obama's determination to achieve his goals set him on the path to the American presidency. **Lexile®** measure: 1200L

Fiction, Nonfiction, and Novels

Chicken Soup for the College Soul by Jack Canfield, et al. Enjoy this collection of funny and encouraging stories that address the many issues surrounding the college experience.

The Everything College Survival Book by Michael S. Malone. Find information about everything there is to know about college, from admissions to graduation.

Fiske Guide to Colleges 2013 by Edward B. Fiske. Use this reference to learn about more than 300 American colleges and universities.

The Insider's Guide to Colleges, 2013: Students on Campus Tell You What You Really Want to Know edited by the Yale Daily News staff. College students share their opinions about life at colleges and trade schools in the United States and Canada.

It's OK If You're Clueless and 23 More Tips for the College Bound by Terry McMillan. A humorous list of tips about how to be successful in college and in life.

The Naked Roommate: And 107 Other Issues You Might Run Into in College by Harlan Cohen. Read advice on how to be successful in college.

Reaching Your Goals: The Ultimate Teen Guide by Anne Courtright. Read five simple steps that will help teens set and reach their goals in life.

What Do You Really Want? How to Set a Goal and Go for It! by Beverly K. Bachel. Read advice from a successful entrepreneur about how to achieve success by defining goals and systematically pursuing them.

Films and TV

College Road Trip (Walt Disney Video, 2008) A high school student and her father have different ideas about which college is best, so they decide to take a college tour. (170 min.)

College: The Big Change (Information Video, 2007) This program offers advice from college educators and students about how to excel in the college setting. (170 min.)

Cracking College: The Seven Secrets of Savvy Students (College Crossroads, LLC, 2007) Gain insight about how to earn good grades and succeed in college. (36 min.)

Dead Poets Society (Walt Disney Video, 1989) An English teacher inspires his high school students to seize the day and pursue their dreams. (128 min.)

October Sky (Universal Studios, 1999) In this film adaptation of a true story, a young man builds a rocket and takes his first steps toward a career in science. (108 min.)

Real Life Teens: Preparing for College (TMW Media Group, 2007) Students can learn different ways they can prepare for college and get more involved with defining their futures. (20 min.)

Rudy (Sony Pictures, 1993) A young man overcomes many obstacles as he pursues his dream of attending and playing football for the University of Notre Dame. (116 min.)

Ten Steps to College (PBS, 2003) This program walks parents and students through the college application process, from finding the right school to planning finances. (60 min.)

Websites

Bureau of Labor Statistics, Occupational Outlook Handbook Use this Web site to find out what kinds of training and education are required for different occupations and careers.

College View Search for statistics and information about U.S. colleges, their academic programs, and student life.

Universities, Colleges, and Trade Schools Follow the links to research different degrees available in trades and skills, such as computer technology.

U.S. Department of Education Find resources that will assist you in applying to and paying for colleges, universities, and vocational or career schools.

Magazines

Choices Students can explore topics that will help them think about the future and develop a sense of personal responsibility for their decisions.

Muse Articles on every topic from science to art and literature allow students to cultivate their interests and consider their future career paths.

The New York Times Upfront Students can read about current events and issues that will affect their goals and choices.

U.S. News and World Report Use the college ranking issue to learn more about colleges, universities, and specialty schools.

SURVIVOR

What inspires the will to survive in an extreme environment?

Unit Introduction

In a short story and a novel excerpt, discover how two authors develop characters who find the strength to survive in extreme environments.

In "The Story of Keesh," by Jack London, a teen boy confronts his elders and proves he can survive and succeed as a lone hunter of polar bears while fulfilling his promise to provide food for the weakest in his village.

In an excerpt from Yann Martel's novel *Life of Pi*, a young man must find within himself the courage and wit to survive in a lifeboat stranded on the ocean with a large tiger as his only companion.

WRITING PERFORMANCE TASK

Write an objective summary of life in the extreme environments portrayed in these two texts. Analyze how the central idea of survival is conveyed through supporting ideas and developed over the course of the text.

SHORT STORY/NOVEL EXCERPT

"The Story of Keesh"
by Jack London

Language
- Academic Vocabulary
- Word Study:
  Context Clues

Reading Fiction
- Identify Evidence
- Key Ideas & Details
- Craft & Structure and
  Writing Assignment

from *Life of Pi* by Yann Martel

Language
- Academic Vocabulary
- Word Study:
  Base Words and Suffixes

Reading Fiction
- Identify Evidence
- Key Ideas & Details
- Craft & Structure and
  Writing Assignment

SPEAKING AND LISTENING

Compare a Book and a Movie
- Collaborate and Present

Checklist: Presentation
- Scoring Guide

WRITING

Writing: Literary Analysis
- Read the Model
- Analyze the Model
- Gather Evidence
- Organize Ideas

- Language Study:
  Supporting a Generalization
- Conventions Study: Verbs in
  Active and Passive Voice
- Revise, Edit, and Publish
- Performance Task Rubric

EXTENDED READING

Novel Excerpt
from *The Lost Island of
Tamarind* by Nadia Aguiar

Academic Vocabulary

"The Story of Keesh" by Jack London

Rate your understanding of each Target Word. Then write its meaning or a sample sentence.

Word	Meaning	Example
abated (v.) p. 65 ① ② ③ ④	became less intense	
apportioned (v.) p. 62 ① ② ③ ④		Sam apportioned the sandwich by cutting it in half and giving one half to Joe.
prophetic (adj.) p. 64 ① ② ③ ④	predicting a future event	
assailed (v.) p. 65 ① ② ③ ④	attacked	
contended (v.) p. 67 ① ② ③ ④	argued	
corroborated (v.) p. 69 ① ② ③ ④	supported a statement	

Rating Scale
① I don't know the word.
② I've seen it or heard it.
③ I know its meaning.
④ I know it and use it.

Word Study

Context Clues

Context clues are words in a text that help you figure out the meaning of an unfamiliar word. Sometimes words are defined in the text or meaning is suggested.

Find context clues to determine the meaning of the bold words in the sentences below.

1. "But the people are **prone** to forget, and they forgot the deed of his father; and he being but a boy, and his mother only a woman, they, too, were swiftly forgotten, and ere long came to live in the meanest of all the *igloos.*"

2. "He sat down, his ears keenly alert to the flood of protest and **indignation** his words had created.

 'That a boy should speak in council!' old Ugh-Gluk was mumbling.

 'Shall the babes in arms tell us men the things we shall do?' Massuk demanded in a loud voice."

THE STORY OF KEESH

¶1 Keesh lived long ago on the rim of the polar sea, was headman of his village through many and prosperous years, and died full of honors with his name on the lips of men. So long ago did he live that only the old men remember his name, his name and the tale, which they got from the old men before them, and which the old men to come will tell to their children and their children's children down to the end of time. And the winter darkness, when the north gales make their long sweep across the icepack, and the air is filled with flying white, and no man may venture forth, is the chosen time for the telling of how Keesh, from the poorest igloo in the village, rose to power and place over them all.

He was a bright boy, so the tale runs, healthy and strong, and he had seen thirteen suns, in their way of reckoning time. For each winter the sun leaves the land in darkness, and the next year a new sun returns so that they may be warm again and look upon one another's faces. The father of Keesh had been a very brave man, but he had met his death in a time of famine, when he sought to save the lives of his people by taking the life of a great polar bear. In his eagerness he came to close grapples with the bear, and his bones were crushed; but the bear had much meat on him and the people were saved. Keesh was his only son, and after that Keesh lived alone with his mother.

Words to Know

gale: (n.) a very strong wind

grapple: (v.) to fight without weapons, wrestle

Close Reading

Writing

1. Describe the setting of the story. How might it become important to the plot?

Setting

The time period and location in which a story takes place.

The story is set ___.

The setting is ___ and the plot might involve ___.

Literary Analysis

2. Locate words and phrases in **paragraphs 1 and 2** that give this story the feel of a folktale or legend.

Close Reading

¶3 But the people are prone to forget, and they forgot the deed of his father; and he being but a boy, and his mother only a woman, they, too, were swiftly forgotten, and ere long came to live in the meanest of all the igloos.

It was at a council, one night, in the big igloo of Klosh-Kwan, the chief, that Keesh showed the blood that ran in his veins and the manhood that stiffened his back. With the dignity of an elder, he rose to his feet, and waited for silence amid the babble of voices.

¶5 "It is true that meat be **apportioned** me and mine," he said. "But it is <u>oft</u> times old and tough, this meat, and, moreover, it has an unusual quantity of bones."

The hunters, grizzled and gray, and lusty and young, were <u>aghast</u>. The like had never been known before. A child, that talked like a grown man, and said harsh things to their very faces!

¶7 But steadily and with seriousness, Keesh went on. "For that I know my father, Bok, was a great hunter, I speak these words. It is said that Bok brought home more meat than any of the two best hunters, that with his own hands he attended to the division of it, that with his own eyes he saw to it that the least old woman and the last old man received fair share."

"Na! Na!" the men cried. "Put the child out!" "Send him off to bed!"
"He is no man that he should talk to men and graybeards!"

¶9 He waited calmly till the uproar died down.

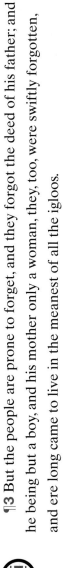

Words and Phrases in Context

3. What is the meaning of *meanest* in **paragraph 3**? Why did the author choose this word to describe Keesh and his mother's igloo?

Literary Analysis

4. What details reveal Keesh as strong, brave, and mature at the council? Explain how he displays these character traits.

Character

A character is someone depicted in narrative or drama. Authors reveal character traits through description, action, and dialogue.

Academic Vocabulary

5. What is Keesh's complaint about the meat that is apportioned to him and his mother?

Literary Analysis

6. Make an inference about the purpose of the council. Who do you think usually speaks there?

Words to Know

<u>oft</u>: *(adj.)* literary form of *often*

aghast: *(adj)* filled with horror, shocked

"Thou hast a wife, Ugh-Gluk," he said, "and for her dost thou speak. And thou, too, Massuk, a mother also, and for them dost thou speak. My mother has no one, save me; wherefore I speak. As I say, though Bok be dead because he hunted over-keenly, it is just that I, who am his son, and that Ikeega, who is my mother and was his wife, should have meat in plenty so long as there be meat in plenty in the tribe. I, Keesh, the son of Bok, have spoken." He sat down, his ears keenly alert to the flood of protest and indignation his words had created.

¶11 "That a boy should speak in council!" old Ugh-Gluk was mumbling.

"Shall the babes in arms tell us men the things we shall do?" Massuk demanded in a loud voice. "Am I a man that I should be made a _mock_ by every child that cries for meat?"

¶13 The anger boiled a white heat. They ordered him to bed, threatened that he should have no meat at all, and promised him sore beatings for his presumption. Keesh's eyes began to flash, and the blood to pound darkly under his skin. In the midst of the abuse he sprang to his feet.

Words to Know

<u>mock</u>: (n.) a joke; the subject of teasing or criticism

<u>presumption</u>: (n.) the act of doing something without the right or permission to do it

Close Reading

7. Why does Keesh feel that he and his mother should have "meat in plenty"?

Words and Phrases in Context

8. What does it mean that Keesh's father hunted "over-keenly"?

Writing

9. Describe the conflict between Keesh and the elders.

At the council, Keesh ____.

The elders become angry because ____.

Keesh, too, becomes angry when ____.

Conflict

The central problem a character struggles with in a narrative.

An **external conflict** is a struggle between the main character and other people or outside forces, such as a natural disaster.

An **internal conflict** is a struggle within the main character's own mind.

"Hear me, ye men!" he cried. "Never shall I speak in the council again, never again till the men come to me and say, 'It is well, Keesh, that thou shouldst speak, it is well and it is our wish.' Take this now, ye men, for my last word. Bok, my father, was a great hunter. I, too, his son, shall go and hunt the meat that I eat. And be it known, now, that the division of that which I kill shall be fair. And no widow nor weak one shall cry in the night because there is no meat, when the strong men are groaning in great pain for that they have eaten overmuch. And in the days to come there shall be shame upon the strong men who have eaten overmuch. I, Keesh, have said it!"

¶15 Jeers and scornful laughter followed him out of the igloo, but his jaw was set and he went his way, looking neither to right nor left.

The next day he went forth along the shoreline where the ice and the land met together. Those who saw him go noted that he carried his bow, with a goodly supply of bone-barbed arrows, and that across his shoulder was his father's big hunting-spear. And there was laughter, and much talk, at the event. It was an *unprecedented* occurrence. Never did boys of his tender age go forth to hunt, much less to hunt alone. Also were there shaking of heads and **prophetic** mutterings, and the women looked pityingly at Ikeega, and her face was grave and sad.

Words to Know

unprecedented: *(adj.)* never done before

Close Reading

Writing

10. How does Keesh respond after the elders scold him and threaten him? What does his reaction reveal about his character?

Keesh leaves the council determined to _____ and to _____.

His plans show that _____ and also that he wants to _____.

Words and Phrases in Context

11. What does *tender* mean in **paragraph 16?** Identify context clues that make its meaning clear.

Literary Analysis

12. Why does Ikeega look "grave and sad"?

¶17 "He will be back ere long," they said cheeringly.

"Let him go; it will teach him a lesson," the hunters said. "And he will come back shortly, and he will be meek and soft of speech in the days to follow."

¶19 But a day passed, and a second, and on the third a wild gale blew, and there was no Keesh. Ikeega tore her hair and put soot of the seal-oil on her face in token of her grief; and the women **assailed** the men with bitter words in that they had mistreated the boy and sent him to his death; and the men made no answer, preparing to go in search of the body when the storm **abated**.

Early next morning, however, Keesh strode into the village. But he came not shamefacedly. Across his shoulders he bore a burden of fresh-killed meat. And there was importance in his step and arrogance in his speech.

¶21 "Go, ye men, with the dogs and sledges, and take my trail for the better part of a day's travel," he said. "There is much meat on the ice—a she-bear and two half-grown cubs."

Words to Know

in token: as a sign or symbol of

arrogance: (n.) an exaggerated sense of one's importance

Close Reading

Academic Vocabulary

13. Identify the "prophetic mutterings" the author references in **paragraph 16.** Are they likely to come true? Explain.

Literary Analysis

14. Why do the men make "no answer" when the women assail them?

Text Structure

15. How does Keesh's successful hunting trip contribute to the rising action of the story's narrative?

Rising Action

A series of events that builds up to the climax, or main confrontation, in a story.

Close Reading

Ikeega was overcome with joy, but he received her demonstrations in manlike fashion, saying: "Come, Ikeega, let us eat. And after that I shall sleep, for I am weary."

¶23 And he passed into their igloo and ate profoundly, and after that slept for twenty running hours. There was much doubt and discussion. The killing of a polar bear is very dangerous, but thrice dangerous is it, and three times thrice, to kill a mother bear with her cubs. The men could not bring themselves to believe that the boy Keesh, single-handed, had accomplished so great a marvel. But the women spoke of the fresh-killed meat he had brought on his back, and this was an overwhelming argument against their unbelief. So they finally departed, grumbling greatly that in all probability, if the thing were so, he had neglected to cut up the <u>carcasses</u>. Now in the north it is very necessary that this should be done as soon as a kill is made. If not, the meat freezes so solidly as to turn the edge of the sharpest knife, and a three-hundred-pound bear, frozen stiff, is no easy thing to put upon a sled and haul over the rough ice. But arrived at the spot, they found not only the kill, which they had doubted, but that Keesh had quartered the beasts in true hunter fashion, and removed the <u>entrails</u>.

Thus began the mystery of Keesh, a mystery that deepened and deepened with the passing of the days. His very next trip he killed a young bear, nearly full-grown, and on the trip following, a large male bear and his mate. He was ordinarily gone from three to four days, though it was nothing unusual for him to stay away a week at a time on the icefield.

Literary Analysis

16. What details show that Keesh is a good hunter? Why do you think the men find that so hard to believe and keep "grumbling greatly" about mistakes they are sure he has made?

Words and Phrase in Context

17. How can a carcass "turn the edge of the sharpest knife"?

Text Structure

18. What is the "mystery of Keesh" in **paragraph 24**? What function does this paragraph serve in the story's narrative?

Words to Know

<u>carcasses:</u> *(n.)* the dead bodies of animals

<u>entrails:</u> *(n.)* the exposed internal organs of an animal, guts

¶25 Always he declined company on these expeditions, and the people marveled. "How does he do it?" they demanded of one another.

"Never does he take a dog with him, and dogs are of such great help, too."

¶27 "Why dost thou hunt only bear?" Klosh-Kwan once ventured to ask him.

And Keesh made fitting answer: "It is well known that there is more meat on the bear," he said.

¶29 But there was also talk of witchcraft in the village. "He hunts with evil spirits," some of the people **contended**, "wherefore his hunting is rewarded. How else can it be, save that he hunts with evil spirits?"

"Mayhap, they be not evil, but good, these spirits," others said. "It is known that his father was a mighty hunter. May not his father hunt with him so that he may attain excellence and patience and understanding? Who knows?"

¶31 Nonetheless, his success continued, and the less skillful hunters were often kept busy hauling in his meat. And in the division of it he was just. As his father had done before him, he saw to it that the least old woman and the last old man received a fair portion, keeping no more for himself than his needs required. And because of this, and of his merit as a hunter, he was looked upon with respect, and even awe; and there was talk of making him chief after old Klosh-Kwan

---

Words to Know

declined: (v.) turned down
merit: (n.) value; worthiness

Close Reading

Literary Analysis

19. How do Keesh's actions add to the air of mystery around him and his hunting trips?

Academic Vocabulary

20. How might some people's **contentions** make trouble for Keesh?

Words and Phrases in Context

21. How is *least* used in **paragraph 31**? Why does Keesh give even "the least old woman" a fair share?

Writing

22. Describe how opinions of Keesh have changed throughout the story.

At first, people in the village _____.
After Keesh spoke in council, _____.
Now, some people _____, while others _____.

Because of the things he had done, they looked for him to appear again in the council, but he never came, and they were ashamed to ask.

¶33 "I am minded to build me an *igloo*," he said one day to Klosh-Kwan and a number of the hunters. "It shall be a large *igloo*, wherein Ikeega and I can dwell in comfort."

"Ay," they nodded gravely.

¶35 "But I have no time. My business is hunting, and it takes all my time. So it is but just that the men and women of the village who eat my meat should build me my *igloo*."

And the *igloo* was built accordingly, on a generous scale which <u>exceeded</u> even the dwelling of Klosh-Kwan. Keesh and his mother moved into it, and it was the first <u>prosperity</u> she had enjoyed since the death of Bok. Nor was material prosperity alone hers, for, because of her wonderful son and the position he had given her, she came to be looked upon as the first woman in all the village; and the women were given to visiting her, to asking her advice, and to quoting her wisdom when arguments arose among themselves or with the men.

¶37 But it was the mystery of Keesh's marvelous hunting that took chief place in all their minds. And one day Ugh-Gluk <u>taxed</u> him with witchcraft to his face.

"It is charged," Ugh-Gluk said ominously, "that thou dealest with evil spirits, wherefore thy hunting is rewarded."

¶39 "Is not the meat good?" Keesh made answer. "Has one in the village yet to fall sick from the eating of it? How dost thou know that witchcraft be concerned? Or dost thou guess, in the dark, merely because of the envy that consumes thee?"

Words to Know

<u>exceeded</u>: (v.) went beyond

<u>prosperity</u>: (n.) wealth; success

<u>taxed</u>: (v.) confronted

Close Reading

Text Structure
23. Why doesn't Keesh go to the council? How does a detail from an earlier part of the story explain this?

Words and Phrases in Context
24. How is *just* used in **paragraph 35**? Why does Keesh think it just that others should build him an igloo?

Literary Analysis
25. How has Keesh's success as a hunter affected his mother?

Text Structure
26. Why does Keesh answer the charge of witchcraft with a series of questions? What does he mean by his final question?

And Ugh-Gluk withdrew **disconfited**, the women laughing at him as he walked away. But in the council one night, after long deliberation, it was determined to put spies on his track when he went forth to hunt, so that his methods might be learned. So, on his next trip, Bim and Bawn, two young men, and of hunters the craftiest, followed after him, taking care not to be seen. After five days they returned, their eyes bulging and their tongues a-tremble to tell what they had seen. The council was hastily called in Klosh-Kwan's dwelling, and Bim took up the tale.

¶41 "Brothers! As commanded, we journeyed on the trail of Keesh, and cunningly we journeyed, so that he might not know. And midway of the first day he picked up with a great he-bear. It was a very great bear."

"None greater," Bawn **corroborated**, and went on himself. "Yet was the bear not inclined to fight, for he turned away and made off slowly over the ice. This we saw from the rocks of the shore, and the bear came toward us, and after him came Keesh, very much unafraid. And he shouted harsh words after the bear, and waved his arms about, and made much noise. Then did the bear grow angry, and rise up on his hind legs, and growl. But Keesh walked right up to the bear."

Words to Know

hastily: (adv.) on short notice, hurriedly
cunningly: (adv.) resourcefully, with skill

Close Reading

Literary Analysis

27. How do Bim and Bawn feel about what they saw? Identify details that reveal their feelings.

Academic Vocabulary

28. What does Bawn corroborate?

Writing

29. What led Bim and Bawn to believe that Keesh was "very much unafraid" of the "very great bear"?

Bim and Bawn knew Keesh was unafraid because he shouted ____

and ____.

Keesh also showed that he was unafraid when he ____.

Close Reading

Literary Analysis

30. How does **paragraph 43** explain why Keesh deliberately angered the bear?

Literary Analysis

31. Describe the effect of the little balls on the bear.

Text Structure

32. How does the author build suspense as Bim and Bawn relate the story of Keesh's hunting techniques? Why does he describe the technique the way Bim and Bawn see it?

¶43 "Ay," Bim continued the story. "Right up to the bear Keesh walked. And the bear took after him, and Keesh ran away. But as he ran he dropped a little round ball on the ice. And the bear stopped and smelled of it, then swallowed it up. And Keesh continued to run away and drop little round balls, and the bear continued to swallow them up."

Exclamations and cries of doubt were being made, and Ugh-Gluk expressed open unbelief.

¶45 "With our own eyes we saw it," Bim <u>affirmed</u>.

And Bawn – "Ay, with our own eyes. And this continued until the bear stood suddenly upright and cried aloud in pain, and thrashed his fore paws madly about. And Keesh continued to make off over the ice to a safe distance. But the bear gave him no notice, being occupied with the misfortune the little round balls had <u>wrought</u> within him."

¶47 "Ay, within him," Bim interrupted. "For he did claw at himself, and leap about over the ice like a playful puppy, save from the way he growled and squealed it was plain it was not play but pain. Never did I see such a sight!"

"Nay, never was such a sight seen," Bawn took up the strain. "And furthermore, it was such a large bear."

¶49 "Witchcraft," Ugh-Gluk suggested.

Words to Know

<u>affirmed</u>: (v.) agreed
<u>wrought</u>: (v.) caused

Close Reading

"I know not," Bawn replied. "I tell only of what my eyes beheld. And after a while the bear grew weak and tired, for he was very heavy and he had jumped about with exceeding violence, and he went off along the shore-ice, shaking his head slowly from side to side and sitting down ever and again to squeal and cry. And Keesh followed after the bear, and we followed after Keesh, and for that day and three days more we followed. The bear grew weak, and never ceased crying from his pain."

¶51 "It was a charm!" Ugh-Gluk exclaimed. "Surely it was a charm!"

"It may well be."

¶53 And Bim relieved Bawn. "The bear wandered, now this way and now that, doubling back and forth and crossing his trail in circles, so that at the end he was near where Keesh had first come upon him. By this time he was quite sick, the bear, and could crawl no farther, so Keesh came up close and speared him to death."

"And then?" Klosh-Kwan demanded.

¶55 "Then we left Keesh skinning the bear, and came running that the news of the killing might be told."

And in the afternoon of that day the women hauled in the meat of the bear while the men sat in council assembled. When Keesh arrived a messenger was sent to him, bidding him come to the council. But he sent reply, saying that he was hungry and tired; also that his *igloo* was large and comfortable and could hold many men.

Words to Know

<u>relieved:</u> *(v.)* took the place of

<u>bidding:</u> *(v.)* asking

Writing

33. Was Bim and Bawn's spy mission a success? Explain.

Bim and Bawn successfully

followed _____ and _____.

However, Bim and Bawn were not

able to _____.

Bim and Bawn did not solve _____.

Literary Analysis

34. Why do the men finally ask Keesh to come to council?

Literary Analysis

35. In the last sentence of **paragraph 56**, why does Keesh point out that "his igloo was large and comfortable and could hold many men"? What message does he want to convey to the people of the village?

Close Reading

¶57 And curiosity was so strong on the men that the whole council, Klosh-Kwan to the fore, rose up and went to the *igloo* of Keesh. He was eating, but he received them with respect and seated them according to their rank. Ikeega was proud and embarrassed by turns, but Keesh was quite **composed**.

Klosh-Kwan recited the information brought by Bim and Bawn, and at its close said in a stern voice: "So explanation is wanted, O Keesh, of thy manner of hunting. Is there witchcraft in it?"

¶59 Keesh looked up and smiled. "Nay, O Klosh-Kwan. It is not for a boy to know aught of witches, and of witches I know nothing. I have but **devised** a means whereby I may kill the ice-bear with ease, that is all. It be headcraft, not witchcraft."

"And may any man?"

¶61 "Any man."

There was a long silence. The men looked in one another's faces, and Keesh went on eating.

¶63 And . . . and . . . and wilt thou tell us, O Keesh?" Klosh-Kwan finally asked in a tremulous voice.

"Yea, I will tell thee." Keesh finished sucking a marrow-bone and rose to his feet. "It is quite simple. Behold!"

Literary Analysis

36. Why does Ikeega feel "proud and embarrassed by turns"?

Literary Analysis

37. Why does Klosh-Kwan speak to Keesh "in a stern voice"? Why does Keesh smile in return?

Words and Phrases in Context

38. What does Keesh mean by "headcraft, not witchcraft"? What is *headcraft*?

Text Structure

39. What is the function of the word *tremulous* in **paragraph 63**? How would the meaning of the sentence change if *tremulous* were replaced with *sarcastic* or with *nonchalant*?

Words to Know

<u>tremulous:</u> *(adj)* timid; nervous; shaky with fear of nervousness

<u>composed:</u> *(adj.)* feeling in control

Close Reading

Text Structure

40. What is the climax of this story's narrative?

Climax

The most exciting or important part of a story, which usually comes near the end.

Literary Analysis

41. How does the ball of blubber make the bear get sick?

Writing

42. Describe the resolution of this story.

Resolution

The outcome of, or solution to, the central conflict, that brings the story to an end.

After Keesh reveals the secret of his hunting technique, everyone _____ and Keesh's "headcraft" leads him to _____ .

¶65 He picked up a thin strip of whalebone and showed it to them. The ends were sharp as needlepoints. The strip he coiled carefully, till it disappeared in his hand. Then, suddenly releasing it, it sprang straight again. He picked up a piece of blubber. "So," he said, "one takes a small chunk of blubber, thus, and thus makes it hollow. Then into the hollow goes the whalebone, so, tightly coiled, and another piece of blubber is fitted over the whalebone. After that it is put outside where it freezes into a little round ball. The bear swallows the little round ball, the blubber melts, the whalebone with its sharp ends stands out straight, the bear gets sick, and when the bear is very sick, why, you kill him with a spear. It is quite simple."

And Ugh-Gluk said "Oh!" and Klosh-Kwan said "Ah!" And each said something after his own manner, and all understood.

¶67 And this is the story of Keesh, who lived long ago on the rim of the polar sea. Because he exercised headcraft and not witchcraft, he rose from the meanest *igloo* to be head man of his village, and through all the years that he lived, it is related, his tribe was prosperous, and neither widow nor weak one cried aloud in the night because there was no meat.

Words to Know

blubber: (*n.*) fat under the skin of a whale, seal or polar animal

Identify Evidence | Analyze Individuals, Events, and Ideas

Reread "The Story of Keesh," highlighting examples and events that London uses to describe life in an extreme Arctic environment and show how it shapes the villagers' way of life.

- In the Evidence column, record details from the text that describes the environment and way the villagers live and survive there.
- In the Explanation column, explain how the evidence introduces, illustrates, or elaborates on individuals, events, and ideas.

	Evidence	Source	Page	Explanation
1.	"when the north gales make their long sweep across the icepack, and the air is filled with flying white, and no man may venture forth.... For each winter the sun leaves the land in darkness"	London	61	The author describes the harsh Arctic winter, so extreme that people cannot even go outside.
2.	"The father of Keesh had been a very brave man, but he had met his death in a time of famine, when he sought to save the lives of his people by taking the life of a great polar bear. In his eagerness he came to close grapples with the bear, and his bones were crushed; but the bear had much meat on him and the people were saved."			Hunting is a dangerous job, but the people of Keesh's village rely on hunters to provide them with food. Without successful hunters, the people would starve.
3.				
4.				

	Evidence	Source	Page	Explanation
5.				
6.				
7.				

Key Ideas and Details

Determining the Central Idea

1. Use the evidence you collected to summarize the key idea of London's short story.

2. List three key individuals that London introduces in this story. Explain why each individual is important to the central idea.

Individuals	Significance

3. List three key events. Explain why each event is important to the central idea.

Events	Significance

Craft and Structure

Structure of a Short Story

1. How does the conflict between Keesh and the village leaders begin?

2. Make a list, in sequential order, of events that develop the conflict.

3. Describe the story's climax. How is the conflict resolved?

Setting

4. Describe the setting of this story. How is it important to the plot?

Narrator's Point of View

5. Identify point of view in this story. Describe what the narrator knows and sees.

Point of View is the lens through which a story is told.

A **first-person narrator** is a character in the story. He or she refers to himself or herself with first-person pronouns: *I, me, my, mine.*

A **third-person narrator** is outside the story.

Third-person omniscient narrators know and see all. They can describe and analyze what every character sees, does, thinks, and feels.

Third-person limited narrators know and see only what one character (usually the main character) knows and sees.

Academic Vocabulary

from *Life of Pi* by Yann Martel

Rate your understanding of each Target Word. Then write either its meaning or a sample sentence.

Word	Meaning	Example
deliberation (n.) p. 80 ① ② ③ ④	the act of considering something carefully before deciding	
agitated (adj.) p. 80 ① ② ③ ④	troubled or nervous	
reprieve (n.) p. 83 ① ② ③ ④	the temporary delay of a punishment or unwanted event	
passivity (n.) p. 83 ① ② ③ ④	lack of resistance or reaction to	
exceptional (adj.) p. 89 ① ② ③ ④		Only an exceptional problem would cause the shop owner to close the shop early.
restrict (v.) p. 91 ① ② ③ ④	limit	

Rating Scale | ① I don't know the word.   ② I've seen it or heard it.
③ I know its meaning.   ④ I know it and use it.

Word Study

Base Words and Suffixes

A **base word** is a word to which prefixes, suffixes, and endings may be added.

A **suffix** is a letter or letters added to the end of a base word to form a new word, such as -*ful* in *careful* or -*ment* in *excitement*.

You can use these word parts to determine the meaning of a word.

The base word *deliberate* means "consider carefully before making a decision."

The suffix -*ion* means "the act, state, or quality of."

Therefore, *deliberation* means "the act of considering something carefully before deciding."

Identify the base word and suffix in each word below.

1. reaction
2. wasteful
3. enjoyment
4. creation
5. resentment
6. harmful

Close Reading

from Life of Pi

by Yann Martel

¶1 I was alone and orphaned, in the middle of the Pacific, hanging on to an oar, an adult tiger in front of me, sharks beneath me, a storm raging about me. Had I considered my <u>prospects</u> in the light of reason, I surely would have given up and let go of the oar, hoping that I might drown before being eaten. But I don't recall that I had a single thought during those first minutes of relative safety. I didn't even notice daybreak. I held onto the oar, I just held on, God only knows why.

The <u>elements</u> allowed me to go on living. The lifeboat did not sink. Richard Parker kept out of sight. The sharks prowled but did not lunge. The waves splashed me but did not pull me off.

¶3 I watched the ship as it disappeared with much burbling and belching. Lights flickered and went out. I looked about for my family, for survivors, for another lifeboat, for anything that might bring me hope. There was nothing. Only rain, <u>marauding</u> waves of black ocean and the flotsam of tragedy.

The darkness melted away from the sky. The rain stopped.

¶5 I could not stay in the position I was in forever. I was cold. My neck was sore from holding up my head and from all the craning I had been doing. My back hurt from leaning against the lifebuoy. And I needed to be higher up if I were to see other lifeboats.

Words to Know

<u>prospects</u>: (*n.*) chances; opportunities

<u>elements</u>: (*n.*) the forces of weather: wind, rain, etc.

<u>marauding</u>: (*adj.*) attacking; invading

Text Structure

1. Identify the narrator's point of view.

Writing

2. Describe the setting of this story.

   As the excerpt begins, the narrator
   is in _____ in _____ during a _____.
   A _____ is in front _____ and sharks _____.
   The setting is so _____ that he thinks
   maybe he should have _____.

Literary Analysis

3. How did Pi, the narrator, become stranded in the ocean?

In the morning I could not move. I was pinned by weakness to the <u>tarpaulin</u>. Even thinking was exhausting. I applied myself to thinking straight. At length, as slowly as a caravan of camels crossing a desert, some thoughts came together....

¶7 I thought of <u>sustenance</u> for the first time. I had not had a drop to drink or a bite to eat or a minute of sleep in three days. Finding this obvious explanation for my weakness brought me a little strength.

Richard Parker was still on board. In fact, he was directly beneath me. Incredible that such a thing should need consent to be true, but it was only after much **deliberation**, upon assessing various mental items and points of view, that I concluded that it was not a dream or a delusion or a misplaced memory or a fancy or any other such falsity, but a solid, true thing witnessed while in a weakened, highly **agitated** state. The truth of it would be confirmed as soon as I felt well enough to investigate.

¶9 How I had failed to notice for two and a half days a 450-pound Bengal tiger in a lifeboat twenty-six feet long was a conundrum I would have to try to crack later, when I had more energy. The feat surely made Richard Parker the largest stowaway, proportionally speaking, in the history of navigation. From tip of nose to tip of tail he took up over a third of the length of the ship he was on.

You might think I lost all hope at that point. I did. And as a result I perked up and felt much better. We see that in sports all the time, don't we? The tennis challenger starts strong but soon loses confidence in his playing. The champion racks up the games. But in the final set, when the challenger has nothing left to lose, he becomes relaxed again, <u>insouciant</u>, daring. Suddenly he's playing like the devil and the champion must work hard to get those last points. So it was with me. To cope with a hyena

---

Words to Know

<u>tarpaulin:</u> *(n.)* heavy-duty waterproof material

<u>sustenance:</u> *(n.)* food and drink; nourishment

<u>insouciant:</u> *(adj.)* having casual lack of concern; being indifferent

---

Close Reading

Words and Phrases in Context

4. What does *sustenance* mean? Find details that help you determine its meaning.

Academic Vocabulary

5. Who is Richard Parker? Why does it require deliberation to decide whether he is a "true thing" and "not a dream or delusion"?

Literary Analysis

6. How is Pi's reaction to losing "all hope" in **paragraph 10** an example of irony?

Irony

Irony is a conflict between what is expected and what actually happens.

seemed remotely possible, but I was so obviously outmatched by Richard Parker that it wasn't even worth worrying about. With a tiger aboard, my life was over. That being settled, why not do something about my parched throat?

¶11 I believe it was this that saved my life that morning, that I was quite literally dying of thirst. Now that the word had popped into my head I couldn't think of anything else, as if the word itself were salty and the more I thought of it, the worse the effect. I have heard that the hunger for air exceeds as a compelling sensation the thirst for water. Only after a few minutes, I say. After a few minutes you die and the discomfort of asphyxiation goes away. ...It was enough to make me go raving mad. I have never known a worse physical hell than this putrid taste and pasty feeling in the mouth, this unbearable pressure at the back of the throat, this sensation that my blood was turning to a thick syrup that barely flowed. Truly, by comparison, a tiger was nothing.

And so I pushed aside all thoughts of Richard Parker and fearlessly went exploring for fresh water.

¶13 The divining rod in my mind dipped sharply and a spring gushed water when I remembered that I was on a genuine, regulation lifeboat and that such a lifeboat was surely outfitted with supplies. That seemed like a perfectly reasonable proposition. What captain would fail in so elementary a way to ensure the safety of his crew? What ship chandler would not thinking of making a little extra money under the noble guise of saving lives? It was settled. There was water aboard. All I had to do was find it.

Which meant I had to move.

Words to Know

<u>parched</u>: (*adj.*) dried out because of intense heat

<u>compelling</u>: (*adj.*) overwhelming

<u>divining rod</u>: (*n.*) a tool used to find underground water sources. It dips down when held above water.

<u>ship chandler</u>: (*n.*) the person who gets the supplies and equipment a ship needs

<u>plausible</u>: (*adj.*) possible; reasonable

Close Reading

Writing

7. How is Pi like the tennis challenger he describes in **paragraph 10**? What does he use this analogy to clarify? Complete the chart to help you analyze Pi's use of an analogy.

Analogy

An analogy is a comparison between two things or ideas. By pointing out how they are similar, the writer hopes to clarify the more complicated or less familiar thing.

Words and Phrases in Context

8. What is *asphyxiation*? Why does Pi say thirst is worse?

Text Structure

9. What is the effect of making the last sentence on the page a paragraph by itself? Explain why Pi is so sure that if he moves, he will find water.

It was three and a half feet deep, eight feet wide and twenty-six feet long, exactly. I know because it was printed on one side of the benches in black letters. It also said that the lifeboat was designed to accommodate a maximum of thirty-two people. Wouldn't that have been merry, sharing it with so many? Instead we were three and it was awfully crowded. …

¶23 It seems orange—such a nice Hindu color—is the color of survival because the whole inside of the boat and the tarpaulin and the life jackets and the lifebuoy and the oars and most every other significant object aboard was orange. Even the plastic, beadless whistles were orange.

The words *Tsimtsum* and *Panama* were printed on each side of the bow in stark, black, roman capitals. …

¶25 I did not grasp all these details—and many more—right away. They came to my notice with time and as a result of necessity. I would be in the direst of dire straits, facing a bleak future, when some small thing, some detail, would transform itself and appear in my mind in a new light. It would no longer be the small thing it was before, but the most important thing in the world, the thing that would save my life. This happened time and again. How true it is that necessity is the mother of invention, how very true.

But that first time I had a good look at the lifeboat I did not see the detail I wanted. The surface of the stern and the sides of the benches was continuous and unbroken, as were the sides of the buoyancy tanks. The floor lay flat against the hull; there could be no cache beneath it. It was certain: there was no locker or box or any other sort of container anywhere. Only smooth, uninterrupted orange surfaces.

Words to Know

Tsimtsum and *Panama:* the name of the ship that sank and the country where it was built

transform: (v.) change

buoyancy tanks: tanks of air used to help the boat stay buoyant, or floating

Close Reading

Literary Analysis

16. Reread the last sentence of **paragraph 22.** Why does Pi say that the lifeboat is "awfully crowded" when it can hold up to 32 people?

Words and Phrases in Context

17. How is it ironic that Pi calls orange the "color of survival"?

Writing

18. Analyze the saying "necessity is the mother of invention." What does it mean? How does it relate to the experiences Pi describes in **paragraph 25?**

This saying means if you _____, you will _____. For Pi, it means that to survive _____, he tells himself that _____.

Literary Analysis

19. What is the detail Pi wanted but did not find in the first sentence of **paragraph 26**? Why did he want it?

¶27 My estimation of captains and ship chandlers wavered. My hopes for survival flickered. My thirst remained.

And what if the supplies were at the <u>bow</u>, beneath the tarpaulin? I turned and crawled back. I felt like a dried-out lizard. I pushed down on the tarpaulin. It was <u>tautly</u> stretched. If I unrolled it, I would give myself access to what supplies might be stored below. But that meant creating an opening onto Richard Parker's den.

¶29 There was no question. Thirst pushed me on.

I unrolled it a little. Immediately I was rewarded. The bow was like the <u>stern</u>; it had an end bench. And upon it, just a few inches from the stern, a hasp glittered like a diamond. There was the outline of a lid. My heart began to pound. I unrolled the tarpaulin further. I peeked under. The lid was shaped like a rounded-out triangle, three feet wide and two feet deep. At that moment I perceived an orange mass. I jerked my head back. But the orange wasn't moving and didn't look right. I looked again. It wasn't a tiger. It was a life jacket. There were a number of life jackets at the back of Richard Parker's den.

Close Reading

Literary Analysis

20. Why does Pi say that his "estimation of captains and ship chandlers wavered"?

Text Structure

21. What does Pi mean when he says "there was no question" in **paragraph 29**? What does this reveal about his priorities?

Literary Analysis

22. Why did Pi jerk his head back when he "perceived an orange mass"?

Close Reading

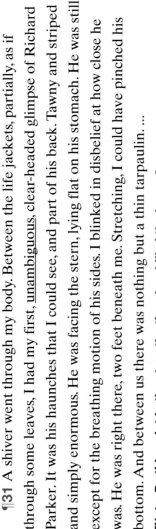

Literary Analysis

23. What does Pi mean when he says his supplication—"God preserve me"—was "gently carried by the breath"? Why was it "passionate yet more gently carried"?

Words and Phrases in Context

24. What is Pi's "moment of material revelation"? Use context clues to help you determine what Pi means.

Literary Analysis

25. Describe Pi's reaction to finding the locker full of water and other goods.

¶31 A shiver went through my body. Between the life jackets, partially, as if through some leaves, I had my first, <u>unambiguous</u>, clear-headed glimpse of Richard Parker. It was his haunches that I could see, and part of his back. Tawny and striped and simply enormous. He was facing the stern, lying flat on his stomach. He was still except for the breathing motion of his sides. I blinked in disbelief at how close he was. He was right there, two feet beneath me. Stretching, I could have pinched his bottom. And between us there was nothing but a thin tarpaulin. …

[Note: By this point in the story the tiger has killed the hyena.]

"God preserve me!" No <u>supplication</u> was ever more passionate yet more gently carried by the breath. I lay absolutely motionless.

¶33 I had to have water. I brought my hand down and quietly undid the hasp. I pulled on the lid. It opened onto a locker. …

I looked down between my legs. I thought I would faint for joy. The open locker glistened with shiny new things. Oh, the delight of the manufactured good, the man-made device, the created thing! That moment of material revelation brought an intensity of pleasure—a heady mix of hope, surprise, disbelief, thrill, gratitude, all crushed into one—unequalled in my life by any Christmas, birthday, wedding, Diwali or other gift-giving occasion. I was positively giddy with happiness.

¶35 My eyes immediately fell upon what I was looking for. Whether in a bottle, a tin can or a carton, water is unmistakably packaged. On this lifeboat, the wine of life was served in pale golden cans that fit nicely in the hand. Drinking Water said the vintage label in black letters. HP Foods Ltd. were the vintners. 500 ml were the contents. There were stacks of these cans, too many to count at a glance.

Words to Know

<u>unambiguous:</u> *(adj.)* not open to other interpretations

<u>supplication:</u> *(n.)* the act of asking or begging in a humble, earnest manner.

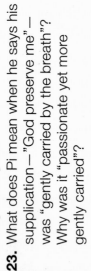

With a shaking hand I reached down and picked one up. It was cool to the touch and heavy. I shook it. The bubble of air inside made a dull *glub glub glub* sound. I was about to be delivered from my hellish thirst. My pulse raced at the thought. I only had to open the can.

¶37 I paused. How would I do that?

I had a can—surely I had a can opener? I looked in the locker. There was a great quantity of things. I rummaged about. I was losing patience. Aching expectations had run its fruitful course. I had to drink *now*—or I would die. I could not find the desired instrument. But there was no time for useless distress. Action was needed. Could I prise it open with my fingernails? I tried. I couldn't. My teeth? It wasn't worth trying. I looked over the gunnel. The tarpaulin hooks. Short, blunt, solid. I kneeled on the bench and leaned over. Holding the can with both my hands, I sharply brought it up against a hook. A good dint. I did it again. Another dint next to the first. By dint of dinting, I managed the trick. A pearl of water appeared. I licked it off. I turned the can and banged the opposite side of the top against the hook to make another hole. I worked like a fiend. I made a larger hole. I sat back on the gunnel. I held the can up to my face. I opened my mouth. I tilted the can.

Words to Know

gunnel: (*n.*) also gunwale; the upper edge of the side of a boat

dint: (*n.*) a dent or hollow in the surface of something

by dint of: through hard work

Close Reading

Text Structure

26. What does Pi realize in **paragraph 37**? How does the author indicate that Pi's thoughts here are important?

Text Structure

27. In **paragraph 38**, why does the author use the words "short, blunt, solid" to form an incomplete sentence.

Writing

28. How do Pi's actions in **paragraph 38** illustrate the saying "necessity is the mother of invention"? **(page 84, paragraph 25)** What do Pi's actions reveal about his character?

In this paragraph, Pi uses a _____ to _____.

His actions illustrate the saying in that Pi needs _____, so he invents _____.

These actions show that Pi is _____.

Close Reading

¶39 My feelings can perhaps be imagined, but they can hardly be described. To the gurgling beat of my greedy throat, pure, delicious, beautiful, crystalline water flowed into my system. Liquid life, it was. I drained that golden cup to the very last drop, sucking at the hole to catch any remaining moisture. I went, "Ahhhhhh!," tossed the can overboard and got another one. I opened it the way I had the first and its contents vanished just as quickly. That can sailed overboard too, and I opened the next one. Which, shortly, also ended up in the ocean. Another can was <u>dispatched</u>. I drank four cans, two liters of that most exquisite of nectars, before I stopped. You might think such a rapid intake of water after prolonged thirst might upset my system. Nonsense! I never felt better in my life. Why, feel my brow! My forehead was wet with fresh, clean, refreshing perspiration. Everything in me, right down to the pores of my skin, was expressing joy.

A sense of well-being quickly overcame me. My mouth became moist and soft. I forgot about the back of my throat. My skin relaxed. My joints moved with greater ease. My heart began to beat like a merry drum and blood started flowing through my veins like cars from a wedding party honking their way through town. Strength and suppleness came back to my muscles. My head became clearer. Truly, I was coming back to life from the dead. It was glorious, it was glorious. I tell you, to be drunk on alcohol is disgraceful, but to be drunk on water is noble and ecstatic. I basked in bliss and <u>plentitude</u> for several minutes.

Words and Phrases in Context

29. What is the "liquid life" Pi speaks of? Why does the author use this metaphor?

Metaphor

A **metaphor** is a figure of speech that compares two unlike things by stating that one *is* (or is *like*) the other.

Writing

30. Analyze the simile Pi uses to describe his blood. What effect does the author create with this simile?

Pi says his blood was flowing like ____. The simile conveys how badly Pi needed ____ and how ____ after drinking it.

Words to Know

dispatched: *(adj.)* dealt with quickly and efficiently

plentitude: *(n.)* the condition of being full or complete

¶41 A certain emptiness made itself felt. I touched my belly. It was a hard and hollow cavity. Food would be nice now. A masala dosai with a coconut chutney—hmmmmmm! Even better: oothappam! HMMMMM! Oh! I brought my hands to my mouth—IDLI! The mere thought of the word provoked a shot of pain behind my jaws and the deluge of saliva in my mouth. My right hand started twitching. It reached and nearly touched the delicious flattened balls of parboiled rice in my imagination. It sank its fingers into their steaming hot flesh . . . it formed a ball soaked with sauce . . . it brought it to my mouth . . . I chewed . . . Oh, it was exquisitely painful!

I looked into the locker for food. I found cartons of Seven Oceans Standard Emergency Ration, from faraway, exotic Bergen, Norway. The breakfast that was to make up for nine missed meals, not to mention odd tiffins that Mother had brought along, came in a half-kilo block, dense, solid and vacuum-packed in silver-colored plastic that was covered with instructions in twelve languages. In English it said the ration consisted of eighteen fortified biscuits of baked wheat, animal fat, and glucose, and that no more than six should be eaten in a twenty-four-hour period. Pity about the fat, but given the **exceptional** circumstances the vegetarian part of me would simply pinch its nose and bear it.

Words to Know

deluge: (n.) flood

tiffins: (n.) light meals, lunches or snacks

Close Reading

Literary Analysis

31. What is the "emptiness" that "made itself felt"? Why didn't Pi notice it before?

Words and Phrases in Context

32. How does Pi describe the food he finds? What effect does the author create with these descriptive details?

Academic Vocabulary

33. What are the exceptional circumstances that make it okay for Pi to eat animal fat? How do Pi's current circumstances make it ironic that he is normally vegetarian?

¶43 At the top of the block were the words *Tear here to open* and a black arrow pointing to the edge of the plastic. The edge gave way under my fingers. Nine wax-paper-wrapped rectangular bars tumbled out. I unwrapped one. It naturally broke into two. Two nearly square biscuits, pale in color and fragrant in smell. I bit into one. Lord, who would have thought? I never suspected. It was a secret held from me: Norwegian cuisine was the best in the world! These biscuits were amazingly good. They were <u>savory</u> and delicate to the <u>palate</u>, neither too sweet nor too salty. They broke up under the teeth with a delightful crunching sound. Mixed with saliva, they made a granular paste that was enchantment to the tongue and mouth. And when I swallowed, my stomach had only one thing to say: Hallelujah!

The whole package disappeared in a few minutes, wrapping paper flying away in the wind. I considered opening another carton, but I thought better. No harm in exercising a little restraint. Actually, with half a kilo of emergency ration in my stomach, I felt quite heavy.

Close Reading

Literary Analysis

34. Does Pi really mean it when he says that "Norwegian cuisine was the best in the world"? What is the effect of using **hyperbole** to describe the emergency food rations?

Text Structure

35. Why do you think Pi says "the whole package disappeared" instead of "I ate the whole package"? What is the effect of phrasing this information this way?

Hyperbole

Figurative Language: Hyperbole

Exaggerated claims that are not meant to be taken literally.

Words to Know

<u>savory:</u> *(adj.)* salty or spicy, not sweet

<u>palate:</u> *(n.)* one's appreciation of taste and flavor

¶45 I decided I should find out what exactly was in the treasure chest before me. It was large locker, larger than its opening. The space <u>extended</u> right down to the hull and ran some little ways into the side benches. I lowered my feet into the locker and sat on its edge, my back against the stem. I counted the cartons of Seven Ocean. I had eaten one; there were thirty-one left. According to the instructions, each 500-gram carton was supposed to last one survivor three days. That meant I had food rations to last me—31 x 3—93 days! The instructions also suggested survivors **restrict** themselves to half a liter of water every twenty-four hours. I counted the cans of water. There were 124. Each contained half a liter. So I had water rations to last me 124 days. Never had simple arithmetic brought such a smile to my face.

What else did I have? I plunged my arm eagerly into the locker and brought up one marvelous object after another. Each one, no matter what it was, <u>soothed</u> me. I was so sorely in need of company and comfort that the attention brought to making each one of these mass-produced goods felt like a special attention paid to me. I repeatedly mumbled, "Thank you! Thank you! Thank you!"

Words to Know

<u>**extended:**</u> (*v.*) stretched; reached

<u>**soothed:**</u> (*v.*) comforted

Close Reading

Literary Analysis

36. Find a **metaphor** Pi uses to show how important the locker is to him.

Words and Phrases in Context

37. Why does "simple arithmetic" bring a smile to Pi's face in **paragraph 45**? Why does the locker contain so much food and water?

Literary Analysis

38. How do the inanimate objects in the locker give Pi a feeling of having "company and comfort"? What do Pi's thoughts in **paragraph 46** reveal about his ability to survive on the lifeboat?

Close Reading

¶47 … It was Richard Parker who calmed me down. It is the **irony** of this story that the one who scared me witless to start with was the very same who brought me peace, purpose, I dare say even wholeness. …

I had to tame him. It was at that moment that I realized this necessity. It was not a question of him or me, but of him *and* me. We were, literally and figuratively, in the same boat. We would live — or we would die — together. He might be killed in an accident, or he could die shortly of natural causes, but it would be foolish to count on such an eventuality. More likely the worst would happen: the simple passage of time, in which his animal toughness would easily outlast my human <u>frailty</u>. Only if I tamed him could I possibly trick him into dying first, if we had to come to that sorry business.

¶49 But there's more to it. I will come clean. I will tell you a secret: a part of me was glad about Richard Parker. A part of me did not want Richard Parker to die at all, because if he died I would be left alone with <u>despair</u>, a foe even more <u>formidable</u> than a tiger. If I still had the will to live, it was thanks to Richard Parker. He kept me from thinking too much about my family and my tragic circumstances. He pushed me to go on living. I hated him for it, yet at the same time I was grateful. I *am* grateful. It's the plain truth: without Richard Parker, I wouldn't be alive today to tell you my story.

Words and Phrases in Context

39. How are Pi and Richard Parker "literally and figuratively, in the same boat?"

Literary Analysis

40. What does Pi mean when he says that only if he tamed the tiger could he "trick him into dying first"?

Writing

41. Why is Pi "glad" that Richard Parker is on the boat with him? Analyze ways the tiger might have helped Pi stay alive to tell his story.

Pi is "glad about Richard Parker" because _____ . Without the tiger, Pi would have _____ . Instead, Pi _____ .

Words to Know

<u>frailty</u>: (*n.*) condition of being fragile or easily breakable

<u>despair</u>: (*n.*) loss of hope

<u>formidable</u>: (*adj.*) powerful, intense

I looked around at the <u>horizon</u>. Didn't I have here a perfect circus ring, inescapably round, without a single corner for him to hide in? I looked down at the sea. Wasn't this an ideal source of treats with which to condition him to obey? I noticed a whistle hanging from one of the life jackets. Wouldn't this make a good whip with which to keep him in line? What was missing here to tame Richard Parker? Time? It might be weeks before a ship sighted me. I had all the time in the world. **Resolve?** There's nothing like extreme need to give you resolve. Knowledge? Was I not a zookeeper's son? Reward? Was there any reward greater than life? Any punishment worse than death? I looked at Richard Parker. My panic was gone. My fear was <u>dominated</u>. Survival was at hand.

¶51 And so it came to be:

Plan Number Seven: Keep Him Alive.

Close Reading

Literary Analysis

42. Describe Pi's plan to tame the tiger.

Literary Analysis

43. What important detail do readers learn about Pi in **paragraph 50**? Why is it important?

Words to Know

<u>horizon</u>: (*n.*) the line at which the sky and Earth seem to meet

<u>dominated</u>: (*v.*) exercised control over

Identify Evidence | Analyze Individuals, Events, and Ideas

Reread the excerpt from *Life of Pi*, locating examples and evidence Martel uses to describe Pi's efforts to survive in extraordinary circumstances after a shipwreck at sea. How does the author introduce, illustrate, and elaborate characters and events?

- In the Evidence column, record details from the text that describe the extreme setting and the actions and skills Pi uses to survive.
- In the Explanation column, explain how the evidence introduces, illustrates, or elaborates on individuals, events, and ideas.

Evidence	Source	Page	Explanation
1. "I was alone and orphaned, in the middle of the Pacific, hanging on to an oar, an adult tiger in front of me, sharks beneath me, a storm raging about me."	Martel/Pi	79	Pi describes his grim and bizarre circumstances in the first sentence of the excerpt.
2.			
3.			
4.			

	Evidence	Source	Page	Explanation
4.				
5.				
6.				
7.				
8.	"I had to tame him."	Martel/Pi	92	Pi reaches a decision about how to deal with the tiger.

Key Ideas and Details

Determining the Central Idea

1. Use the evidence you collected to summarize the key idea of this excerpt from Martel's novel.

2. List the three characters that appear in this excerpt. Explain how each is important to the central idea.

Character	Significance

Craft and Structure

Structure of the Narrative

1. Setting

The setting of this novel excerpt is unusual and extreme. Describe the setting below. Then list three problems Pi faces that arise from this extreme setting.

Description

Problems

2. Character

List three character traits that help Pi survive in this extreme setting. For each trait, provide an example from the text in which Pi's thoughts or actions revealed this trait.

Trait	Example

3. Narrator's Point of View

Compare and contrast narrator's point of view in this expert from *Life of Pi* with the point of view in "The Story of Keesh."

Collaborate and Present

Plan and Deliver a Presentation

Assignment: Work with a group to analyze the extent to which the film *Life of Pi* stays faithful to or departs from the text in portraying the character's relationship to his environment.

Compare and Contrast

1. Consider the following questions:
   - How is the setting described in the book excerpt? What challenges does the setting present to Pi?
   - How does the movie portray these same elements?

2. Go back to the book excerpt and choose one scene that illustrates the environment and the problem it poses for Pi. Describe the scene in the chart below. Then describe the same scene as it is portrayed in the film.

Text Excerpt	Film

Organize Your Presentation

3. Work with a group to create a presentation that compares and contrasts the same scene in the text and the movie. Use the information you noted in the chart.
   - Draft an outline of the information to present to the class.

Present

4. Present the results of your group's discussion to the class.

Seeking Clarification

- Are you saying that…
- Do you mean…
- How does this differ from…

Reporting Ideas

- _____ pointed out
- _____ indicated that
- _____ emphasized

Presentation

- Be still and use good posture.
- Speak loudly and clearly.
- Make eye contact with your audience.

Presentation Checklist

Use the checklist below to evaluate your collaboration skills, reasoning, and final presentation.
Think carefully about your work. If you know you completed an item thoroughly, give yourself a check (✓).

COLLABORATE AND PRESENT CHECKLIST

Comprehension & Collaboration

☐ Engage in group discussions with diverse partners on topics and issues that you read about.

☐ Come to discussions prepared, having read and researched the material, and viewed the movie.

☐ Refer to evidence to probe and reflect on and contribute to the discussion.

☐ Follow rules for discussions and decision-making.

☐ Ask and respond to specific questions.

☐ Make informed comments about topics that are being discussed.

☐ Demonstrate understanding of the key ideas presented by classmates by reflection and paraphrasing.

Number of ✓ s in this category: ___

Evidence & Reasoning

☐ Explain the purpose of the presentation.

☐ Present information relevant to the task.

☐ Explain how the setting is portrayed in the book excerpt. Use at least one example from the text.

☐ Explain how the setting is portrayed in the movie. Use at least one example.

☐ Compare and contrast the examples cited for the movie and the book.

☐ Synthesize your key ideas with a conclusion.

Number of ✓ s in this category: ___

Presentation of Knowledge & Ideas

☐ Adapt language to a variety of contexts and tasks to demonstrate knowledge of formal English.

☐ Include multimedia components (e.g., graphics, images, music, sound) and visual displays.

☐ Use appropriate volume/tone (clear, not too fast, too slow, or too loud) and avoid using "like" or "ummm."

☐ Have strong posture, a confident stance, and make frequent eye contact.

☐ Occasionally move from one spot to another without fidgeting.

☐ Smile and act relaxed.

Number of ✓ s in this category: ___

Total # of ✓ s: ___

Add up the total number of checks (✓) in each category. Then use the scoring guide below to calculate your final score.

Scoring Guide

④ Exemplary	③ Meets Standards	② Needs Work	① Does Not Meet Standards
16 to 19 ✓ s	13 to 15 ✓ s	11 to 12 ✓ s	10 or less ✓ s

Read the Model

The writer of this literary analysis examines how an author uses characters' thoughts and actions to develop the theme of survival in an extreme environment. Read and discuss the model essay below.

Informative Essay

A literary analysis is a type of informative essay that examines an element of a text, such as character, theme, plot, or setting.

- The **introduction** states the title and author of the text that the writer will analyze, and includes the thesis statement.

- The **body paragraphs** express the writer's main points about the text.

- The **conclusion** sums up or restates the thesis. It also explains why the information in the essay matters.

Survival at Sea   by Steve Patel

Survival in an extreme environment requires a sense of hope and the intelligence to use all available resources. In the story *The Lost Island of Tamarind*, author Nadia Aguiar describes characters who use hope and resourcefulness to survive at sea.

The story centers on three children, Maya, Simon, and Penny, who have hope, even though they are stranded in the ocean after a fierce storm. When Maya discovers that the safety harness line on the family's sailboat has snapped, she realizes that their parents have been washed overboard. At this moment, "her throat and chest began to tighten and she felt her limbs going numb and the world blackening around her" (111). The children look out over the water and see that "for miles around them there was nothing. . . . They were completely alone" (111–112). Amidst this isolated, dangerous setting, Maya sees that the rowboat is missing. This leads her to hope that their parents are safe. She tells Simon, "They were wearing life jackets . . . And they have the rowboat. And we know they're both strong swimmers" (112). Hope helps Maya move beyond her emotions and take action to help herself and her siblings survive.

The characters use the resources they have available to survive. For instance, Maya and Simon put up the sails and read the logbook to figure out their location. Simon fishes, while Maya finds tinned milk to feed Penny. During the day, they mend torn sails and make repairs. At night, Simon sets off the boat's emergency flares, but there are no ships nearby to see. Though they are taking action, Maya begins to give into her fears as she settles into the first night's watch. She realizes, "if they didn't find land in a day or two they would be out of food for Penny" (116). Maya and Simon comfort each other with the hope that they will reach land the next day.

The author effectively conveys the challenges of this extreme environment through details of the characters' reactions. The children's hope and resourcefulness will help them survive. Hope and resourcefulness are powerful tools to survive any challenge!

Analyze the Model

Use the outline below to examine how the writer of this literary analysis examines the theme of survival.

Introduction

¶ Thesis Statement

Topic Sentence/Main Idea	Relevant Evidence
¶2 Body	
¶3 Body	

Conclusion

¶ Why it Matters

Step 1 | Gather Evidence

Write an objective summary of life in the extreme environments portrayed in these two texts. **Analyze how the central idea of survival is conveyed through supporting ideas and developed over the course of the text.**

What You Need to Know | Evidence from both texts describes how the idea of survival in an extreme environment is developed. (See pages 61 and 79.)

What You Need to Write | Use the note-taking guide to list details from each text that show how the idea of survival in an extreme environment is developed and supported.

"The Story of Keesh"

Environment:

Evidence/Details:

Page # _____

Environment:

Evidence/Details:

Page # _____

Environment:

Evidence/Details:

Page # _____

Life of Pi

Environment:

Evidence/Details:

Page # _____

Environment:

Evidence/Details:

Page # _____

Environment:

Evidence/Details:

Page # _____

Step 2 | Organize Ideas

Use the outline below to record your thesis statement and organize your evidence into paragraphs.

Introduction		
¶ Thesis Statement		

Topic Sentence/Main Idea	Relevant Evidence	
¶2		
¶3		

Conclusion	
¶ Why it Matters	

Step 3 | Draft

Language Study | Supporting a Generalization

See It

A generalization is a broad statement about something. Specific supporting details help make a generalization clear and convincing. In a literary analysis, include specific ideas and details from text evidence that support the generalization. Related ideas and details may be grouped under a subtopic.

- **Generalization:** Survival in an extreme environment requires a sense of hope and the intelligence to use all available resources.

- **Details:** Maya and Simon find hope in the idea that their parents have the rowboat. They put up the sails and read the logbook to figure out their location. Simon fishes while Maya finds tinned milk to feed Penny. They mend torn sails and make repairs.

Try It

Put a check in the box next to each detail that supports the generalization.
Generalization: A champion knows that winning does not always mean finishing first.

1. ☐ Martin spent hours not only training for the race but also coaching new members of the track team.

2. ☐ Qualifying for the Olympics was a goal that all of the runners were striving toward.

3. ☐ Martin loved to run and often did even when he wasn't training for a competition.

4. ☐ Near the finish line, the runner who had been in front slowed down, mistakenly thinking he had already crossed the line and won. Martin slowed down along with him.

5. ☐ Instead of taking advantage of the runner's mistake and sprinting out in front, Martin ran next to the runner to signal to him that the race wasn't finished.

6. ☐ Olympic trials are difficult to prepare for, both physically and mentally.

Apply It | Think about the broad statement you wrote in your draft about survival. Use the frames below to practice using relevant text evidence to support your statement.

1. The central idea or theme of _____ and _____ is survival in extreme environments.
    (title of text)   (title of text)

2. In _____ by _____, the _____ is described by the author as _____.
    (title of text)   (author's name)   (extreme environment)

3. Survival in _____ means _____.
    (name of text or extreme environment)   (generalization)

4. _____ develops the central idea through _____ who _____.
    (author's name)   (main character)   (what the character does)

5. For instance, _____ must _____.
    (character's name)   (supporting idea or detail)

6. The resources _____ makes available for _____ are _____.
    (author's name)   (character's name)   (supporting idea or detail)

7. _____ takes charge of his survival when _____.
    (character's name)   (supporting idea or detail)

8. _____ shows the character's response to the environment through _____.
    (author's name)   (supporting idea or detail)

Conventions Study | Active and Passive Voice

See It

In the active voice, the subject of a sentence does the action of the verb. In the passive voice, the subject does not act. Instead, it receives the action of the verb. To express passive voice, use a form of "to be" with the main verb. Commonly, a verb in the passive voice is followed by a phrase beginning with *by*. For example:

Active: *Maya sailed the boat into the harbor. The storm had damaged the boat.* **Passive:** *The boat was sailed into the harbor. The boat was damaged by the storm.*

Active Voice

The subject performs the action of the verb, or the action is done by the subject.

Passive Voice

The action of the verb is performed upon the subject or the action is done to the subject.

Try It

Circle each verb phrase. Then rewrite the sentence in active voice and underline the verb.

1. The airport was crowded with fans who came to catch a glimpse of the actor.

_____

2. Our attic has been taken over by a family of raccoons.

_____

3. The tree house is held in place by nails and wood screws.

_____

Apply It

Write *A* for Active or *P* for Passive. Then rewrite the sentence in the opposite voice.

4. The driver of the speeding car was given a ticket by the state trooper.

_____

5. Lawyers can't divulge the secrets of clients.

_____

6. The author gave a reading at my local bookstore.

_____

Step 4 | Revise and Edit   Revise your draft with a partner.

Organization and Clarity					
State the authors and titles of the texts in the introduction.	Self	1	2	3	4
	Partner	1	2	3	4
State a generalization about the theme of survival in the introduction.	Self	1	2	3	4
	Partner	1	2	3	4
Include a key idea in the topic sentence of each body paragraph.	Self	1	2	3	4
	Partner	1	2	3	4
Wrap up ideas in a concluding paragraph with a final thought about the theme.	Self	1	2	3	4
	Partner	1	2	3	4

Evidence and Reasoning					
Cite the author and text page number for each quotation from an author's text.	Self	1	2	3	4
	Partner	1	2	3	4
Include three or more pieces of evidence in each body paragraph to support the analysis of the theme.	Self	1	2	3	4
	Partner	1	2	3	4

Language and Conventions					
Use appropriate active and passive voice.	Self	1	2	3	4
	Partner	1	2	3	4
Use academic and interesting vocabulary from the texts.	Self	1	2	3	4
	Partner	1	2	3	4
Establish and maintain a formal style and objective tone throughout the essay.	Self	1	2	3	4
	Partner	1	2	3	4

Step 5 | Publish   Publish your story either in print or digital form.

Scoring Guide | ① needs improvement   ② average   ③ good   ④ excellent

Publish

Publish your essay either in print or digital form. Use the rubric below to assess your final performance task.

PERFORMANCE TASK RUBRIC

Score Point	Organization and Clarity	Evidence and Reasoning	Language and Conventions
Exemplary ④	• introductory paragraph identifies the **topic clearly** and **previews** points for analysis • body paragraphs include **relevant examples** to **strongly develop** how writers use story elements to develop a theme • includes **well-chosen** text evidence, quotations, precise language, and specific details to support generalizations • concluding statement **restates the theme** analyzed in the essay and summarizes strategies and techniques the writers used to develop the theme	• **accurately explains and convincingly analyzes** how the writers use story elements to convey the central idea of survival • includes **several examples of relevant** text evidence that **supports** the analysis	• demonstrates a **strong command** of the conventions of standard English grammar and usage, as well as of standard English capitalization, punctuation, and spelling • vocabulary is **appropriate** to the topic (vocabulary about survival and extreme environments; accurate terms for referring to story elements; correct usage of verbs in the active and passive voice)
Meets Standards ③	• introductory paragraph identifies the **topic clearly** • body paragraphs include **examples** to **develop** how writers use story elements to develop a theme • includes **some** text evidence, quotations, precise language, and details to support generalizations • concluding statement **restates the theme** analyzed in the essay and summarizes strategies and techniques the writers used to develop the theme	• **accurately explains and generally analyzes** how the writers use story elements to convey the central idea of survival • includes **relevant** text evidence that **supports** the analysis	• demonstrates a **near command** of the conventions of standard English grammar and usage, as well as of standard English capitalization, punctuation, and spelling **with some errors** • vocabulary is **appropriate** to the topic (vocabulary about survival and extreme environments; accurate terms for referring to story elements; correct usage of verbs in the active and passive voice)

PERFORMANCE TASK RUBRIC

Score Point	Organization and Clarity	Evidence and Reasoning	Language and Conventions
Needs Work ②	• introductory paragraph identifies the **topic** • body paragraphs include **some examples** that **somewhat develop** how writers use story elements to develop a theme • includes **a limited amount** of text evidence, quotations, precise language, and details to support generalizations • concluding statement **refers to the theme** analyzed in the essay and attempts to summarize the strategies and techniques the writers used to develop the theme	• **accurately explains** how the writers use story elements to convey the central idea of survival with **limited analysis** • includes **some** text evidence that **supports** the analysis	• demonstrates a **marginal command** of the conventions of English grammar and usage, as well as of standard English capitalization, punctuation, and spelling • there **are many errors, but the text is still understandable** • includes only **one or two examples** of vocabulary that is appropriate to the topic (vocabulary about survival and extreme environments; accurate terms for referring to story elements; correct usage of verbs in the active and passive voice)
Does Not Meet Standards ①	• introductory paragraph is **unclear** • body paragraphs do **not include examples** and/or **do not develop** how writers use story elements to develop a theme • includes **little text evidence** and few details to support generalizations • concluding statement is **unclear or does not relate back to the theme** analyzed in the essay	• response is **partial or unsubstantiated explanation** of how writers use story elements to convey the central idea of survival • includes **no analyses of textual evidence**	• demonstrates **almost no command** of the conventions of standard English grammar and usage, as well as of standard English capitalization, punctuation, and spelling • there **are many errors that disrupt** the reader's understanding of the text • **does not include** vocabulary that is appropriate to the topic (vocabulary about survival and extreme environments; accurate terms for referring to story elements; correct usage of verbs in the active and passive voice)

Questions

Literary Analysis

1. What is the mood—or overall atmosphere—in **paragraph 1**? What descriptive details does the author use to create this mood?

Literary Analysis

2. How does the author create suspense in **paragraphs 3 and 4**?

from **The Lost Island of Tamarind**

by Nadia Aguiar

¶1 When Maya awoke, her head was throbbing and Penny was crying. Sunlight streamed in the hatch, which was knocking brokenly against the deck, one of its hinges missing. Maya wriggled her fingers and toes. Everything was stiff and sore, but it worked. From on deck, she could hear the sound of the breeze through tattered sails. Simon was lying on the floor near her.

"Simon," she whispered, shaking his shoulder until his eyes opened.

¶3 He sat up and looked groggily around him as the events of the previous night flooded back to him. Maya picked Penny up from the hanging crib and went down the hall to her parents' cabin. Simon followed her. They looked in the doorway but no one was there. Objects had been tossed around during the storm and the floor was strewn with paper and clothes. They looked into each cabin but they were all empty. Her step quickening, Maya went back through the cabin and up the companionway to the deck. The sun was bright and she had to hold her hand over her eyes to protect them from the glare off the wet boards. The sea was calm and flat. Their parents were nowhere in sight.

Simon ran back down to check the cabin again but came right back up, an astonished look on his face. "They're gone," he said.

¶5 He walked to the railing and gazed out over the water in disbelief.

Maya walked forward a few steps, up to the closed chock where the line from the safety harnesses would have been fastened. There was only a stump of the line left— after that the fibers were shredded. The rope holding their parents to the deck had snapped. A sharp, cold feeling came over her.

¶7 The sea looked sweet, docile, the light dazzling off points of tiny waves. Maya's eyes hurt from searching it. The boat rocked slowly and a metal clip on one of the halyards clacked forlornly against the mast. The ocean had never looked so vast and

Words to Know

halyards: (n.) ropes used to raise or lower a sail

forlornly: (adv.) in a sad and lonely way

empty. Her throat and chest began to tighten and she felt her limbs going numb and the world blackening around her. Her head still hurt from where she had struck it the night before. She had not been sick during the storm but now she felt dizzy and ill. Afraid she would fall with Penny in her arms, she sat down for a moment.

"We have to radio for help," she said to Simon when the blackness receded. Her voice felt like it was coming from very far away.

¶9 They went back down into the main cabin, and Maya put Penny back in the hanging crib. Maya followed Simon into the captain's quarters. The first thing that she noticed was that the GPS screen was black and lifeless. She pressed the reset button but nothing happened. And nothing happened when she pressed other buttons on it either. From the corner of her eye she caught sight of the old compass. A thousand spidery cracks blurred its glass face. Beneath the glass the needle had snapped in half. Maya looked over at Simon. He had his ear to the radio and was turning its knob. But there was no familiar crackle of static. It was silent.

"It's dead," he said. "Everything here is broken."

¶11 In a daze they went back on deck. Maya felt the blackness seeping in around the corners of her vision again, but just then she noticed that the rowboat was missing. She turned to her brother.

"They've got the rowboat," she said. "They're okay."

¶13 Her words were swallowed into the blue void of sky and sea.

"They've got the rowboat, they're okay," she repeated loudly as if to ward off any creeping thought that they were not. "They're probably not even that far away from us."

¶15 The two children could not have said how long they stood there. The sun reflecting off the sea scalded Maya's eyes. There was only a faint touch of a breeze now and then. The ocean was deserted. For miles around them there was nothing, not the smudge of another boat on the horizon, not a school of flying fish being chased by a bigger fish, not the friendly squeak of a dolphin.

They were completely alone.

Questions

Literary Analysis

3. What does the dialogue on this page reveal about how Maya deals with challenges?

Words and Phrases in Context

4. What does the author mean when she says that Maya's "words were swallowed into the blue void of sea and sky" in **paragraph 13**?

Questions

Literary Analysis

5. What is the central conflict of this novel excerpt? How does Maya suggest they resolve this conflict?

Words and Phrases in Context

6. What does the author mean by the phrase "out of her fog" in **paragraph 25**?

¶17 Simon sat down cross-legged and stared out bleakly.

Maya wanted to sit down, too, to sit down and not move and pretend that what was happening wasn't happening, that there had never been a storm, that there were still five people instead of only three on the *Pamela Jane.*

¶19 Simon had begun to cry very softly.

"Wait," Maya said finally. Her throat was dry and her voice felt rusty, almost as if it were someone else's voice and not her own. She paused, sorting out her thoughts. Her brain seemed to be working more slowly than usual. "They were wearing life jackets—I saw them putting them on before they went on deck. And they have the rowboat. And we know they're both strong swimmers. They're probably in the row-boat right now, waiting for help."

¶21 As she spoke, Maya began to feel more convinced that everything really might still be alright.

"Right?" she said. "We have every reason to think they're okay. We just have to figure out what to do now."

¶23 Simon sniffled and wiped his eyes with the back of his hand.

"Since the radio is broken and we can't call for help, we're going to have to sail to land ourselves so that we can have rescue boats sent out for them," Maya said. "Okay?"

¶25 But neither of them wanted to move. Maya's head ached. From the cabin they heard Penny begin to cry. The sound of her baby sister brought Maya out of her fog.

"Simon," she said firmly. "You start rigging the sails. I'm going to feed Penny and then I'll be out to help you." She stood up. Simon slowly began to get to his feet. Maya stopped before she went down the ladder into the cabin and looked back at him. "If it were us who'd gotten swept overboard, would they just sit here?" she asked. "No—they'd do something to find us!" she answered triumphantly. "So get going."

¶27 Maya heated a bottle of formula on the stove and fed Penny. When she

Words to Know

rigging: (v.) making ready for sailing
triumphantly: (adv.) victoriously

came back out, Simon was finishing rigging the mainsail. Even though their parents had fitted the *Pamela Jane* with winches and levers so that the children could do everything on it themselves, the sail was still heavy enough that it took both of them to hoist it. They each grabbed the main halyard and began to pull, sinking all their weight into it. The runner whined as it slid up the mast and slowly the sail began to lift. They didn't think about anything else for the next few minutes as they worked. The sail sounded like thunder as it rose and then with one last haul it was up, brilliant white and standing seventy feet above them.

Beads of sweat had sprung up on Maya's brow. She stood back, heart pounding, and wiped the sweat off with her shirt. The physical exertion had given her new energy.

¶29 "Maybe we won't even make it to land before we find them," she said. "We'll be sailing and we'll see them in the water. The storm couldn't have blown us that far away from one another. And even if we don't find them ourselves, it's just a matter of getting to land so that search boats can go out to pick them up."

Looking out at the endless <u>fathoms</u> of blue <u>encircling</u> them, Simon could have said that Maya was crazy. But instead he nodded.

¶31 "I'll get the logbook," said Simon. "So we can figure out where we are." They had been drifting, hardly moving at all, when out of the blue the wind shifted and a shiver passed over the water. Maya felt a surge of adrenaline—or perhaps it was hope—course through her arms and legs. She looked at Simon and she saw that he had felt it, too.

¶33 Simon sat down and rested the logbook in front of him. He looked at it for a moment before he opened it. The pages inside were creamy white and their edges were gilt. The log entries began several months ago, and his father's handwriting filled the book with notes about the weather and their position at sea.

"Can it help us?" asked Maya.

Words to Know

fathoms: (*n.*) units of length used mainly to measure the depth of water; one fathom is equal to six feet

encircling: (*v*) surrounding someone or something completely

---

Questions

Words and Phrases in Context

7. Why would the author use phrases like "the runner whined" and "the sail sounded like thunder" to describe the mechanics of hoisting a sail in **paragraph 27**?

Literary Analysis

8. What does the interaction between Maya and Simon in **paragraphs 29–31** reveal about them?

¶35 Simon nodded. "I think so," he said. "All the coordinates are still here."

Simon pored over the logbook and began reconstructing the path the *Pamela Jane* had been on before the storm. . . .

¶37 "We've been sailing northwest since we left St. Alban's," he said. "According to this, we were sailing northwest at 6 knots at 11 degrees north latitude, 52 degrees west longitude when the storm struck," he said. "The storm was blowing from the north and we were caught in it for about six hours, would you say?"

"I don't know," Maya said. "At least!"

¶39 "Well, let's see," said Simon. "Papi notes that there were signs the storm was approaching at twenty-four hundred hours last night. He made a note here that he and Mami were going onto the deck at oh one hundred hours. You were awake then and I woke up right after—we know the storm was pretty bad by then. By the time we woke up this morning, at seven hundred hours, the storm had probably passed about two hours earlier, which would mean the storm winds were blowing us south for six hours, which, I think, would probably put us somewhere near here. . . Now if the sun is here. . ."

Maya found it hard to pay attention. The whole thing was too much like a math problem for her. Maya didn't like charts and numbers and calculations so she just watched as Simon worked.

¶41 "If my calculations are correct," he said finally. "We should sail due west. That's our closest point to land." He smiled triumphantly at Maya.

"Great," she said. "Thank you. Now, I'm going to start cleaning up the cabin. Can you get us on course?"

¶43 "Aye, aye," said Simon.

The jib mast had been damaged in the storm and some sheets needed to be replaced so for the next hours Maya and Simon worked to repair everything and keep the *Pamela Jane* on course. They took turns on watch. The one off watch sat with Penny and mended torn sails. Penny seemed puzzled that their parents weren't there and she kept looking around the deck for them. Every time she did,

Questions

Words and Phrases in Context

9. What does *coordinates* mean in **paragraph 35**? Use context clues to determine the meaning.

Literary Analysis

10. Review **paragraphs 39–42**. How do Maya and Simon reverse roles in this scene?

Maya felt a lump rise in her throat.

¶45 Simon caught a red snapper and cooked it for their lunch. When Penny was hungry, they fed her tinned milk and brought her out to sit in the shade. Simon complained, but Maya wouldn't let him have any of the milk so that she could save it for the baby. When a swell caught her off balance and she spilled half of it on the deck he sighed and made a big production of the whole thing. Maya had to grit her teeth to stop herself from getting into an argument.

In the evening, Maya tucked Penny into her little hanging cot in the cabin and sang to her until she fell asleep. On her way back to the deck, she stopped in the doorway to her parents' quarters. She could only bear to look in their room for a moment, but she took one of her mother's sweaters and put it on, less because she was cold than she thought it would be comforting. Outside, an orange glow was seeping through the water, sinking into the ocean depths. Darkness came suddenly and then they were moving along beneath a tapestry of stars, new ones popping out every minute. She pulled the sweater more tightly around her.

¶47 "We'll have to take turns on watch tonight," she said.

Simon nodded and they sat there quietly, staring into the darkness.

¶49 "Wait," said Simon excitedly. Something had occurred to him that might be able to help. "We forgot about the flares!"

"Right!" said Maya. She felt excited, too. The flares could be seen for miles— maybe a nearby ship would see their distress signal and they would be rescued.

¶51 They had never shot distress flares before, but their parents had taught them how in case there was ever an emergency. Simon found the flares and brought them onto the deck. He lit the first one and stood back as it rocketed into the sky, leaving a train of sparks that were quickly snuffed out by the damp air. A couple of hundred feet up they exploded, illuminating the *Pamela Jane* and the sea around her.

Words to Know

distress: (*adj.*) having to do with a situation in which a ship, airplane, etc. is in danger and needs help

illuminating: (*v.*) filling with light

Questions

Literary Analysis

11. Why do Maya and Simon argue in **paragraph 45**? What can you infer from this argument about the conditions on the boat?

Literary Analysis

12. What is Penny's purpose in this story?

The sky and the water blazed orange for a moment, and the dark backs of fish were visible beneath the surface of the sea. Then the salty blackness swallowed the flare, and Maya and Simon stood there on the gently rolling deck, waiting for their eyes to adjust again after the brief, sudden brilliance.

They waited a while before they lit the second flare, turning and squinting at the horizon all around them in hopes of seeing a ship's light or an answering flare. But there was nothing, just the sound of a fish jumping out of the water. They fired the second flare, but still there was nothing. The smell of smoke lingered in the air, and Maya's disappointment as she scanned the darkness was bitter.

¶53 They sat in silence for a while.

"I could stay up with you," offered Simon.

¶55 Maya shook her head. "Get some sleep. We'll switch in a few hours. There's no point in both of us trying to stay awake at the same time and then falling asleep and missing seeing a ship. Or land."

Simon sat there for a few minutes before he went below deck. Without him, sitting in the darkness, a <u>keen</u> sense of aloneness overwhelmed Maya. She missed her parents sharply, as she had not when she had been busy all day. She felt the <u>enormity</u> of the sea around her. Her little brother and sister were in the cabin, young and in need of her protection. She was the eldest; she was in charge. She was responsible for them until they found their parents. Until they found their parents . . . Maya felt another stab of fear. She had no idea where they were or where they were sailing. If they didn't find land in a day or two they would be out of food for Penny. What were they going to do? The night was hot and humid but Maya shivered. She was so deep in her thoughts that she didn't see Simon until he was standing right in front of her, holding a blanket and pillow.

¶57 "I checked on Penny," he said. "She's still sleeping. I thought I would come

---

Words to Know

keen: *(adj.)* very strong and deep

enormity: *(n.)* the large size or scale of something

Questions

Literary Analysis

13. How does the author's point of view help you to better understand Maya in **paragraph 56**?

Text Structure

14. In **paragraph 56**, the author makes a connection between two seemingly different ideas when she writes, "The night was hot and humid but Maya shivered." What does this say about why Maya is shivering?

and sleep out here with you. For the fresh air."

"Oh," said Maya. "All right." She was touched—she knew that she would be lonely and afraid out there by herself. Tears burned her eyes. She was happy that he couldn't see them in the dark. She wanted to say something, anything to him, about the day, about how frightened she had been and how glad she was that he had been there with her.

¶59 "I think we're making good time," she said instead.

"Yes," said Simon from beneath the blanket. "The wind has really picked up. We'll definitely reach land by tomorrow."

¶61 Maya murmured <u>affirmatively</u>, as if of course this was true.

"Maya?"

¶63 "Go to sleep."

Simon sighed.

¶65 "Good night, Maya."

"Good night."

¶67 Soon Simon was asleep. Maya sat awake on watch. She was an experienced sailor, and she kept her eye on the horizon for the lights of land or another ship, and she got up to adjust the sails every now and then. But as fine a sailor as she was, she was too <u>preoccupied</u> to notice that they were <u>veering</u> ever so slightly off course, just a few degrees with every mile of ocean they left behind. With her brother asleep beside her and her sister safely tucked in the cabin below, Maya struggled to keep her eyes open as the *Pamela Jane*—her yellow hull and crisp white sails illuminated in the moonlight—plowed through the warm sea.

Words to Know

affirmatively: *(adv.)* in a way that shows agreement

preoccupied: *(adj.)* thinking about something so much that you do not pay attention to other things

veering: *(v.)* changing direction

Questions

Text Structure

15. What detail in the last paragraph suggests what will happen next in the story? How is this an effective way to end the chapter?

Literature Circle Leveled Novels

***Shackleton's Stowaway** by Victoria McKernan*
Teenage stowaway Perce Blackborow gets more than he bargained for when he stows away on Shackleton's ship, which is crushed in the ice and leaves its passengers stranded for months. **Lexile®** measure: 740L

***Hatchet** by Gary Paulsen*
Brian survives a plane crash in the Canadian wilderness with only his clothes and a small hatchet. Can he endure the challenges of nature and his own mistakes until help comes? **Lexile®** measure: 1020L

***Out of the Dust** by Karen Hesse*
Written in first-person free verse, this story follows a young girl as she deals with the Depression, catastrophic dust storms, and her growing talent at the piano. When personal tragedy threatens to steal her musical ability, she must learn how to work through her grief. **Lexile®** measure: NP

Fiction, Nonfiction, and Novels

***North** by Donna Jo Napoli.* Travel with twelve-year-old Alvin on his harrowing journey to the North Pole, where he meets a group of Inuit people who help him survive the tough Arctic winter. **Lexile®** measure: 600L

***Holes** by Louis Sachar.* Stanley Yelnats has landed at Camp Green Lakes, a juvenile detention facility in Texas where boys spend all day digging five-by-five-foot holes in the middle of a dried-up lake. **Lexile®** measure: 660L

***First Light** by Rebecca Stead.* When his family travels to Greenland, Peter meets Thea, who is part of an underground civilization called Gracehope. **Lexile®** measure: 760L

***Shabanu: Daughter of the Wind** by Suzanne Fisher Staples.* Shabanu is a free-spirited desert girl who must act for the good of her family and marry a powerful landowner when their water supply is threatened. **Lexile®** measure: 970L

***The 10 Most Extreme Sports** by Kimberly Mitchell.* Find out about surfing, mountain climbing, and other exciting but risky sports. **Lexile®** measure: IG970L

***My Season with Penguins: An Antarctic Journal** by Sophie Webb.* Glimpse the scientific method in action as you read biologist and artist Sophie Webb's diary and see her illustrations. **Lexile®** measure: 1040L

***Shipwreck at the Bottom of the World** by Jennifer Armstrong.* After being shipwrecked in Antarctica, Shackleton and his men survived to tell the tale. Find out how. **Lexile®** measure: 1090L

***Vanishing World: The Endangered Arctic** by Fredrik Granath and Mireille de la Lez.* Understand life in the Arctic with this book, which features stunning photos of polar animals.

Films and TV

Antarctic Wildlife Adventure (National Geographic, 2005) Set sail with a family of explorers to observe the stark beauty of Antarctica. (76 min.)

Everest: Beyond the Limit (Discovery Channel, 2007) Join the breathless struggle of mountaineers climbing toward the summit of Everest. (287 min.)

Exploring the Deserts of the Earth (Koch Vision, 2007) Hop on a motorcycle and visit deserts around the world on the ultimate road trip. (357 min.)

Life in the Freezer (BBC Warner, 2005) Gaze at the pristine glaciers of Antarctica and find out how humpback whales, penguins, killer whales, and seabirds make their homes there. (180 min.)

Masters of the Arctic Ice (National Geographic, 2007) Journey to the top of the world and follow polar bears, ringed seals, and other animals as they make their homes amidst the ice. (52 min.)

Mountain of Ice (NOVA, 2006) Follow a group of mountain climbers up the east side of Vinson Massif, the highest mountain in Antarctica. (56 min.)

Return to Penguin City (Animal Planet, 2008) Storm the beaches of Antarctica with the Adélie penguins, and find out how climate change has begun to affect their lives. (49 min.)

World's Last Great Places Collection (National Geographic, 2007) Visit some of the most extreme habitats in the world, including the Everglades, Africa, and the Namib Desert. (60 min.)

Websites

PBS: Journey into Amazonia Learn about the animals and organisms that populate the forest from top to bottom.

National Geographic: Discover Antarctica Explore the wildlife and terrain of Antarctica with this virtual map, and then determine your Antarctica IQ with an interactive quiz.

PBS: Under Antarctic Ice View photos and research from McMurdo Station, and hear interviews from people who have visited.

National Geographic: Everest 50 Celebrate the 50th anniversary of the first scaling of Everest with a virtual climb, a 360-degree view from the top, and news about Everest today.

Magazines

American Way Search for "Everest" in this magazine's Web site, and find out about people who have conquered the mountain.

Backpacker Find out how to survive in cold, harsh environments, and hear from people who have done it.

National Geographic Search for articles about how ice shapes the world.

National Parks Explore the extreme environments in the national parks located throughout the United States.

The Power of Art

How does art influence your everyday life?

WRITING PERFORMANCE TASK

Does a person need knowledge and empathy to create great art? Consider the arguments and evidence in at least one selection as you develop your claim.

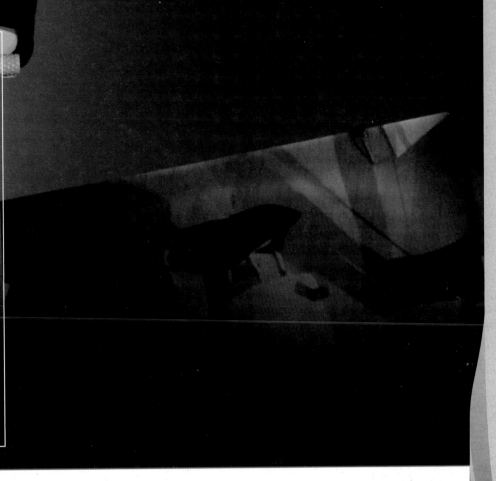

Unit Introduction

In these two selections, writers discuss and describe the role art plays in the lives of developing young artists.

In an excerpt from *Letters to a Young Artist*, Anna Deavere Smith offers ideas and advice about how to get started and to continue growing as an artist.

In "Zebra," a short story by Chaim Potok, we meet a young boy who discovers that drawing and sculpting are the keys to recovering from a devastating accident.

📖 LETTERS/SHORT STORY

from *Letters to a Young Artist* by Anna Deavere Smith

"Zebra" by Chaim Potok

Language
- Academic Vocabulary
- Word Study:
  Context Clues

Reading Literature
- Identify Evidence
- Key Ideas and Details
- Craft and Structure and Writing Assignment

Language
- Academic Vocabulary
- Word Study
  Word Families

Reading Literature
- Identify Evidence
- Key Ideas and Details
- Craft and Structure and Writing Assignment

🎤 SPEAKING AND LISTENING

Present a Multi-Media Presentation
- Collaborate and Present

Checklist: Presentation
- Scoring Guide

✍ WRITING

Writing: Argumentative Essay
- Read the Model
- Analyze the Model
- Gather Evidence
- Organize Ideas

- Language Study: Supporting Evidence
- Conventions Study: Verb Mood
- Revise, Edit, and Publish
- Performance Task Rubric

📖 EXTENDED READINGS

Poem
"I Want to Write" by Margaret Walker

Academic Vocabulary

From *Letters to a Young Artist*
by Anna Deavere Smith

Rate your understanding of each word. Then write its meaning and a sample sentence.

Word	Meaning	Example
chaotic (*adj.*) p. 125 ① ② ③ ④	confused and disordered	
discipline (*n.*) p. 126 ① ② ③ ④		Juan has become a better guitar player through the discipline of playing in public.
fundamental (*adj.*) p. 123 ① ② ③ ④	basic and essential	
rigor (*n.*) p. 124 ① ② ③ ④	strictness and exactness; attention to detail	
empathy (*n.*) p. 124 ① ② ③ ④	the ability to identify with and understand someone else's feelings and thoughts	
mentor (*n.*) p. 128 ① ② ③ ④		The soccer player's mentor taught her to be a better team player.

Rating Scale | ① I don't know the word. ② I've seen it or heard it.
③ I know its meaning. ④ I know it and use it.

Word Study

A word family is a group of words that shares the same base word and have related meanings. Word webs help you visualize how to find base words.

chaotic

chaotically

chaos

Complete each sentence using the correct word form from the *chaos* word family.

1. A terrible storm left the town in _____ .

2. The club meeting ended _____ with members yelling and arguing.

3. I never ride my bike on that street because the traffic is too _____ .

from
Letters to a
Young Artist

by Anna Deavere Smith

¶1 Dear BZ:

¶2 Being "in it, and out of it, at the same time," is a sort of **fundamental** first exercise one should do as one develops as an artist.

¶3 Did you take ballet when you were younger, or do you now? You know how in the beginning of the class you go through all the positions in the warm-up, and the positions become the foundation, or the <u>basis</u> of ballet? It's a basic vocabulary. Like when you bake, you need flour, butter, sugar, some kind of liquid, etc. The fundamental ingredients.

¶4 Well, I believe that fundamental to becoming an artist is understanding the <u>position</u> of an artist, rehearsing that position, and practicing that position. It is from that position that you will develop an eye, an ear, and a heart. These three organs are essential. Yes, as a painter you will need a hand, and as an actor I need a voice and a body—but before getting to those, we need to develop the eye, the ear, the heart.

Words to Know

<u>basis</u>: (n.) the root, or basic structure

<u>position</u>: (n.) place or role in society or the world

Close Reading

Text Structure

1. How do the ballet and baking analogies in **paragraph 3** help to clarify the ideas the author discusses in **paragraph 4**?

Writing

2. What does Smith believe is fundamental to being an artist? Explain.

According the author, an artist must _____ and _____ the position of an artist. The author explains that _____ and _____. She means that an artist must _____ and _____.

Close Reading

Key Ideas and Details

3. Explain the difference between sympathy and empathy, as described here. Why is empathy "more useful and more important"? Why does it require more rigor?

Words and Phrases in Context

4. What does *suspend* mean in **paragraph 6**? Identify clues that helped you determine how *suspend* is used in this paragraph.

Anecdote

An **anecdote** is a short and amusing or interesting account, which may depict a real incident or person.

Key Ideas And Details

5. What does it mean to "step outside a situation"? How does the anecdote about the accident scene illustrate Smith's ideas about stepping outside?

¶5 We do that by learning how to step outside of given situations to watch, to listen, and to feel, and to feel as others as much as to feel things about others. Feeling as others is **empathy**. Feeling for others is sympathy. Empathy is more useful and more important. It requires more **rigor**. That rigor will make you stronger of heart and spirit. Empathy requires a very highly developed imagination. It is more active than sympathy. It requires more intellectual development. Sympathy, to me, is just tears. Empathy is potentially very productive.

¶6 Stepping outside gives you the space to watch, listen, feel. To step outside, you must suspend opinions and judgments. It doesn't mean that you are <u>devoid</u> of them. It means that you can control them long enough to watch, listen, and feel. You store what you have learned, and then you do what you will with what you have gathered. You may even try to influence how others watch, listen, and feel. But first and foremost you must be able to step outside.

¶7 Read an essay by Bertolt Brecht, the mid-twentieth-century German playwright, called "Street Scene." In it he describes an accident scene, where people come out into the street and describe an accident. They all give their version. He calls the telling — the storytelling that happens — a kind of "natural theater." It will remind you that you have to be available to watch and listen and feel for all scenes.

Words to Know

<u>devoid</u>: *(adj.)* completely lacking; having none

¶8 To me, artists are students of the human condition, potentially. Being outside does not mean being without <u>compassion</u>. But it does mean that you may sometimes become clinical.

¶9 Years ago I interviewed the head of pediatric surgery at Sloan-Kettering Hospital in New York. I asked him what had moved him to become a cancer surgeon for children. I thought he would tell me a moving story about having seen a child suffering, but instead he replied, "I wanted to do bigger operations."

¶10 What was driving him was his desire to be a very good surgeon, and to discover things. I think as artists we too should want to do "bigger operations."

¶11 Standing in and out at the same time is a structural matter. It is a way of bringing order to the otherwise **chaotic** situation of life. I say chaotic because as an artist you are both in life and commenting on life. That's your position.

¶12 ADS
New York City
February 2000

Words to Know

<u>compassion</u>: (n.) feelings of sadness for and desire to help someone who is suffering; pity

---

Close Reading

Writing

6. What is the "human condition"? Why does Smith say that artists are "students of the human condition, potentially"?

The human condition is _____. Artists who _____ learn more about _____, so these artists _____.

Text Structure

7. How does the anecdote in **paragraph 9**, about Smith's meeting with a surgeon, help to illustrate the ideas in **paragraph 8**?

Key Ideas And Details

8. In **paragraph 10**, the author draws an analogy between the surgeon and artists. What might be an artist's version of "bigger operations"?

Text Structure

9. What position is the author referring to when she says, "That's your position"? Why does she conclude her letter with this statement?

Close Reading

Text Structure

10. Why does Smith begin this letter with the one-word question: "Jealousy?"

Key Ideas and Details

11. Why does Smith say that artists, unlike athletes, can't really compete with each other? What does she suggest that artists do instead?

Words and Phrases in Context

12. What is the meaning of *essence* in **paragraph 15**? Find context clues that helped you determine its meaning.

Writing

13. In **paragraph 15**, how does Smith suggest that artists go about finding out the "true nature" or "essence" of their art? Where does this knowledge and "real communion" with the soul come from?

According to Smith, this knowledge does not come _____ . It comes from being one with _____ , from _____ , and from your ability to _____ with what you are _____ .

¶13 Dear BZ:

¶14 Jealousy? Hmmm. Jealousy links up with competition. It's hard to compete, really compete, in the art world. That's why award ceremonies are a little <u>suspect</u>. Athletes can compete; businesses can compete. I don't know how much you can really compete as an artist. You can compete with yourself.

¶**15** You are an explorer. You understand that every time you go into the studio, you are after something that does not yet exist. Maybe it's the same for a runner. I don't know. But with running or swimming or gymnastics or tennis, the achievement is measurable. Forget about the competition. Rather, commit yourself to find out the true nature of your art. How does it really work; what's the essence of it? Go for that thing that no one can teach you. Go for that <u>communion</u>, that real communion with your soul, and the **discipline** of expressing that communion to others. That doesn't come from competition. That comes from being one with what you are doing. It comes from concentration and from your own ability to be fascinated endlessly with the story, the song, the jump, the color you are working on.

Words to Know

<u>suspect</u>: *(adj.)* sketchy or dodgy; worthy of suspicion

<u>communion</u>: *(n.)* communication; sharing of thoughts and feeling

¶16 I know this sounds a little monkish or even sort of "holier than thou," but I really do believe it. And that said, jealousy is a human sentiment. Few of us are above it. John Lahr, a writer, told me that the major emotion in Los Angeles is envy. I have to say, he's probably right. And a lot of it has to do with how close to or how far from an Academy Award one is. And L.A., the capital of smoke and mirrors, would have some believe that the award is just a step away. When you drive down Hollywood Boulevard, some of those dreamers look as though the dream ate them alive.

¶17 Keep it real. Even jealousy is based on fantasies: a fantasy that someone else has what belongs to you.

¶18 ADS

Los Angeles

Words to Know

<u>sentiment</u>: (*n.*), feeling, emotion

Close Reading

Words and Phrases in Context

14. What does the expression "holier than thou" mean? Why does Smith suggest that her comments about jealousy might sound "sort of 'holier than thou'"?

Key Ideas and Details

15. What does Smith mean when she says "some of those dreamers look as though the dream ate them alive"? What is the dream that "ate them alive"? What message about jealousy is she conveying through this use of figurative language?

Close Reading

Academic Vocabulary

16. How is the author herself serving as a mentor though these letters?

Key Ideas and Details

17. Why does Smith say that many of her mentors were "unexpected"?

Words and Phrases in Context

18. How does Smith define the difference between a mentor and a teacher? Identify how she uses figurative language to explain what mentors do.

Key Ideas and Details

19. Why does Smith consider Studs Terkel a mentor?

¶19 Dear BZ:

¶20 Your question "How did you find your **mentors**?" is a good one. I sought them out on my own, and they came from all sorts of backgrounds. Many of them were unexpected. They are not all actors, or writers, or artists, for that matter. Tonight I had dinner with someone I consider a mentor: Studs Terkel. More on that in a moment.

¶21 Mentors are different from teachers in general because you pick them. You seek them out, or sometimes they declare themselves as your mentor. I suppose in the <u>strict</u> sense of the word, a mentor is someone who takes the responsibility of "schooling you," showing you the ropes, bringing you through the system. I think of them also as inspirational people who have broken ground or lit a path.

¶22 And now Studs. I consider Studs Terkel, the great radio man, a mentor. I don't know very many people who are as truly <u>learned</u> as he is. He is now ninety years old. He has interviewed thousands of people, from regular working people to Martin Luther King. One of his best friends was the great gospel singer Mahalia Jackson. When I visit him in Chicago, all kinds of people approach him — he's a part of the community. Just the fact that he's out there puts me on a path and lights the way.

Words to Know

<u>strict</u>: *(adj.)* adhering to rules, as in a dictionary definition
<u>learned</u>: *(adj.)* well educated; very knowledgeable

¶23 Although it's important to make communities with like-minded people—people who are your age, your generation, who are working on projects that have resonance with yours—I am a firm believer in crossing generations to find mentorship and inspiration and a sense of furthering the craft. So I'd say that as you begin to seek mentorship, be creative about where you look. Look in unlikely places. It will enrich your work. It will broaden your work and make it more likely that you will cross boundaries and reach a wider, more culturally and intellectually diverse audience.

¶24 ADS
Chicago
February 2002

Close Reading

Words and Phrases in Context

20. What does the word "broaden" mean in **paragraph 23**? Why would looking "in unlikely places" for mentors "broaden your work"? What are the likely results of broadening your work?

Writing

21. Why do artists need mentors? Summarize what Smith says artists can learn from their mentors.

According to Smith, a mentor can ____ and ____. Artists also need mentors to help them ____ and ____.

Words to Know

resonance: (n.) richness and meaning; the ability to evoke strong emotions.

enrich: (v.) make something richer or more meaningful

Identify Evidence | Analyze Individuals, Events, and Ideas

Reread *Letters to a Young Artist*, highlighting details that show what Anna Deavere Smith thinks young people must know and do in order to become good artists.

- As you read, use the Evidence column to record examples from the text of Smith's advice to young artists.
- In the Explanation column, explain how each piece of evidence introduces, illustrates, or elaborates Smith's advice and ideas about becoming and improving as an artist.

Evidence	Source	Page	Explanation
1. "Well, I believe that fundamental to becoming an artist is understanding the position . . ." It is from that position that you will develop an eye, an ear, a heart."	Smith	123	The author argues that it's important for artists to grasp their role in life. She says this will result in learning to watch, listen, and feel.
2.			
3.			
4.			

	Evidence	Source	Page	Explanation
5.				
6.				
7.				
8.				

Key Ideas and Details

Determining the Central Idea

1. Use the evidence you collected to summarize the key idea of these letters.

2. This reading includes three letters. Identify the topic of each letter and explain its significance to Smith's central idea.

Topic	Significance

Craft and Structure

Structure of a Letter

1. Greeting: Letters begin with a greeting. What greeting does Smith use in each letter?

2. Introduction: Like essays, each of Smith's letters has an introductory paragraph, in which she introduces a claim or idea. Choose a letter. Identify the idea Smith introduces in the introductory paragraph.

3. Body: How does Smith develop her ideas?Sum up what she discusses in each body paragraph of the letter you chose.

4. Conclusion: How does Smith conclude the letter you chose? How does she summarize or add to her ideas?

5. Signature: How does Smith sign each letter? What information does she include in addition to her name?

Author's Purpose

6. Describe the author's purpose in writing.

Academic Vocabulary

"Zebra"
by Chaim Potok

Rate your understanding of each word. Then write either its meaning or a sample sentence.

Word	Meaning	Example
encountered (v.) p. 144 ① ② ③ ④	experienced something unexpectedly	
emerged (v.) p. 137 ① ② ③ ④	came out of something or some place	
vacant (adj.) p. 138 ① ② ③ ④		The abandoned house on the corner had been vacant for years.
intricate (adj.) p. 146 ① ② ③ ④	having a lot of fine detail; complex	
sensation (n.) p. 147 ① ② ③ ④	a mental feeling, often a strange or excited feeling	
situated (adj.) p. 154 ① ② ③ ④	located; built or placed in a particular location	

Rating Scale
① I don't know the word.
② I've seen it or heard it.
③ I know its meaning.
④ I know it and use it.

Word Study

Context Clues

Context Clues are words or phrases in a text that help you figure out the meaning of an unfamiliar word.

Make inferences to determine the meaning of the boldface words in the sentences below:

1. "There was a hill on Franklin Avenue, a steep hill. By the time he reached that hill, he would feel his legs so light it was as if he had no legs at all and was flying. He would begin to **descend** the hill, certain as he ran that he needed only to give himself the slightest push and off he would go."

2. "He wore a khaki army jacket, a blue denim shirt, blue jeans, and brown cowboy boots. His gaunt face and muscular neck were reddened by **exposure** to the sun.

Zebra

By Chaim Potok

¶1 His name was Adam Martin Zebrin, but everyone in his neighborhood knew him as Zebra.

He couldn't remember when he began to be called by that name. Perhaps they started to call him Zebra when he first began running. Or maybe he began running when they started to call him Zebra.

¶3 He loved the name and he loved to run.

Close Reading

Writing

1. Who is Zebra? What do readers learn about him in **paragraphs 1–3**?

Zebra is the main _____. His real name was _____. Zebra loved _____. Both began since before _____.

Close Reading

Literary Analysis

2. Zebra first sees zebras in a zoo, but he only begins to identify with zebras after he sees them in a movie. Why? Contrast the zoo zebras in **paragraph 4** with the movie zebras in **paragraph 5** and explain.

Literary Analysis

3. What is the mood in **paragraphs 6–10** as Zebra runs through his neighborhood? Identify descriptive details and sensory language the author uses to create this mood.

Mood

The **mood** is the atmosphere the author creates in a story or a scene. It is the feeling a reader gets from reading. Authors create a mood through word choices, descriptive details, dialogue, and sensory language.

When he was very young, his parents took him to a zoo, where he saw zebras for the first time. They were odd-looking creatures, like stubby horses, short-legged, thick-necked, with dark and white stripes.

¶5 Then one day he went with his parents to a movie about Africa, and he saw zebras, hundreds of them, thundering across a grassy plain, dust rising in boiling brown clouds.

Was he already running before he saw that movie, or did he begin to run afterward? No one seemed able to remember. He would go running through the neighborhood for the sheer joy of feeling the wind on his face. People said that when he ran he arched his head up and back, and his face kind of flattened out. One of his teachers told him it was clever to run that way, his balance was better. But the truth was he ran that way, his head thrown back, because he loved to feel the wind rushing across his neck.

¶7 Each time, after only a few minutes of running, his legs would begin to feel wondrously light. He would run past the school and the homes on the street beyond the church. All the neighbors knew him and would wave and call out, "Go, Zebra!" And sometimes one or two of their dogs would run with him awhile, barking.

He would imagine himself a zebra on the African plain. Running.

¶9 There was a hill on Franklin Avenue, a steep hill. By the time he reached that hill, he would feel his legs so light it was as if he had no legs at all and was flying. He would begin to descend the hill, certain as he ran that he needed only to give himself the slightest push and off he would go, and instead of a zebra he would become the bird he had once seen in a movie about Alaska, he would swiftly change into an eagle, soaring higher and higher, as light as the gentlest breeze, the cool wind caressing his arms and legs and neck.

Words to Know

<u>wondrously:</u> *(adv.)* with wonder or amazement

<u>caressing:</u> *(v.)* softly stroking or touching

<u>thundering:</u> *(v.)* to run in a loud, rapid way that makes a noise like thunder

Then, a year ago, racing down Franklin Avenue, he had given himself that push and had begun to turn into an eagle, when a huge rushing shadow appeared in his line of vision and crashed into him and plunged him into a darkness from which he **emerged** very, very slowly....

¶11 "Never, never, never run down that hill so fast that you can't stop at the corner," his mother had warned him again and again.

His schoolmates and friends kept calling him Zebra even after they all knew that the doctors had told him he would never be able to run like that again.

¶13 His leg would heal in time, the doctors said, and perhaps in a year or so the brace would come off. But they were not all certain about his hand. From time to time his injured hand, which he still wore in a sling, would begin to hurt. The doctors said they could find no cause for the pain.

One morning, during Mr. Morgan's geography class, Zebra's hand began to hurt badly. He sat staring out the window at the sky. Mr. Morgan, was a stiff-mannered person in his early fifties, given to smart suits and dapper bow ties, called on him to respond to a question. Zebra stumbled about in vain for the answer. Mr. Morgan told him to pay attention to the geography inside the classroom and not the geography outside.

¶15 "In this class, young man, you will concentrate your attention upon the earth, not upon the sky," Mr. Morgan said.

Later, in the schoolyard during the midmorning recess, Zebra stood near the tall fence, looking out at the street and listening to the noises behind him.

¶17 His schoolmates were racing about, playing exuberantly, shouting and laughing with full voices. Their joyous sounds went ringing through the quiet street.

Words to Know

brace: (n.) a stiff device to hold or protect a body part, usually for healing purposes

exuberantly: (adv.) with joy and enthusiasm

Close Reading

Literary Analysis

4. Identify the "huge rushing shadow" that "crashed into" Zebra and the "darkness" he emerged from afterward. Why doesn't the author identify these things directly?

Writing

5. Describe the conflict in this story. Explain how it is an example of situational irony.

The conflict in this story began when Zebra _____ so fast that he _____ and a car _____. As a result, he will never _____. His situation is ironic because _____

Situational Irony

Situational irony is a great difference between the purpose of an action and its results.

Most times Zebra would stand alongside the basketball court or behind the wire screen at home plate and watch the games. That day, because his hand hurt so badly, he stood alone behind the chain-link fence of the school yard.

¶19 That's how he happened to see the man. And that's how the man happened to see him.

One minute the side street on which the school stood was strangely empty, without people or traffic, without even any of the dogs that often roamed about the neighborhood — **vacant** and silent, as if it were already in the full heat of summer. The red-brick ranch house that belonged to Mr. Morgan, and the white clapboard two-story house in which Mrs. English lived, and the other homes on the street, with their columned front porches and their back patios, and the tall oaks — all stood curiously still in the warm golden light of the mid- morning sun.

¶21 Then a man emerged from wide and busy Franklin Avenue at the far end of the street.

Zebra saw the man stop at the corner and stand looking at a public trash can. He watched as the man poked his hand into the can and fished about but seemed to find nothing he wanted. He <u>withdrew</u> the hand and, raising it to shield his eyes from the sunlight, glanced at the street sign on the lamppost.

Words to Know

<u>withdrew</u>: (v.) took out

Close Reading

Literary Analysis

6. How have Zebra's life, and the mood of the story, changed since the accident? What is the effect, in **paragraph 18**, of the description of Zebra standing behind a chain-link fence?

Text Structure

7. Why are the two sentences that form **paragraph 19** set apart as a paragraph by themselves?

Academic Vocabulary

8. Why does the author establish that the street was "strangely empty . . . vacant and silent" as the man emerged from Franklin Avenue?

¶23 He started to walk up the street in the direction of the school.

He was tall and wiry, and looked to be about forty years old. In his right hand he carried a bulging brown plastic bag. He wore a khaki army jacket, a blue denim shirt, blue jeans, and brown cowboy boots. His <u>gaunt</u> face and muscular neck were reddened by exposure to the sun. Long brown hair spilled out below his dark-blue farmer's cap. On the front of the cap, in large orange letters, were the words LAND ROVER.

¶25 He walked with his eyes on the sidewalk and the curb, as if looking for something, and he went right past Zebra without noticing him.

Zebra's hand hurt very much. He was about to turn away when he saw the man stop and look around and peer up at the red-brick wall of the school. The man set down the bag and took off his cap and stuffed it into a pocket of his jacket. From one of his jeans pockets he removed a handkerchief, with which he then wiped his face. He shoved the handkerchief back into the pocket and put the cap back on his head.

¶27 Then he turned and saw Zebra.

He picked up the bag and started down the street to where Zebra was standing. When the man was about ten feet away, Zebra noticed that the left sleeve of his jacket was empty.

¶29 The man came up to Zebra and said in a low, friendly, shy voice, "Hello."

Zebra answered with a cautious "Hello," trying not to look at the empty sleeve, which had been tucked into the man's jacket pocket.

¶31 The man asked, with a <u>distinct</u> Southern accent, "What's your name, son?"

Zebra said, "Adam."

¶33 "What kind of school is this here school, Adam?"

Words to Know

<u>gaunt</u>: *(adj.)* very thin

<u>distinct</u>: *(adj.)* noticeable

Close Reading

Words and Phrases in Context

9. What is the meaning of *exposure* in the third sentence of **paragraph 24**? Use the descriptive details that the author provides in this paragraph to visualize the man. What can you infer about him from his appearance?

Literary Analysis

10. Why is the left sleeve of the man's jacket empty? Why does Zebra try not to look at it?

Close Reading

Text Structure

11. Why does **paragraph 41** begin with the sentence "Zebra's hand had to begin to tingle and throb"? How does the sentence relate to the rest of the information in the paragraph?

Text Structure

12. Reread the last sentence in **paragraph 41**. The author uses the word *yet* to connect two contradictory ideas. What are these ideas?

Literary Analysis

13. Why does it take Zebra "by surprise" when the man begins to talk about teaching an art class?

"It's a good school," Zebra answered.

¶35 "How long before you-all begin your summer vacation?"

"Three days," Zebra said.

¶37 "Anything special happen here during the summer?"

"During the summer? Nothing goes on here. There are no classes."

¶39 "What do you-all do during the summer?"

"Some of us go to camp. Some of us hang around. We find things to do."

¶41 Zebra's hand had begun to tingle and throb. Why was the man asking all those questions? Zebra thought maybe he shouldn't be talking to him at all. He seemed vaguely <u>menacing</u> in that army jacket, the dark-blue cap with the words LAND ROVER on it in orange letters, and the empty sleeve. Yet there was kindness in his gray eyes and <u>ruddy</u> features.

The man gazed past Zebra at the students playing in the yard. "Adam, do you think your school would be interested in having someone teach an art class during the summer?"

¶43 That took Zebra by surprise. "An art class?"

"Drawing, sculpting, things like that."

¶45 Zebra was trying very hard not to look at the man's empty sleeve. "I don't know. . . ."

"Where's the school office, Adam?"

¶47 "On Washington Avenue. Go to the end of the street and turn right."

Words to Know

menacing: *(adj.)* threatening

ruddy: *(adj.)* reddened, usually by the sun

"What happened to you, Adam?"

Thanks," the man said. He hesitated a moment. Then he asked, in a quiet voice,

¶49 "A car hit me," Zebra said. "It was my fault."

The man seemed to <u>wince</u>.

¶51 For a flash of a second, Zebra thought to ask the man what had happened to him. The words were on his tongue. But he kept himself from saying anything.

The man started back up the street, carrying the brown plastic bag.

¶53 Zebra suddenly called, "Hey, mister."

The man stopped and turned. "My name is John Wilson," he said softly.

¶55 "Mr. Wilson, when you go into the school office, you'll see signs on two doors. One says 'Dr. Winter,' and the other says 'Mrs. English.' Ask for Mrs. English."

Dr. Winter, the principal, was a <u>disciplinarian</u> and a grump. Mrs. English, the assistant principal, was generous and kind. Dr. Winter would probably tell the man to call his secretary for an appointment. Mrs. English might invite him into her office and offer him a cup of coffee and listen to what he had to say.

¶57 The man hesitated, looking at Zebra.

"Appreciate the advice," he said.

¶59 Zebra watched him walk to the corner.

Under the lamppost was a trash can. Zebra saw the man set down the plastic bag and stick his hand into the can and haul out a battered umbrella.

Words to Know

<u>wince</u>: (v.) to flinch, move back suddenly due to shock or surprise

<u>disciplinarian</u>: (n.) a person who is interested in disciplining others

---

Close Reading

Literary Analysis

14. In **paragraph 50** why does the man seem "to wince"?

Writing

15. Why does Zebra tell the man to speak to Mrs. English? Why do you think he suddenly decides to help the man?

Zebra tells the man to see Mrs. English because _____. At the last minute, he helps the man because _____.

Close Reading

Common Core Code X

Literary Analysis

16. In **paragraph 61**, why does the man put a broken umbrella into his bag? Why does the author let us know that the umbrella is broken?

Literary Analysis

17. Reread **paragraph 65**. What is the significant about the way the school nurse addresses Zebra?

¶61 The man tried to open the umbrella, but its metal ribs were broken. The black fabric dangled flat and limp from the pole. He put the umbrella into the plastic bag and headed for the entrance to the school.

A moment later, Zebra heard the whistle that signaled the end of recess. He followed his classmates at a distance, careful to avoid anyone's bumping against his hand.

¶63 He sat through his algebra class, copying the problems on the blackboard while holding down his notebook with his left elbow. The sling chafed his neck and felt warm and clumsy on his bare arm. There were sharp pains now in the two curled fingers of his hand.

Right after the class he went downstairs to the office of Mrs. Walsh, a cheerful, gray-haired woman in a white nurse's uniform.

¶65 She said, "I'm sorry I can't do very much for you, Adam, except give you two Tylenols."

Words to Know

chafed: *(v.)* rubbed uncomfortably

He swallowed the Tylenols down with water.

¶67 On his way back up to the second floor, he saw the man with the dark-blue cap emerge from the school office with Mrs. English. He stopped on the stairs and watched as the man and Mrs. English stood talking together. Mrs. English nodded and smiled and shook the man's hand.

The man walked down the corridor, carrying the plastic bag, and left the school building.

¶69 Zebra went slowly to his next class.

The class was taught by Mrs. English, who came hurrying into the room some minutes after the bell had rung.

¶71 "I apologize for being late," she said, sounding a little out of breath. "There was an important matter I had to attend to."

Mrs. English was a tall, gracious woman in her forties. It was common knowledge that early in her life she had been a journalist on a Chicago newspaper and had written short stories, which she could not get published. Soon after her marriage to a doctor, she had become a teacher.

¶73 This was the only class Mrs. English taught.

Ten students from the upper school—seventh and eighth grades—were chosen every year for this class. They met for an hour three times a week and told one another stories. Each story would be discussed and analyzed by Mrs. English and the class.

¶75 Mrs. English called it a class in the imagination.

Zebra was grateful he did not have to take notes in this class. He had only to listen to the stories.

¶77 That day, Andrea, the freckle-faced, redheaded girl with very thick glasses who sat next to Zebra, told about a woman scientist who discovered a method of healing trees that had been blasted apart by lightning.

Words to Know

gracious: *(adj.)* kind and pleasant

Close Reading

Literary Analysis

18. In **paragraph 67**, why does Zebra identify the John Wilson as "the man with the dark-blue cap"? Why does he not think of Wilson by name, for instance, or in terms of his missing arm?

Words and Phrases in Context

19. In **paragraph 72**, what does "common knowledge" mean? Why does the author include the information about Mrs. English's earlier career?

Mark, who had something wrong with his upper lip, told in his quavery voice about a selfish space cadet who stepped into a time machine and met his future self, who turned out to be a hateful person, and how the cadet then returned to the present and changed himself.

¶79 Kevin talked in blurred, high-pitched tones and often related parts of his stories with his hands. Mrs. English would quietly repeat many of his sentences. Today he told about an explorer who set out on a journey through a valley filled with yellow stones and surrounded by red mountains, where he **encountered** an army of green shadows that had been at war for hundreds of years with an army of purple shadows. The explorer showed them how to make peace.

When it was Zebra's turn, he told a story about a bird that one day crashed against a closed windowpane and broke a wing. A boy tried to heal the wing but couldn't. The bird died, and the boy buried it under a tree on his lawn.

¶81 When he had finished, there was silence. Everyone in the class was looking at him.

"You always tell such sad stories," Andrea said.

¶83 The bell rang. Mrs. English dismissed the class. In the hallway, Andrea said to Zebra, "You know, you are a very gloomy life form."

"Andrea, get off my case," Zebra said.

¶85 He went out to the schoolyard for the mid afternoon recess. On the other side of the chain-link fence was the man in the dark-blue cap. Zebra went over to him.

"Hello again, Adam," the man said. "I've been waiting for you."

¶87 "Hello," said Zebra.

"Thanks much for suggesting I talk to Mrs. English."

Words to Know

<u>quavery</u>: *(adj.)* shaky

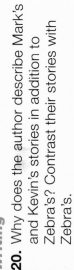

Close Reading

Writing
20. Why does the author describe Mark's and Kevin's stories in addition to Zebra's? Contrast their stories with Zebra's.

The other boys' stories _____, while Zebra's story _____.

The author describes the other stories to make the point _____

Literary Analysis
21. Why do you think everyone but Andrea stayed silent after Zebra told his story?

Words and Phrases in Context
22. What does Andrea mean when she calls Zebra "a very gloomy life form"?

¶89 "You're welcome."

"Adam, you at all interested in art?"

¶91 "No."

"You ever try your hand at it?"

¶93 "I've made drawings for class. I don't like it."

"Well, just in case you change your mind, I'm giving an art class in your school during the summer."

¶95 "I'm going to camp in August," Zebra said.

"There's the big long month of July."

¶97 "I don't think so," Zebra said.

"Well, okay, suit yourself. I'd like to give you something, a little thank-you gift."

¶99 He reached into an inside pocket and drew out a small pad and a pen. He placed the pad against the fence.

"Adam, you want to help me out a little bit here? Put your fingers through the fence and grab hold of the pad."

¶101 Extending the fingers of his right hand, Zebra held the pad to the fence and watched as the man began to work with the pen. He felt the pad move slightly.

Words to Know

suit: (v.) be convenient or acceptable to something

extending: (v.) stretching out

Close Reading

Literary Analysis

23. What can you infer from **paragraph 94** about Mr. Wilson's conversation with Mrs. English?

Literary Analysis

24. Why is Mr. Wilson so interested in getting Zebra to take his class?

Close Reading

"I need you to hold it real still," the man said.

¶103 He was standing bent over, very close to Zebra. The words LAND ROVER on his cap shone in the afternoon sunlight. As he worked, he glanced often at Zebra. His tongue kept pushing up against the insides of his cheeks, making tiny hills rise and fall on his face. Wrinkles formed **intricate** spidery webs in the skin below his gray eyes. On his smooth forehead, in the blue and purple shadows beneath the peak of his cap, lay glistening beads of sweat. And his hand—how dirty it was, the fingers and palm smudged with black ink and encrusted with colors.

Then Zebra glanced down and noticed the plastic bag near the man's feet. It lay partly open. Zebra was able to see a large pink armless doll, a dull metallic object that looked like a dented frying pan, old newspapers, strings of cord, crumpled pieces of red and blue cloth, and the broken umbrella.

¶105 "One more minute is all I need," the man said.

He stepped back, looked at the pad, and nodded slowly. He put the pen back into his pocket and tore the top page from the pad. He rolled up the page and pushed it through the fence. Then he took the pad from Zebra.

¶107 "See you around, Adam," the man said, picking up the plastic bag.

Zebra unrolled the sheet of paper and saw a line drawing, a perfect image of his face.

¶109 He was looking at himself as if in a mirror. His long straight nose and thin lips and sad eyes and gaunt face; his dark hair and smallish ears and the scar on his forehead where he had hurt himself years before while roller skating.

In the lower right-hand corner of the page the man had written: "To ADAM, with thanks, John Wilson."

Literary Analysis

25. What is Wilson drawing? Why is his hand so dirty? Explain.

Literary Analysis

26. Where did the items in Wilson's plastic bag come from? Why does the author keep mentioning this bag?

Words to Know

<u>encrusted:</u> *(adj.)* crusted over

¶111 Zebra raised his eyes from the drawing. The man was walking away.

Zebra called out, "Mr. Wilson, all my friends call me Zebra."

¶113 The man turned, looking surprised.

"From my last name," Adam said. "Zebrin. Adam Martin Zebrin. They call me Zebra."

¶115 "Is that right?" the man said, starting back toward the fence. "Well, in that case you want to give me back that piece of paper."

He took the pad and pen from his pocket, placed the page on the pad, and, with Zebra holding the pad to the fence, did something to the page and then handed it back.

¶117 "You take real good care of yourself, Zebra," the man said. He went off toward Franklin Avenue.

Zebra looked at the drawing. The man had crossed out Adam and over it had drawn an animal with a stubby neck and short legs and a striped body.

¶119 A zebra!

Its legs were in full gallop. It seemed as if it would gallop right off the page.

¶121 A strong breeze rippled across the drawing, causing it to flutter like a flag in Zebra's hand. He looked out at the street.

The man was walking slowly in the shadows of the tall oaks. Zebra had the odd **sensation** that all the houses on the street had turned toward the man and were watching him as he walked along. How strange that was: the windows and porches and columns and front doors following intently the slow walk of that tall, one-armed man—until he turned into Franklin Avenue and was gone.

Words to Know

rippled: (v.) to move in a way that ripples in water do

Close Reading

Literary Analysis

27. Explain why Zebra decides to tell Mr. Wilson his nickname, and then his full name.

Text Structure

28. What does the exclamation point in **paragraph 119** indicate?

Literary Analysis

29. In **paragraph 122**, why does Zebra have the "odd sensation" that "all the houses on the street" were watching John Wilson?

¶123 The whistle blew, and Zebra went inside. Seated at his desk, he slipped the drawing carefully into one of his notebooks.

From time to time he glanced at it. Just before the bell signaled the end of the school day, he looked at it again.

¶125 Now *that* was strange! He thought he remembered that the zebra had been drawn directly over his name: the head over the A and the tail over the M. Didn't it seem now to have moved a little beyond A?

Probably he was running a fever again. He would run mysterious fevers off and on for about three weeks after each operation on his hand. Fevers sometimes did that to him: excited his imagination.

¶127 He lived four blocks from the school. The school bus dropped him off at his corner. In his schoolbag he carried his books and the notebook with the drawing.

Words to Know

signaled: (v.) indicated; gave a signal

operation: (n.) surgery

Close Reading

Writing

30. Describe Zebra's growing feelings about the drawing. Cite details from the text that reveal how he feels.

Zebra has become _____ . All day, he cannot stop _____ . In fact, he is so _____ the zebra drawing that he imagines that _____ .

Literary Analysis

31. Why does Zebra ride the bus home from school when he lives only four blocks away? Why does the author include these details?

His mother offered him a snack, but he said he wasn't hungry. Up in his room, he looked again at the drawing and was astonished to discover that the zebra had reached the edge of his name and appeared <u>poised</u> to leap off.

¶129 It had to be a fever that was causing him to see the zebra that way. And sure enough, when his mother took his temperature, the thermometer registered 102.6 degrees.

She gave him his medicine, but it didn't seem to have much effect, because when he woke at night and switched on his desk light and peered at the drawing, he saw the little zebra galloping across the page, along the <u>contours</u> of his face, over the hills and valleys of his eyes and nose and mouth, and he heard the tiny clickings of its hooves as cloudlets of dust rose in its wake.

¶131 He knew he was asleep. He knew it was the fever working upon his imagination.

But it was so real.

¶133 The little zebra running . . .

When he woke in the morning the fever was gone, and the zebra was quietly in its place over Adam.

¶135 Later, as he entered the school, he noticed a large sign on the bulletin board in the hallway:

SUMMER ART CLASS

¶137 The well-known American artist Mr. John Wilson will conduct an art class during the summer for students in 7th and 8th grades. For details, speak to Mrs. English. There will be no tuition fee for this class.

Words to Know

<u>poised</u>: (adj.) ready; in position

<u>contours</u>: (n.) edges

Close Reading

Text Structure

32. What effect does the author create with the series of short paragraphs, **131–133**? Why is **paragraph 133** an incomplete sentence?

Literary Analysis

33. Examine **paragraph 136**. Why do these three words appear in all capital letters, and set apart as a paragraph?

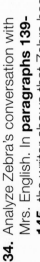

Close Reading

Text Structure

34. Analyze Zebra's conversation with Mrs. English. In **paragraphs 139-145**, the writer shows that Zebra has a hard time asking her questions. How does the writer convey this difficulty? What does it imply when Zebra tells her, in **paragraph 141**, that he can't draw?

Literary Analysis

35. Why does Zebra want to know where Vietnam is? What does it imply that he is willing to ask Mr. Morgan?

During the morning, between classes, Zebra ran into Mrs. English in the second-floor hallway.

¶139 "Mrs. English, about the summer art class . . . is it okay to ask where—um—where Mr. Wilson is from?"

"He is from a small town in Virginia. Are you thinking of signing up for his class?"

¶141 "I can't draw," Zebra said.

"Drawing is something you can learn."

¶143 "Mrs. English, is it okay to ask how did Mr. Wilson—um—get hurt?"

The school corridors were always crowded between classes. Zebra and Mrs. English formed a little island in the <u>bustling</u>, student-jammed hallway.

¶145 "Mr. Wilson was wounded in the war in Vietnam," Mrs. English said. "I would urge you to join his class. You will get to use your imagination."

For the next hour, Zebra sat impatiently through Mr. Morgan's geography class, and afterward he went up to the teacher.

¶147 "Mr. Morgan, could I—um—ask where is Vietnam?"

Mr. Morgan smoothed down the jacket of his beige summer suit, touched his bow tie, rolled down a wall map, picked up his pointer, and cleared his throat.

Words to Know

<u>bustling</u>: *(adj.)* busy

¶149 "Vietnam is this long, narrow country in southeast Asia, bordered by China, Laos, and Cambodia. It is a land of valleys in the north, coastal plains in the center, and marshes in the south. There are <u>barren</u> mountains and tropical rain forests. Its chief crops are rice, rubber, fruits, and vegetables. Between 1962 and 1973, America fought a terrible war there to prevent the south from falling into the hands of the communist north. We lost the war."

"Thank you."

¶151 "I am impressed by your suddenly awakened interest in geography, young man, though I must remind you that your class is studying the Mediterranean," said Mr. Morgan.

During the afternoon recess, Zebra was watching a heated basketball game, when he looked across the yard and saw John Wilson walk by, carrying a <u>laden</u> plastic bag. Some while later, he came back along the street, empty-handed.

¶153 Over supper that evening, Zebra told his parents he was thinking of taking a summer art class offered by the school.

His father said, "Well, I think that's a fine idea." "Wait a minute. I'm not so sure," his mother said.

¶155 "It'll get him off the streets," his father said. "He'll become a Matisse instead of a lawyer like his dad. Right, Adam?"

"Just you be very careful," his mother said to Adam. "Don't do anything that might injure your hand."

¶157 "How can drawing hurt his left hand, for heaven's sake?" said his father.

Words to Know

<u>barren</u>: *(adj.)* empty of plants or animals

<u>laden</u>: *(adj.)*. weighted down

Close Reading

Literary Analysis

36. Why might a reader see Mr. Morgan's response to Zebra as humorous, even though Mr. Morgan doesn't intend it to be? What does the reader know that Mr. Morgan does not?

Words and Phrases in Context

37. Based on what Zebra has observed Mr. Wilson doing already, what do you think his bag is "laden" with?

Words and Phrases in Context

38. In **paragraph 155**, why does Zebra's father suggest that Zebra will become a Matisse?

Close Reading

Word and Phrases in Context

39. What does it mean that Zebra's hand was a "dread and a mystery" to him? Identify what's unusual about this use of *dread*.

Literary Analysis

40. Why does Zebra feel he has been "stupid, stupid, stupid"? How is this feeling connected to his observation that "the galloping little zebra stood very still"?

That night, Zebra lay in bed looking at his hand. It was a dread and a mystery to him, his own hand. The fingers were all there, but like dead leaves that never fell, the ring and little fingers were <u>rigid</u> and curled, the others barely moved. The doctors said it would take time to bring them back to life. So many broken bones. So many torn muscles and <u>tendons</u>. So many injured nerves. The dark shadow had sprung upon him so suddenly. How stupid, stupid, stupid he had been!

¶159 He couldn't sleep. He went over to his desk and looked at John Wilson's drawing. The galloping little zebra stood very still over Adam.

Early the following afternoon, on the last day of school, Zebra went to Mrs. English's office and signed up for John Wilson's summer art class.

¶161 "The class will meet every weekday from ten in the morning until one," said Mrs. English. "Starting Monday."

Zebra noticed the three plastic bags in a corner of the office.

¶163 "Mrs. English, is it okay to ask what Mr. Wilson—um—did in Vietnam?"

He told me he was a helicopter pilot," Mrs. English said. "Oh, I neglected to mention that you are to bring an unlined notebook and a pencil to the class."

¶165 "That's all? A notebook and a pencil?"

Mrs. English smiled. "And your imagination."

¶167 When Zebra entered the art class the next Monday morning, he found about fifteen students there—including Andrea from his class with Mrs. English.

The walls of the room were bare. Everything had been removed for the summer. Zebra noticed two plastic bags on the floor beneath the blackboard.

¶169 He sat down at the desk next to Andrea's.

Words to Know

<u>rigid</u>: *(adj.)* stiff

<u>tendons</u>: *(n.)* fibrous tissues that attach muscle to bone

She wore blue jeans and a yellow summer blouse with blue stripes. Her long red hair was tied behind her head with a dark-blue ribbon. She gazed at Zebra through her thick glasses, leaned over, and said, "Are you going to make gloomy drawings, too?"

¶171 Just then John Wilson walked in, carrying a plastic bag, which he put down on the floor next to the two others.

He stood alongside the front desk, wearing a light-blue long-sleeved shirt and jeans. The left shirtsleeve had been folded back and pinned to the shirt. The dark-blue cap with the words LAND ROVER sat jauntily on his head.

¶173 "Good morning to you-all," he said with a shy smile. "Mighty glad you're here. We're going to do two things this summer. We're going to make paper into faces and garbage into people. I can see by your expressions that you don't know what I'm talking about, right? Well, I'm about to show you."

He asked everyone to draw the face of someone sitting nearby.

¶175 Zebra hesitated, looked around, then made a drawing of Andrea. Andrea carefully drew Zebra.

He showed Andrea his drawing. "It's awful." She grimaced. "I look like a mouse."

¶177 Her drawing of him was good. But was his face really so sad?

Words to Know

jauntily: *(adv.)* cheerfully

Close Reading

Literary Analysis

41. In **paragraph 170**, why does Andrea ask Zebra if he's "going to make gloomy drawings, too?"

Writing

42. What does expressions mean in **paragraph 173**? Discuss context clues that indicate its meaning; then, identify another way you could use "expression" when talking about art.

In this paragraph, expression means
_____ . *I can tell because* John Wilson
_____ . *In art class, you might also use*
expression _____ .

Literary Analysis

43. Consider the relationship between Zebra and Andrea. How does her drawing of Zebra sum it up?

Close Reading

Academic Vocabulary

44. Why does it matter where a drawing is "situated in relation to the edge of the paper"?

John Wilson went from desk to desk, peering intently at the drawings. He paused a long moment over Zebra's drawing. Then he spent more than an hour <u>demonstrating</u> with chalk on the blackboard how they should not be thinking *eyes* or *lips* or *hands* while drawing, but should think only *lines* and *curves* and *shapes*; how they should be looking at where everything was **situated** in relation to the edge of the paper; and how they should not be looking *directly* at the edges of what they were drawing but at the space *outside* the edges.

¶**179** Zebra stared in wonder at how fast John Wilson's hand raced across the blackboard, and at the empty sleeve rising and falling lightly against the shirt.

"You-all are going to learn how to see in a new way," John Wilson said.

¶**181** They made another drawing of the same face.

"Now I look like a horse," Andrea said. "Are you going to add stripes?"

¶**183** "You are one big pain, Andrea," Zebra said.

Shortly before noon, John Wilson laid out on his desk the contents of the plastic bags: a clutter of junked broken objects, including the doll and the umbrella.

¶**185** Using strips of cloth, some lengths of string, crumpled newspaper, his pen, and his one hand, he swiftly transformed the battered doll into a red-nosed, umbrella-carrying clown, with baggy pants, a tattered coat, a derby hat, and a somber smile. Turning over the battered frying pan, he made it into a <u>pedestal</u>, on which he placed the clown.

Literary Analysis

45. How is John Wilson teaching the students to see in a new way? Locate examples that explain what he means.

Words to Know

<u>demonstrating:</u> (*v.*) showing how to do something

<u>pedestal:</u> (*n.*) a stand upon which something is placed

"That's a sculpture," John Wilson said, with his shy smile. "Garbage into people."

¶187 The class burst into applause. The clown on the frying pan looked as if it might take a bow.

"You-all will be doing that, too, before we're done," John Wilson said. "Now I would like you to sign and date your drawings and give them to me."

¶189 When they returned the next morning the drawings were on a wall. Gradually, in the days that followed, the walls began to fill with drawings.

Sculptures made by the students were looked at with care, discussed by John Wilson and the class, and then placed on shelves along the walls: a miniature bicycle made of wire; a parrot made of an old sofa cushion; a cowboy made of rope and string; a fat lady made of a dented metal pitcher; a zebra made of glued-together scraps of cardboard.

¶191 "I like your zebra," Andrea said.

"Thanks," Zebra said. "I like your parrot."

¶193 One morning John Wilson asked the class members to make a contour drawing of their right or left hand. Zebra felt himself sweating and trembling as he worked.

"That's real nice," John Wilson said, when he saw Andrea's drawing.

¶195 He gazed at the drawing made by Zebra.

"You-all were looking at your hand," he said. "You ought to have been looking at the edge of your hand and at the space outside."

Words to Know

<u>miniature:</u> *(adj.)* a small object that resembles something that is usually much bigger

Close Reading

Literary Analysis

46. Identify two questions that are answered in **paragraphs 185–188** in the text. What does Zebra learn that he has been wondering about since he met Wilson? What does Wilson explain to the class?

Literary Analysis

47. Reread **paragraph 196**. What is the literal meaning of Wilson's comment to Zebra? What is the figurative interpretation? On what levels is Wilson qualified to give this advice?

Close Reading

Words and Phrases in Context

48. Why does Zebra find it astonishing that his drawing looks like a hand?

Text Structure

49. Why are the words *felt deeply* italicized in **paragraph 198** and again in **paragraph 204**?

¶197 Zebra drew his hand again. Strange and ugly, the two fingers lay rigid and curled. But <u>astonishingly</u>, it looked like a hand this time.

One day, a few minutes before the end of class, John Wilson gave everyone an assignment: draw or make something at home, something very special that each person *felt deeply* about. And bring it to class.

¶199 Zebra remembered seeing a book titled *Incredible Cross-Sections* on a shelf in the family room at home. He found the book and took it into his room.

There was a color drawing of a rescue helicopter on one of the Contents pages. On pages 30 and 31, the helicopter was shown in pieces, its complicated insides displayed in detailed drawings. Rotor blades, control rods, electronics equipment, radar scanner, tail rotor, engine, lifeline, winch — all its many parts.

¶201 Zebra sat at his desk, gazing intently at the space outside the edges of the helicopter on the Contents page.

He made an outline drawing and brought it to class the next morning.

¶203 John Wilson looked at it. Was there a stiffening of his muscular neck, a sudden tensing of the hand that held the drawing?

He took the drawing and tacked it to the wall. The next day he gave them all the same home assignment: draw or make something they *felt very deeply* about.

Words to Know

<u>astonishingly</u> *(adv.)* very surprisingly

¶205 That afternoon, Zebra went rummaging through the trash bin in his kitchen and the garbage cans that stood near the back door of his home. He found some sardine cans, a broken eggbeater, pieces of cardboard, chipped buttons, bent bobby pins, and other odds and ends.

With the help of epoxy glue, he began to make of those bits of garbage a kind of helicopter. For support, he used his desktop, the floor, his knees, the elbow of his left arm, at one point even his chin. Struggling with the last piece— a button he wanted to position as a wheel—he realized that without thinking he had been using his left hand, and the two curled fingers had straightened slightly to his needs.

¶207 His heart beat thunderously. There had been so many hope-filled moments before, all of them ending in bitter disappointment. He would say nothing. Let the therapist or the doctors tell him. . . .

The following morning, he brought the helicopter to the class.

¶209 "Eeewwww, what is *that*?" Andrea grimaced.

"Something to eat you with," Zebra said.

¶211 "Get human, Zebra. Mr. Wilson will have a laughing fit over that."

But John Wilson didn't laugh. He held the helicopter in his hand a long moment, turning it this way and that, nodded at Zebra, and placed it on a windowsill, where it shimmered in the summer sunlight.

Words to Know

rummaging: *(v.)* messily searching through something in no particular order
shimmered: *(v.)* shined with a quavery light

Cl[...]

LITERATURE

Literary A[...]

50. Why is [...] as a p[...] Why c[...] to make it[...]

Literary Analysis

51. Explain what is happening to Zebra in **paragraph 207**? Why does his heart "beat thunderously"? What does he decide to say nothing about?

Writing

52. How does Zebra feel about his art class? Cite details from the short story that reveal his feelings.

Zebra _____ his art class. Details that reveal this include _____.
I can also infer _____.

3c

Lit[...]
5[...]

Close Reading

Literary Analysis

53. Why is it hard for Zebra to decide what to draw for John Wilson?

¶**213** The next day, John Wilson informed everyone that three students would be leaving the class at the end of July. He asked each of those students to make a drawing for him that he would get to keep. Something to remember them by. All their other drawings and sculptures they could take home.

Zebra lay awake a long time that night, staring into the darkness of his room. He could think of nothing to draw for John Wilson.

¶**215** In the morning, he sat gazing out the classroom window at the sky and at the helicopter on the sill.

"What are you going to draw for him?" Andrea asked.

¶**217** Zebra shrugged and said he didn't know.

"Use your imagination," she said. Then she said, "Wait, what am I seeing here? Are you able to move those fingers?"

¶**219** "I think so."

"You think so?"

¶**221** "The doctors said there was some improvement."

Her eyes glistened behind the thick lenses. She seemed genuinely happy.

¶**223** He sat looking out the window. Dark birds wheeled and soared. There was the sound of traffic. The helicopter sat on the windowsill, its eggbeater rotor blades ready to move to full throttle.

Literary Analysis

54. How has Zebra's relationship with Andrea evolved? Locate details in the text that reflect their growing friendship.

Literary Analysis

55. What did Zebra notice as "he sat looking out the window"?

Words to Know

glistened: (*v.*) shone wetly

wheeled: (*v.*) turned

Later that day, Zebra sat at his desk at home, working on a drawing. He held the large sheet of paper in place by pressing down on it with the palm and fingers of his left hand. He drew a landscape: hills and valleys, forests and flatlands, rivers and plateaus. Oddly, it all seemed to resemble a face.

¶225 Racing together over that landscape were a helicopter and a zebra. It was all he could think to draw. It was not a very good drawing. He signed it: "To John Wilson, with thanks. Zebra."

The next morning, John Wilson looked at the drawing and asked Zebra to write on top of the name "John Wilson" the name "Leon."

¶227 "He was an old buddy of mine, an artist. We were in Vietnam together. Would've been a much better artist than I'll ever be."

Zebra wrote in the new name.

¶229 "Thank you kindly," John Wilson said, taking the drawing. "Zebra, you have yourself a good time in camp and a good life. It was real nice knowing you."

He shook Zebra's hand. How strong his fingers felt!

Close Reading

Text Structure

56. Reread the last sentence in **paragraph 224**. Replace *oddly* with *unsurprisingly*. How does the new adverb change the meaning of the sentence? Which sentence would John Wilson be most likely to write? Explain.

Literary Analysis

57. What does John Wilson think of Zebra's drawing? Does he agree with Zebra that it is not very good? Identify details that reveal how he feels.

Text Structure

58. What does the sentence "would've been a much better artist than I'll ever be" imply about Wilson's Vietnam buddy, Leon?

Words to Know

plateaus: (n.) high, flat areas

¶231 "I think I'm going to miss you a little," Andrea said to Zebra after the class.

"I'll only be away a month."

¶233 "Can I help you carry some of those drawings?"

"Sure. I'll carry the helicopter."

¶235 Zebra went off to a camp in the Adirondack Mountains. He hiked and read and watched others playing ball. In the arts and crafts program he made some good drawings and even got to learn a little bit about watercolors. He put together clowns and airplanes and helicopters out of <u>discarded</u> cardboard and wood and clothing. From time to time his hand hurt, but the fingers seemed slowly to be coming back to life.

"Patience, young man," the doctors told him when he returned to the city. "You're getting there."

¶237 One or two additional operations were still necessary. But there was no urgency. And he no longer needed the leg brace.

Close Reading

Writing

59. What does Andrea's dialogue in **paragraphs 231 and 233** reveal about how her attitude toward Zebra has changed?

Andrea used to say mostly ____ things to Zebra; for example, ____ and ____. Recently, she is mostly ____ to Zebra; for example, ____ and ____.

60. Text Structure

Compare and contrast Zebra at camp with Zebra on the school playground at the beginning of the story, when he first met Wilson. How has Zebra changed since then?

Words to Know

<u>**discarded:**</u> *(adj.)* thrown away

Close Reading

Literary Analysis

61. Zebra tells Mrs. Wilson that his summer was okay. Do you think that assessment is accurate? Why do you think he puts it that way? Explain.

Literary Analysis

62. Why did Mr. Wilson send Zebra the photograph? Identify the detail that explains why he sent it.

On the first day of school, one of the secretaries found him in the hallway and told him to report to Mrs. English.

¶239 "Did you have a good summer?" Mrs. English asked.

"It was okay," Zebra said.

¶241 "This came for you in the mail."

She handed him a large brown envelope. It was addressed to Adam Zebrin, Eighth Grade, at the school. The sender was John Wilson, with a return address in Virginia.

She helped Zebra open the envelope.

¶243 "Adam, I admit I'm very curious to see what's inside," Mrs. English said.

¶245 Between two pieces of cardboard were a letter and a large color photograph.

The photograph showed John Wilson down on his right knee before a glistening dark wall. He wore his army jacket and blue jeans and boots, and the cap with the words LAND ROVER. Leaning against the wall to his right was Zebra's drawing of the helicopter and the zebra racing together across a facelike landscape. The drawing was enclosed in a narrow frame.

¶247 The wall behind John Wilson seemed to glitter with a strange black light.

Zebra read the letter and showed it to Mrs. English.

Close Reading

Text Structure

63. What new information do we learn about Wilson from this letter? How does reading Wilson's letter in the first person add to readers' understanding of this character?

Words and Phrases in Context

64. Where did John Wilson take the photo he sent to Zebra? What similar phrases does the author use both here and **paragraph 247** to let readers know?

Literary Analysis

65. What prompts Zebra to take a walk on Franklin Avenue?

¶**249** *Dear Zebra,*

 One of the people whose names are on this wall was among my very closest friends. He was an artist named Leon Kellner. Each year I visit him and leave a gift— something very special that someone creates and gives me. I leave it near his name for a few hours, and then I take it to my <u>studio</u> in Virginia, where I keep a collection of those gifts. All year long I work in my studio, but come summer I go looking for another gift to give him.
Thank you for your gift.

  Your friend, John Wilson

  P.S. I hope your hand is healing.

Mrs. English stood staring awhile at the letter. She turned away and touched her eyes. Then she went to a shelf on the wall behind her, took down a large book, leafed through it quickly, found what she was searching for, and held it out for Zebra to see.

¶**251** Zebra found himself looking at the glistening black wall of the Vietnam Memorial in Washington, D.C. And at the names on it, the thousands of names.

Later, in the school yard during recess, Zebra stood alone at the chain-link fence and <u>gazed</u> down the street toward Franklin Avenue. He thought how strange it was that all the houses on this street had seemed to turn toward John Wilson that day, the windows and porches and columns and doors, as if saluting him.

¶**253** Had that been only his imagination?

Maybe, Zebra thought, just maybe he could go for a walk to Franklin Avenue on

---

Words to Know

<u>studio</u>: *(n.)* a room where an artist works

Saturday or Sunday. He had not walked along Franklin Avenue since the accident; had not gone down that steep hill. Yes, he would walk carefully down that hill to the corner and walk back up and past the school and then the four blocks home.

¶255 Andrea came over to him.

"We didn't get picked for the story class with Mrs. English," she said. "I won't have to listen to any more of your gloomy stories."

¶257 Zebra said nothing.

"You know, I think I'll walk home today instead of taking the school bus," Andrea said.

¶259 "Actually, I think I'll walk, too," Zebra said. "I was thinking maybe I could pick up some really neat stuff in the street."

"You are becoming a pleasant life form," Andrea said.

Close Reading

Writing

66. Why does Zebra plan to "pick up some really neat stuff in the street"?

Zebra has become _____.

He plans to use the "neat stuff" to _____. Zebra can no longer _____ but now he has a new _____.

Text Structure

67. Reread the last sentence of this story. Is Andrea's statement a fitting way to end the story? Explain.

Identify Evidence | Analyze Individuals, Events, and Ideas

Reread "Zebra," highlighting examples and events Potok includes that describe how the power of art and his empathetic friendship with Mr. Wilson help Zebra heal after his accident.

- In the Evidence column, record examples from the text that describe Zebra's difficulties post-accident, and how he discovers and is transformed by art.
- In the Explanation column, explain how the evidence introduces, illustrates, or develops characters, events, and ideas.

Evidence	Source	Page	Explanation
1. "That day, because his hand hurt so badly, he stood alone behind the chain-link fence of the school yard."	Potok	138	After a car accident, Zebra's whole life changes. His hand hurts all the time, he feels sad and isolated from his friends, and he can no longer do the thing he loves best.
2.			
3.			
4.			

	Evidence	Source	Page	Explanation
5.				
6.				
7.				

Key Ideas and Details

Determining the Central Idea

1. Use the evidence you collected to summarize the key idea of Potok's short story. What is the central idea of the text? Use evidence.

2. List three key characters from this story. Explain why each is important to the central idea.

Character	Significance

3. List three events from this story. Explain why each event is important to the central idea.

Event	Significance

Craft and Structure

Structure of a Letter

1. Identify the **greeting** in Mr. Wilson's letter to Zebra on page 162.

2. What does Mr. Wilson write about in the **body** of the letter?

3. Identify the **signature** of Mr. Wilson's letter.

4. Sometimes, a personal letter includes a "P.S." The letters *P.S.* stand for "postscript." A postscript is a message that the letter writer forgot to include in the body of the letter. What is Mr. Wilson's "P.S." to Zebra?

Purpose of a Letter

5. What is the purpose of Wilson's letter from the character's perspective? Why did he write to Zebra?

6. What is the author's purpose in including this letter in the short story?

7. Compare and contrast Wilson's letter to Anna Deavere Smith's letters in Text 1.

Collaborate and Present

Plan and Deliver a Multi-Media Presentation

Assignment: Work with a group to discuss the role mentors play in the letters from *Letters to a Young Artist* and in "Zebra." Then create a poem, story, artwork, or video to represent a mentor in your own life.

Analyze the Content

1. Consider the following questions:
   - What did Anna Deavere Smith suggest that mentors do? How does their guidance help young artists grow?
   - What did Mr. Wilson do for Zebra? How did his actions affect Zebra's life?

2. Return to the texts and find examples of things mentors did or could do. Then explain how each example did or could affect someone's life.

Example	Effect

Create Your Presentation

3. Use your chart to help you determine who your mentors are and how they have guided or inspired you.
   - Choose a mentor and a format. How will your project represent your mentor?
   - Create a sketch, draft, or outline of your presentation.

Present

4. Share your completed project with the class.

Seeking Clarification

- I think you are saying that in the text . . . .
- If I understand you correctly, you mean . . . .
- So what you are saying is . . . .

Reporting Ideas

- _____ noted that
- _____ gave evidence that
- _____ emphasized

Presentation

- Confirm that your ideas are sensible and comprehensible.
- Make sure that your writing and/or artwork is legible.
- Determine that your sound and video are in a format that viewers and listeners will be able to view, hear, and understand.

Project Checklist

Use the checklist below to evaluate your collaboration skills, reasoning, and final presentation. Think carefully about your work. If you know you completed an item thoroughly, give yourself a check (✓).

COLLABORATE AND PRESENT CHECKLIST

Comprehension & Collaboration

- ☐ Come to discussions prepared, having read and studied material.
- ☐ Refer to evidence when contributing to the discussion.
- ☐ Follow rules for discussions and lead by example.
- ☐ Ask and answer specific questions.
- ☐ Make comments that contribute to the topic under discussion.
- ☐ Review the key ideas under discussion and demonstrate understanding of multiple perspectives through reflection and paraphrasing.

Number of ✓s in this category: ____

Evidence and Reasoning

- ☐ Explain the purpose of the presentation.
- ☐ Present information relevant to the task.
- ☐ Explain whom your art represents.
- ☐ Explain why that person is your mentor.
- ☐ Use at least one example from each text that helped you define the role of a mentor and identify a mentor in your own life.
- ☐ Synthesize the key ideas of your project in a conclusion.

Number of ✓s in this category: ____

Presentation of Knowledge & Ideas

- ☐ Adapt language to a variety of contexts and tasks to demonstrate knowledge of formal English.
- ☐ Include multimedia components (e.g., graphics, images, music, sound) and visual displays.
- ☐ Use appropriate volume/tone (clear, not too fast, too slow, or too loud) and avoid using *like* or *ummm*.
- ☐ Have strong posture, a confident stance, and make frequent eye contact.
- ☐ Occasionally move from one spot to another without fiddling.
- ☐ Smile and act relaxed.

Number of ✓s in this category: ____

Total # of ✓s: ____

Add up the total number of checks (✓) in each category. Then use the scoring guide below to calculate your final score.

Scoring Guide

16 to 18 ✓s	13 to 15 ✓s	11 to 12 ✓s	10 or less ✓s
④ Exemplary	③ Meets Standards	② Needs Work	① Does Not Meet Standards

Read the Model

Writers use many strategies to craft ideas and persuade readers. The writer of this argumentative essay explains why an artist needs knowledge and empathy in order to create great works of art. Read and discuss the model essay below.

Argumentative Essay

An argumentative essay provides a clearly stated claim that is supported with logical reasoning and relevant evidence.

The introduction states the claim.

- **Identify the claim.**

The body paragraphs provide logical reasons in support of the claim.

- **Identify two reasons that support the claim.**

- **Identify examples of text citations.**

- **Verb voice can be active or passive.**

- **Identify examples of active and passive voice.**

The conclusion sums up or restates the claim.

- **Identify the conclusion.**

Requirement for Artists   By David Quinn

Art comes in many forms—painting, drawing, acting, making music, and writing. While the forms vary greatly, the works themselves often share a similar purpose: to interpret and comment on the world around us. In order to achieve this goal and create great art, artists need empathy and knowledge.

Some people might claim that true artists can create art spontaneously with little special knowledge or understanding. As Anna Deavere Smith points out in *Letters to a Young Artist*, this is not the case. "I believe that fundamental to becoming an artist is understanding the position of an artist, rehearsing that position, and practicing that position," Smith writes (123). While hours of studying for an advanced degree may not contribute to creating great art, knowledge and practice of the artist's role is critical components to creating a great art."

Empathy, or the ability to understand another person's feelings or perspective, is another important trait of a great artist. Critics may claim just the opposite and say that art is entirely based on the artist's own experiences and perspective. But as Deavere Smith states, "artists are students of the human condition," and empathy is "important" and "potentially very productive" because "it requires a very highly developed imagination" and intellect (124).

There is no set prescription to follow for creating great art. However, it is clear that an artist with knowledge and empathy, combined with a rich imagination and a creative spirit, is on a path to creating great art. If artists have knowledge and empathy, they can channel these traits into their creative works, creating art for many to appreciate and enjoy.

Analyze the Model

An argumentative essay states a claim and supports it with logical reasons and evidence from the text.

Structuring an Argument

In an **argumentative essay**, the writer uses an organizational structure that effectively and logically sequences claims, counterclaims, reasons and evidence.

The **claim** presents a clear plan for the essay.

- Evaluate the claim.

The **topic sentence** of each body paragraph clearly states reasons in support of the claim.

- Evaluate whether each topic sentence supports the claim.

Relevant **evidence** includes logical reasoning, such as direct quotations from the text, that supports the writer's ideas and/or addresses related counterclaims

- Evaluate whether all sentences in each body paragraph support the topic sentence or address a related counterclaim.

Introduction

Thesis:

Body Paragraph 1

Supporting Evidence:

Reason:

Counterclaim:

Body Paragraph 2

Supporting Evidence:

Reason:

Counterclaim:

Conclusion

Step 1 | Gather Evidence

Does a person need knowledge and empathy to create great art? Consider the arguments and evidence in at least one selection as you develop your claim.

What You Need to Know | Examine the evidence from the excerpt from *Letters to Young Artists* and "Zebra" that supports your claim about the need for artists to have knowledge and empathy to create great art.

What You Need to Write | Use a note-taking guide to list evidence from the text(s) that illustrates and supports your claim and reasons and refutes counterclaims.

Letters to a Young Artist

> Reason:
>
> Counterclaim:
>
> Evidence:
>
> Page # _____

> Reason:
>
> Counterclaim:
>
> Evidence:
>
> Page # _____

> Reason:
>
> Counterclaim:
>
> Evidence:
>
> Page # _____

"Zebra"

> Reason:
>
> Counterclaim:
>
> Evidence:
>
> Page # _____

> Reason:
>
> Counterclaim:
>
> Evidence:
>
> Page # _____

> Reason:
>
> Counterclaim:
>
> Evidence:
>
> Page # _____

Step 2 | Organize Ideas

What You Need to Know | In order to write a successful argument, you need to support your claim with reasons and evidence.

To develop your claim:
1. Review the reasons you have listed and be sure you can support each with specific details and evidence from the text.
2. Prepare to present analysis of both sides of the claim.

What You Need to Write | Study the evidence you have gathered and organize the reasons and evidence that best support your claim.

Introduction

Thesis:

Body Paragraph 1

Counterclaim:
Reason:
Supporting Evidence:

Body Paragraph 2

Counterclaim:
Reason:
Supporting Evidence:

Conclusion

Step 3 | Draft

Write a draft of your essay on the computer or on paper.

Language Study | Select Strong Supporting Evidence

See It | Good writers support claims with convincing reasons and relevant evidence. Examine paragraph two of the model essay.

Try It | Only four of the eight statements below support the following claim: All students should study the arts in high school. Read each carefully and then write the four you select. Be prepared to defend your choice of statements.

1. In addition to supporting reading, math, and language skills, the arts develop critical thinking and social skills.

2. Some high school art classes offered today are drawing, design, art history, music appreciation, voice, orchestra, drama, and dance.

3. High school students who enroll in arts classes have higher math and verbal SAT scores than students who do not take arts classes.

4. A recent Harris Poll reports that 93% of Americans believe the arts are a vital part of a well-rounded education.

5. There are not many career paths that utilize art skills.

6. States do not formally assess students' art skills, so teachers should not focus on teaching them.

7. Teaching art in school wastes precious instruction time that could be used for more important skills.

8. Art teaches children to think critically by requiring them to make choices about colors, balance, shading, and other elements of design, according to the National PTA.

All students should study the arts in high school.

1.

2.

3.

4.

Apply It | Do people need knowledge and empathy to create great art? Choose a frame to revise the claim in your argumentative essay.

1. One reason artists _____ need empathy is _____.
   (do / do not)

2. According to _____, knowledge _____ necessary to create great art.
   (author's name)   (is / is not)

3. Many people believe _____, but this is incorrect because _____.
   (counterclaim)   (claim)

4. After analyzing the evidence, I maintain that _____.

5. _____ uses empathy to _____.
   (author's name)

Now, **go back to your draft** and reread your evidence. Remember that strong evidence supports the claim. Revise one paragraph of your essay to better support your claim.

_____

_____

_____

_____

Conventions Study | Use Correct Verb Mood

See It | Writers choose verb mood according to the purpose of a sentence.

- **Indicative mood** is use to state a fact or ask a question. These **students take** art classes. Have **you studied** art?
- **Imperative mood** is used to give a command or make a direct request. Please **draw** a picture. **Stop** that right now!
- **Subjunctive Mood** is used to express doubts, desires, suggestions, suppositions, and thoughts about conditions contrary to fact. If **I were** taller, **I could** reach the shelf. They wish **you were** here. I suggest **you take** that art class.

Try It | Identify the mood of each sentence below.

1. Yesterday, I finished my project for art class.
   Mood: _____

2. If it were sunny, we could go to the beach.
   Mood: _____

3. Did you hear that sound?
   Mood: _____

4. Shut the door!
   Mood: _____

5. I can't go to the game tonight.
   Mood: _____

Apply It | Write one sentence in each of the three verb moods.

Step 4 | Revise and Edit Revise your draft with a partner.

Organization and Clarity

Introduce a claim and support it with clear, organized reasons and relevant evidence.		Self	1	2	3	4	Partner	1	2	3	4
Use words, phrases, and clauses to clarify the relationship between the claim and supporting reasons.		Self	1	2	3	4	Partner	1	2	3	4
Establish and maintain a formal style.		Self	1	2	3	4	Partner	1	2	3	4
Provide a concluding statement that follows from the evidence presented.		Self	1	2	3	4	Partner	1	2	3	4

Evidence and Reasoning

Criteria		Self					Partner				
Develop or refute the claim that mental strength and agility are just as important as physical prowess in sports.		Self	1	2	3	4	Partner	1	2	3	4
Support claim using evidence from the Unit texts, correctly citing the author and page number for each piece of evidence.		Self	1	2	3	4	Partner	1	2	3	4

Language and Convention

Criteria		Self					Partner				
Recognize and adjust variations from standard English.		Self	1	2	3	4	Partner	1	2	3	4
Correctly punctuate, capitalize, and spell all words and phrases.		Self	1	2	3	4	Partner	1	2	3	4
Vary sentence patterns for meaning, reader interest, and variety.		Self	1	2	3	4	Partner	1	2	3	4

Step 5 | Publish Publish your essay either in print or digital form.

Scoring Guide | ① needs improvement ② average ③ good ④ excellent

Publish

Publish your argument either in print or digital form. Use the rubric below to assess your final performance task.

PERFORMANCE TASK RUBRIC

Score Point	Organization and Clarity	Evidence and Reasoning	Language and Conventions
Exemplary ④	• introductory paragraph includes a **strong thesis statement** that **identifies the topic** and effectively **states a claim** • body paragraphs **focus on each part of the author's claim** and present claims, counterclaims, reasons, and evidence in a **logical sequence** • includes **well-chosen** text evidence, precise language, and consistent verb voice and mood • concluding statement **restates the author's claim**	• **accurately explains and convincingly argues** whether great art requires knowledge and empathy • includes **relevant** evidence from the letters or short story to support each logical reason	• demonstrates a strong command of the conventions of standard English grammar and usage, as well as of standard English capitalization, punctuation, and spelling • vocabulary is appropriate to the topic (vocabulary about the arts; accurate vocabulary for writing a strong thesis statement and convincing argument; vocabulary for defending an opinion or claim)
Meets Standards ③	• introductory paragraph includes **an adequate thesis statement** that **identifies the topic** and **states a claim** • body paragraphs address **each part of the author's claim** and present claims, counterclaims, reasons, and evidence in a **fairly logical sequence** • includes **some** text evidence, precise language, and consistent verb voice and mood • concluding statement **restates the author's claim**	• **adequately explains and argues** whether great art requires knowledge and empathy • includes **some relevant** evidence from the letters or short story to support each logical reason	• demonstrates a near command of the conventions of standard English grammar and usage, as well as of standard English capitalization, punctuation, and spelling with some errors • vocabulary is appropriate to the topic (vocabulary about the arts; accurate vocabulary for writing a strong thesis statement and convincing argument; vocabulary for defending an opinion or claim)

PERFORMANCE TASK RUBRIC

Score Point	Organization and Clarity	Evidence and Reasoning	Language and Conventions
Needs Work ②	• introductory paragraph includes **a weak thesis statement that attempts to identify** the topic and claim • body paragraphs **address some parts of the claim** and present claims, counterclaims, reasons, and evidence • includes **a limited amount of** text evidence, precise language and consistent verb voice and mood • concluding statement **restates the author's claim**	• **partially explains and minimally argues** whether great art requires knowledge and empathy • includes **one or two examples of relevant** evidence from the letters or short story to support each logical reason	• demonstrates a **marginal command** of the conventions of English grammar and usage, as well as of standard English capitalization, punctuation, and spelling • there **are many errors, but the text is still understandable** • includes only **one or two examples** of vocabulary that is appropriate to the topic (vocabulary about the arts; accurate vocabulary for writing a strong thesis statement and convincing argument; vocabulary for defending an opinion or claim)
Does Not Meet Standards ①	• introductory paragraph is **unclear** and does not include a thesis statement that identifies the topic or states a claim • body paragraphs do **not address the parts of the claim** and/ or **do not present claims, counterclaims, reasons, and evidence** • essay includes **little text evidence** and inconsistent verb voice and mood • concluding statement is **unclear**	• response is **partial or inaccurate argument** about whether great art requires knowledge and empathy • includes **no textual evidence** from the letters and short story	• demonstrates **almost no command** of the conventions of standard English grammar and usage, as well as of standard English capitalization, punctuation, and spelling • there **are many errors that disrupt** the reader's understanding of the text • **does not include** vocabulary that is appropriate to the topic (vocabulary about the arts; accurate vocabulary for writing a strong thesis statement and convincing argument; vocabulary for defending an opinion or claim)

I Want to Write

by Margaret Walker

I want to write

I want to write the songs of my people.

I want to hear them singing melodies in the dark.

I want to catch the last floating strains from their sob-torn throats.

Line 5   I want to frame their dreams into words; their souls into notes.

I want to catch their sunshine laughter in a bowl;

fling dark hands to a darker sky

and fill them full of stars

then crush and mix such lights till they become

Line 10   a mirrored pool of brilliance in the dawn.

Words to Know

<u>strains:</u> (n.) sounds of music

Questions

Text Structure

1. What is the purpose of the text below the photograph?

Literary Analysis

2. Why does the poet want to write? Who are her people?

Text Structure

3. Poetry is written in many different forms, from ballads to sonnets to limericks to haiku. What do you notice about the form and structure of this poem? How is it similar to or different from other poems you have read?

Born in 1915, in Birmingham, Alabama, poet and novelist Margaret A. Walker graduated from Northwestern University when she was only 19. She was one of the youngest Black writers to publish a volume of poetry. Her first collection of poems For My People won the prestigious Yale Series of Younger Poets Award in 1942. Walker is also well-known as the author of Jubilee, a historical novel that tells the story of a slave family during and after the Civil War. Walker often wrote about the lives and experiences of African Americans.

Questions

Words and Phrases in Context

4. Examine the imagery and descriptive language the poet uses to describe her people. What tone does her language convey? What is the poet's perspective on her subject?

Literature Circle Leveled Novels

Down a Dark Hall *by Lois Duncan*
Kit is accepted to a boarding school with only three other students. All are gifted with ESP and are being used to channel dead artists who produce "original" work for the profit of the headmasters. Will the girls be able to escape? **Lexile**® measure: 750L

Bronx Masquerade *by Nikki Grimes*
The students of Bronx High School are studying the Harlem Renaissance. They write poems of their own and read them to their classmates, revealing their private thoughts and deepest fears. **Lexile**® measure: 670L

Drums, Girls, and Dangerous Pie *by Jordan Sonnenblick*
Steven's younger brother is diagnosed with leukemia, and Steven turns to his drums and music to get him through the pain. In the end, he and his family learn to lean on each other, too. **Lexile**® measure: 940L

Fiction, Nonfiction, and Novels

What a Song Can Do: 12 Riffs on the Power of Music *Edited by Jennifer Armstrong.* Twelve short stories offer a unique perspective on the different ways that music can influence a person's life. **Lexile**® measure: 780L

Runaway Girl: The Artist Louise Bourgeois *by Jan Greenberg and Sandra Jordan.* View the work of one of the best-known living sculptors and learn about how her life experiences influenced the themes of her sculptures. **Lexile**® measure: 980L

Angela Weaves a Dream: The Story of a Young Maya Artist *by Michele Sola.* Read about a young Maya woman who learns to weave in the Maya tradition, and view photographs of her work. **Lexile**® measure: 1010L

Savion: My Life in Tap *by Savion Glover.* An innovative dancer and choreographer combines rap and hip-hop with traditional tap-dancing styles. **Lexile**® measure: 1010L

Jacques-Henri Lartigue: Boy With a Camera *by John Cech.* Learn how the young photographer mastered photography when it was still a new technology, and view some of his early photographs. **Lexile**® measure: 1060L

Filmmaking for Teens: Pulling Off Your Shorts *by Troy Lanier and Clay Nichols.* Learn about the important aspects of making your first film, including writing scripts, using equipment, and setting deadlines.

To the Young Writer *by Hank Nuwer.* Professional writers provide instruction, advice, and inspiration for aspiring writers.

Vincent Van Gogh: Portrait of an Artist *by Jan Greenberg and Sandra Jordan.* A biography of the famous artist that chronicles the evolution of his style and his struggles with depression and self-doubt.

Films and TV

African Weaving (CustomFlix, 2006) Learn about the traditional weaving methods of the Asante and Ewe people of Ghana, and view the elaborate textiles that reflect their cultural heritage. (25 min.)

Captured Light: The Invention of Still Photography (The History Channel, 1998) Explore the history of photography, from its earliest technology to a celebrated art form. (50 min.)

Free to Dance (PBS, 2001) Follow the development of modern American dance and the role that African-American dancers and choreographers played in shaping this art form. (180 min.)

Freedom Writers (Paramount, 2007; PG-13) Follow a group of students who discover their own talents and form unexpected bonds when a teacher challenges them to write in a daily journal. (122 min.)

In the Mix: Self-Expression, Self-Esteem . . . Around the World (PBS) Explore the different ways that teens around the world are expressing their ideas and emotions through writing, painting, and music. (30 min.)

Music of the Heart (Miramax, 1999; PG) In this film adaptation of a true story, a dedicated teacher works to keep alive her music program for struggling students. (124 min.)

Salvador Dali (A&E Home Video, 2004) Learn about the life and eclectic work of the world-famous artist, whose imagination inspired him to work in different media. (50 min.)

Stomp Out Loud (HBO Home Video, 1997) A troupe of unique performers makes music out of everyday objects and creates an intricate rhythm and dance routine. (50 min.)

Websites

Heilbrunn Timeline of Art History Explore groundbreaking art through the ages by searching according to time period or region of the world on this site sponsored by the Metropolitan Museum of Art.

Nuttin' but Stringz Find more information about Damien and Tourie Escobar and their music. This site includes videos that feature their music and the brothers telling their story.

Poets.org Search for classic and contemporary poets to find biographical information and selected works.

Vincent van Gogh Gallery Learn more about the life and works of Vincent van Gogh and the impact his work has had on the world.

Magazines

Art Explore different topics about art history, current artists, and ideas for projects in different artistic media.

Cicada Students can read fiction and poetry that touches on many ideas and subjects.

Dance Read articles about current dance trends, great performances, and dancers' biographies.

Scope Read contemporary and classic fiction, plays, nonfiction articles, and personal narratives written by teens.

DESIGNING THE FUTURE

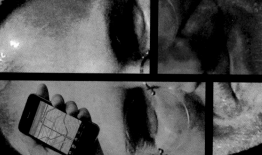

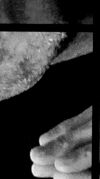

What makes a good team worth more than the sum of its individual parts?

Unit Introduction

In these excerpts from two informational texts, learn ways that different technology teams balance individual talents to form an effective team.

In "La Vida Robot," Joshua Davis offers background about the members of a high school robotics team from an impoverished community, and details how they managed to defeat a team from the Massachusetts Institute of Technology (MIT).

In an excerpt from *Steve Jobs*, Walter Isaacson explores how a team of individuals with complementary skills created one of the best-known, most influential technology companies today.

WRITING PERFORMANCE TASK

Determine Davis's perspective on the factors necessary for building a strong team. Then write an essay that analyzes his perspective, and either compares or contrasts it with Isaacson's perspective.

MAGAZINE ARTICLE/BIOGRAPHY EXCERPT

"La Vida Robot"
by Joshua Davis from *Wired*

Language
- Academic Vocabulary
- Word Study:
  Using References

Reading Informational Text
- Identify Evidence
- Key Ideas and Details
- Craft and Structure and
  Writing Assignment

SPEAKING AND LISTENING

Present Findings
- Collaborate and Present

WRITING

Writing: Informative Essay
- Read the Model
- Analyze the Model
- Gather Evidence
- Organize Ideas
- Language Study:
  Organizing a Paragraph

EXTENDED READING

"Building the Future Spacesuit"
by Dava Newman from *NASA.gov*

from ***Steve Jobs***
by Walter Isaacson

Language
- Academic Vocabulary
- Word Study:
  Context Clues

Reading Informational Text
- Identify Evidence
- Key Ideas and Details
- Craft and Structure and
  Writing Assignment

Checklist: Presentation
- Scoring Guide

- Conventions Study:
  Using Verbs for
  Specific Effects
- Revise, Edit, and Publish
- Performance Task Rubric

Academic Vocabulary

from "La Vida Robot" by Joshua Davis

Rate your understanding of each Target Word. Then read its meaning and write a sample sentence.

Word	Meaning	Example
functional *(adj.)* p. 187 ① ② ③ ④	working correctly; useful	I wasn't looking for a pretty coat, just something functional and warm for winter.
engineer *(n.)* p. 187 ① ② ③ ④	someone whose job is to design or build machines, bridges, roads, etc.	
accomplishment *(n.)* p. 190 ① ② ③ ④		Richard's great accomplishment was winning the karate tournament after hurting his leg earlier this year.
obstacle *(n.)* p. 193 ① ② ③ ④	something blocking the way or that makes it difficult to achieve something	
innovative *(adj.)* p. 194 ① ② ③ ④		The company is looking for employees who will find innovative solutions to old problems.

Rating Scale | ① I don't know the word.   ② I've seen it or heard it.
 ③ I know its meaning.   ④ I know it and use it.

Word Study

Using References

When you encounter a word you don't know, sometimes you can't figure out how to pronounce it. Dictionaries include a pronunciation guide for all the words they list.

"Stinky now buzzed through the water, dodging all <u>obstacles</u>."

1. How is obstacle pronounced?

"Just getting them to the Santa Barbara contest in June with a robot would be an <u>accomplishment</u>."

2. How is accomplishment pronounced?

"MIT had designed an <u>innovative</u> system of bladders and pumps to carry out this task."

3. How is innovative pronounced?

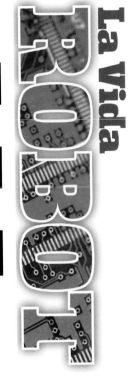

La Vida ROBOT

from **WIRED** magazine

by Joshua Davis

¶1 The winter rain makes a mess of West Phoenix. It turns dirt yards into mud and forms reefs of garbage in the streets. Junk food wrappers, diapers, and Spanish-language magazines are swept into the gutters. On West Roosevelt Avenue, security guards, two squad cars, and a handful of cops watch teenagers file into the local high school. A sign reads, *Carl Hayden Community High School: The Pride's Inside.*

¶2 Across campus, in a second-floor windowless room, four students huddle around an odd, 3-foot-tall frame constructed of PVC pipe [a plastic pressure pipe]. They have equipped it with <u>propellers</u>, cameras, lights, a laser, depth detectors, pumps, an underwater microphone, and an articulated pincer, a type of claw. It's a cheap but very **functional** underwater robot capable of recording sounds and <u>retrieving</u> objects 50 feet below the surface.

¶3 The four teenagers who built it are all undocumented Mexican immigrants who came to this country through tunnels or hidden in the backseats of cars. They live in sheds and rooms without electricity. But over three days last summer, these kids from the desert proved they are among the smartest young underwater **engineers** in the country.

Words to Know

<u>propellers:</u> (*n.*) pieces of equipment with two or more blades that spin around, making an object move

<u>retrieving:</u> (*v.*) finding something and bringing it back

---

Close Reading

Text Structure

1. What is the purpose of boldfacing the name of the high school in **paragraph 1**?

> **Typeface** is a set of characters that share a common design feature. **Boldface** and *italic* fonts are some examples of typeface.

Typeface

Writing

2. What details in **paragraph 3** does Davis use to help introduce the four students from Carl Hayden Community High School? What can you infer about the students from these details?

Davis states that the four students _____. In addition, Davis writes that _____. These details suggest that _____.

Close Reading

Text Structure

3. What will the writer describe in the section called "The Master Mechanic"? How do you know?

Words and Phrases in Context

4. What does the word *eviction* mean in **paragraph 4**? Use context clues to determine the meaning.

Key Ideas and Details

5. What details does the author provide about Lorenzo's appearance in **paragraph 4**? What does the author mean when he states, "The bling wasn't fooling anyone"?

Key Ideas and Details

6. Why didn't Cameron expect "a kid like Lorenzo" to be interested in the ROV competition? Use details in **paragraph 6** to support your answer.

The Master Mechanic

¶4 It was the end of June. Lorenzo Santillan, 16, sat in the front seat of the school van and looked out at the migrant farm workers in the fields along Interstate 10. Lorenzo's face still had its baby fat, but he'd recently sprouted a mustache and had taken to wearing a fistful of gold rings, a gold chain, and a gold medallion pierced through the upper part of his left ear. The bling wasn't fooling anyone. His mother had been fired from her job as a hotel maid, and his father had trouble paying the rent as a gardener. They were on the <u>verge</u> of eviction for nonpayment of rent. He could see himself having to quit school to work in those fields.

¶5 "What's a PWM cable?" The sharp question from the van's driver, Allan Cameron, snapped Lorenzo out of his <u>reverie</u>. Cameron was the computer science teacher sponsoring Carl Hayden's robotics program. Together with his fellow science teacher Fredi "Ledge" Lajvardi, Cameron had put up flyers around the school a few months earlier, offering to sponsor anyone interested in competing in the third annual Marine Advanced Technology Education Center's Remotely Operated Vehicle (ROV) Competition. Lorenzo was one of the first to show up to the after-school meeting last spring.

¶6 Cameron hadn't expected many students to be interested, particularly not a kid like Lorenzo, who was failing most of his classes and perpetually looked like he was about to fall asleep. But Lorenzo didn't have much else to do after school. He didn't want to walk around the streets. He had tried that—he'd been a member of a gang. When his friends started to get arrested for theft, he dropped out. He didn't want to go to jail. That's why he decided to come to Cameron's meeting.

Words to Know

<u>verge:</u> *(n.)* point where something is about to happen

<u>reverie:</u> *(n.)* state of being lost in thought

Close Reading

Words and Phrases in Context

7. What does the word *flourished* mean in **paragraph 8**? What context clues help you determine its meaning?

Writing

8. What makes Lorenzo a "mechanics man"? What can you infer from this about the type of responsibilities he will have on the team? Use details in **paragraphs 7 and 8** to support your answer.

Since Lorenzo can _____ and _____, he is a good "mechanics man."

I can infer from this information that Lorenzo will be responsible for _____.

¶7 "PWM," Lorenzo replied automatically from the van's passenger seat. "Pulse width modulation. *Esto* controls analog circuits with digital output."

¶8 Over the past four months, Lorenzo had flourished, learning a new set of acronyms and raising his math grade from an F to an A. He had grown up rebuilding car engines with his brother and cousin. Now he was ready to build something of his own. The team had found its mechanics man.

The Brains

¶9 Ever since his younger sister demanded her own room four years ago, Cristian Arcega had been living in a 30-square-foot plywood shed attached to the side of his parents' trailer. He liked it there. It was his own space. He was free to <u>contemplate</u> the <u>acceleration</u> of a raindrop as it leaves the clouds above him. He could hear it hit the roof and slide toward the puddles on the street outside. He imagined that the puddles were oceans and that the underwater robot he was building at school could explore them.

The team included (L–R): Teacher Allan Cameron, Lorenzo Santillan, Oscar Vazquez, Cristian Arcega, Luis Aranda, and teacher Fredi Lajvardi.

Words to Know

<u>esto</u>: (*n.*) Spanish for "this"

<u>contemplate</u>: (*v.*) think about seriously

<u>acceleration</u>: (*n.*) an increase in the rate or speed of something

NONFICTION

Close Reading

Key Ideas and Details

9. What qualities set Cristian apart from the other students at Carl Hayden? Use details from **paragraph 10** to support your answer.

Key Ideas and Details

10. In **paragraph 11**, why did the teachers "figure their students would lose"? What was the purpose of entering them into the competition?

Academic Vocabulary

11. In **paragraph 12**, why would "just getting" the students to the contest with a robot be an *accomplishment*?

Writing

12. What makes Cristian the team's "genius"? Use details in **paragraph 13** to support your answer. What can you infer from these details about the responsibilities Cristian will have on the team?

According to the author, Cristian is a "genius" because _____.

Cristian's responsibilities will probably _____.

¶10 Cameron and Ledge formed the robotics group for kids like Cristian. He was probably the smartest 16-year-old in West Phoenix—without even trying, he had one of the highest GPAs in the school district. His brains and diminutive stature (5' 4", 135 pounds) kept him apart at Carl Hayden. That, and the fact that students socialized based on Mexican geography: in the cafeteria, there were Guanajuato tables and Sonora tables [Guanajuato and Sonora are Mexican states]. Cristian was from Mexicali [another state], but he'd left Mexico in the back of a station wagon when he was 6. He thought of himself as part American, part Mexican, and he didn't know where to sit. So he ate lunch in the storage room the teachers had commandeered for the underwater ROV club.

¶11 The robot competition (sponsored in part by the Office of Naval Research and NASA) required students to build a robot that could survey a sunken mock-up of a submarine—not easy stuff. For the competition, the teachers had entered the club in the expert-level Explorer division instead of the beginner Ranger division. They figured their students would lose anyway, and there was more honor in losing to the college kids in the Explorer division than to the high schoolers in Ranger. Their real goal was to show the students that there were other opportunities outside West Phoenix. The teachers wanted to give their kids hope.

¶12 Just getting them to the Santa Barbara contest in June with a robot would be an **accomplishment**, Cameron thought. He and Ledge had to gather a group of students who, in four months, could raise money, build a robot, and learn how to pilot it. They had no idea they were about to assemble the perfect team.

¶13 "We should use glass syntactic flotation foam [a lightweight foam that can stand the pressure of very deep water]," Cristian said excitedly at that first meeting. "It's got a really high compressive strength."

¶14 Cameron and Ledge looked at each other. Now they had their genius.

Words to Know

<u>survey</u>: *(n.)* examine and measure a geographical area

<u>opportunities</u>: *(n.)* chances to do something

Born Leader

¶15 Oscar Vazquez was a born leader. A senior, he'd been in ROTC since ninth grade and was planning on a career in the military. But when he was called to schedule a recruitment meeting at the end of his junior year, the officer in charge told him he was ineligible for military service. Because he was undocumented—his parents had brought him to the U.S. from Mexico without proper immigration papers—he couldn't join, wouldn't get any scholarships, and had to start figuring out what else to do with his life. Oscar felt aimless until he heard about the robot club from Ledge, who was teaching his senior biology seminar. Maybe, he thought, engineering could offer him a future.

¶16 ROTC had trained Oscar well: he knew how to motivate people. He made sure that all of his team members were in the room and focused when he contacted experts to explain tough science concepts. He also helped persuade a handful of local businesses to donate money to the team. Oscar and his team raised a total of about $800.

Team Work

¶17 Now it was up to Cristian and Lorenzo to figure out what to do with the newfound resources. They spoke with Luis Aranda, who was now the fourth member of the team. Luis was the tether man, responsible for the pickup and release of what would be a 100-pound robot. The conversation resulted in Luis going to a hardware store to buy PVC pipe. Despite the donations, they were still on a tight budget. Cristian would have to keep dreaming about glass syntactic flotation foam; PVC pipe was the best they could afford.

Words to Know

seminar: (n.) a class in which a topic is discussed by a teacher and a small group of students

motivate: (v.) to make someone want to achieve something

tether: (n.) rope or chain that is used to tie something to something else

---

Close Reading

Words and Phrases in Context

13. What does the word *ineligible* mean in **paragraph 15**? Use context clues to help determine the meaning.

Writing

14. Based on the information in **paragraph 16**, what does the author believe are qualities of a good leader? Why is Oscar a "born leader"?

The author believes that _____ and _____ are qualities of a good leader.

Oscar is a born leader because _____.

Close Reading

Key Ideas and Details

15. What "bold idea" does the team make use of in **paragraphs 18 and 19**?

Academic Vocabulary

16. Why is Stinky the robot "the type of machine only an *engineer* would describe as beautiful" as noted in **paragraph 20**?

Key Ideas and Details

17. In **paragraph 20**, the author states that the Carl Hayden team used "rubber glue" to put together their robot. How was this method different from the method used by the other teams? What does this detail suggest about the Carl Hayden team?

¶18 But PVC had benefits. The air inside the pipe would create buoyancy as well as provide a waterproof housing for wiring. Cristian calculated the volume of air inside the pipes and realized immediately that they'd need a <u>ballast</u>. He proposed housing the battery system on board, in a heavy waterproof case.

¶19 It was a bold idea. If they didn't have to run a power line down to the robot, their tether could be much thinner, making the robot more mobile. Since the competition required that their robot run through a series of seven exploration tasks, mobility was key. Most of the other teams wouldn't even consider putting their power supplies in the water. A leak could take the whole system down. But if they couldn't figure out how to waterproof their case, Cristian argued, then they shouldn't be in an underwater contest.

¶20 While other teams machined and welded metal frames, the guys broke out the rubber glue and began assembling the PVC pipe. They did the whole thing in one night, and dubbed their new creation Stinky. Lorenzo painted it garish shades of blue, red, and yellow to designate the functionality of specific pipes. Every inch of PVC had a clear purpose. It was the type of machine only an engineer would describe as beautiful.

Test Run

¶21 Carl Hayden Community High School doesn't have a swimming pool, so one weekend in May, after about six weeks of work in the classroom, the team took Stinky to a scuba training pool in downtown Phoenix. Luis lifted the machine up and gently placed it in the water. The team powered it up. Cristian had <u>hacked</u> together off-the-shelf joysticks, a motherboard, motors, and an array of onboard finger-sized video cameras, which now sent flickering images to black-and-white monitors on a folding picnic table. Using five small electric trolling motors, the robot could spin

---

Words to Know

<u>ballast:</u> *(n.)* a substance that provides stability

<u>hacked:</u> *(v.)* put together in a clever and improvised way

and tilt in any direction. To move smoothly, two drivers had to <u>coordinate</u> their commands. The first thing they did was smash the robot into a wall.

¶22 "This is good, this is good," Oscar kept repeating, buying himself a few seconds to come up with a positive spin. "Did you see how hard it hit the wall? This thing's got power. Once we figure out how to drive it, we'll be the fastest team there."

¶23 By early June, as the contest neared, the team had the hang of it. Stinky now buzzed through the water, dodging all **obstacles**. The drivers, Cristian and Oscar, could make the robot hover, spin in place, and angle up or down. They could send enough power to Stinky's small engines to pull Luis around the pool. They felt like they had a good shot at not placing last.

Facing the Competition

¶24 The team arrived at the Olympic-size University of California at Santa Barbara pool on a sunny Thursday afternoon. The pool was concealed under a black tarp—the contest organizers didn't want the students to get a peek at the layout of the mission. Students from cities across the country—Miami, Florida; New Haven, Connecticut; Galveston, Texas; Long Beach, California; and half a dozen others—milled around the water's edge. The Carl Hayden teammates tried to hide their nervousness, but they were <u>intimidated</u>. Lorenzo had never seen so many white people in one place. He was also new to the Pacific Ocean. He had seen it for the first time several months earlier on a school trip to San Diego.

¶25 It still <u>unnerved</u> him to see so much water. He said it was incredible and terrifying at the same time.

Words to Know

<u>coordinate</u>: (v.) work together

<u>intimidated</u>: (v.) made someone feel worried and not confident

<u>unnerved</u>: (adj.) upset or frighten someone so they lose their confidence or ability to think clearly

---

Close Reading

Writing
18. What does the author use to illustrate that Oscar is a good leader?

The author illustrates that Oscar is a good leader when he describes _____.

Anecdote

An anecdote is a short entertaining account of some happening that is used to bring humor or to illustrate a particular characteristic or trait.

Key Ideas and Details
19. What are the team's expectations going into the competition, as described in **paragraph 23**? What can you infer about them from this attitude?

Words and Phrases in Context
20. What does the word *concealed* mean in **paragraph 24**? What context clues help to determine the meaning?

Close Reading

Key Ideas and Details

21. What details does the author provide about the MIT students in **paragraph 26**? Why would Lorenzo be "scared" of them?

Words and Phrases in Context

22. How do the similes used in **paragraph 27** help illustrate the differences among the robots?

Simile

A simile is a figure of speech that uses like, as, or as if to make a direct comparison between two essentially different objects, actions, or qualities.

Writing

23. How does MIT's robot do in the first task of the competition in **paragraph 29**? What can you infer about Davis's point of view about what makes a successful team from this anecdote?

During the first task of the competition, MIT's robot _____.

I can infer that the author thinks teams are successful because _____.

¶26 Even though Lorenzo had never heard of their school — Massachusetts Institute of Technology (MIT) — the students from Cambridge, Massachusetts scared him. There were 12 of them — six ocean-engineering students, four mechanical engineers, and two computer science majors. Their robot was small, densely packed, and had a large ExxonMobil sticker emblazoned on the side. The largest corporation in the U.S. had kicked in $5,000. Other donations brought the MIT team's total budget to $11,000.

¶27 As Luis hoisted Stinky to the edge of the practice side of the pool, Cristian heard <u>repressed</u> snickering. It didn't give him a good feeling. He was proud of his robot, but he could see that it looked like a budget car compared to the luxury sports cars around the pool. Luis had thought that Lorenzo's paint job was nice. Now it just looked clownish.

MIT Makes a Move

¶28 The first task of the contest was to withdraw 500 milliliters of fluid from a container 12 feet below the surface. Its only opening was a small, half-inch pipe fitted with a one-way valve. Though the Carl Hayden team didn't know it, MIT had designed an **innovative** system of bladders and pumps to carry out this task. MIT's robot was supposed to land on the container, create a seal, and pump out the fluid. On three test runs in Boston, the system worked fast and flawlessly.

¶29 MIT's ROV motored smoothly down and quickly located the 5-gallon drum inside the plastic submarine mock-up at the bottom of the pool. But as the robot approached the container, its protruding mechanical arm hit a piece of the submarine frame, blocking it from going farther. They tried a different angle but still couldn't reach the drum. The robot wasn't small enough to slip past the gap in the frame, making their pump system useless. There was nothing they could do — they had to move on to the next assignment.

Words to Know

<u>repressed</u>: *(adj.)* held back, stifled

¶30 Next up was the Carl Hayden team. Luis slowly lowered Stinky into the water for their run. The robot careened wildly as it dived toward the bottom. Luis stood at the pool's edge, paying out the tether cable. Meanwhile, Cristian, Oscar, and Lorenzo monitored Stinky's <u>descent</u> on their video screens in the control tent.

¶31 "*Vámonos*, Cristian, this is it!" Oscar said, pushing his control too far forward. They were nervous and overcompensated for each other's joystick movements, causing Stinky to veer off course.

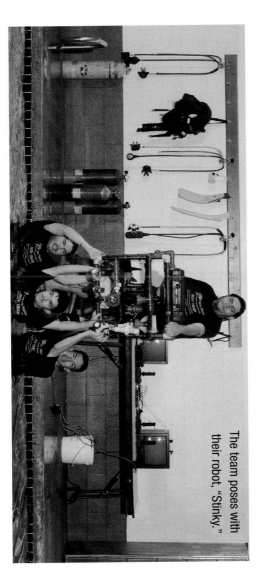

The team poses with their robot, "Stinky."

¶32 Finally, they settled down and reached the submarine. They saw the drum and tried to steady the robot. Stinky had a bent copper nose, a bilge pump, and a dime-store balloon. First, they had to fit the nose into a half-inch pipe. Then they had to fill the balloon for exactly 20 seconds to get 500 milliliters of water. They had practiced a dozen of times at the scuba pool in Phoenix, and it had taken them, on average, 10 minutes to stab the copper structure into the narrow tube. Now they had 30 minutes total to complete all seven tasks on the checklist.

Words to Know

<u>descent</u>: (*n.*) the process of going down

<u>vámonos</u>: (*v.*) Spanish for "let's go"

Close Reading

Words and Phrases in Context

24. What does the word veer mean in **paragraph 31**? What context clues help you determine the meaning of the word?

Key Ideas and Details

25. What can you infer about the team's chances of completing the task from the details in **paragraph 32**? Explain your answer.

¶33 It was up to Oscar and Cristian. They readjusted their grip on the joysticks and leaned into the monitors. Stinky hovered in front of the submarine framing that had frustrated the MIT team. Because Stinky's copper pipe was 18 inches long, it was able to reach the drum. The control tent was silent. Now that they were focused on the mission, both pilots relaxed and made almost imperceptibly small movements with their joysticks. Oscar tapped the control forward while Cristian gave a short backward blast on the vertical propellers. As Stinky floated forward a half inch, its rear raised up and the sampling pipe sank perfectly into the drum.

¶34 "*Díos mío,*" Oscar whispered, not fully believing what he saw.

¶35 Oscar backed Stinky out of the sub. They spun the robot around, piloted it back to Luis at the edge of the pool, and looked at the judges, who stood in the control tent behind them.

¶36 "Can we make a little noise?" Cristian asked Pat Barrow, a NASA lab operations manager supervising the contest.

¶37 "Go on ahead," he replied.

¶38 Cristian started yelling, and all three ran out to hug Luis, who held the now-filled blue balloon. Luis stood there with a silly grin on his face while his friends danced around him.

Words to Know

<u>imperceptibly:</u> *(adv.)* unable to be seen

Close Reading

Key Ideas and Details

26. What was the Carl Hayden team's robot able to achieve in **paragraph 33** that the MIT team's robot could not?

Writing

27. How do Oscar and Cristian work together? What details in **paragraph 33** illustrate this?

Oscar and Cristian _____.

The details that illustrate this include _____.

¶39 The awards ceremony took place over dinner, and the Carl Hayden team was glad for that. They hadn't eaten well over the past two days, and even flavorless iceberg lettuce looked good to them. Their nerves had calmed. After completing all the required tasks, they decided that they had probably placed somewhere in the middle of the pack, maybe fourth or fifth overall. Privately, each of them was hoping for third.

¶40 The announcer took to the stage and leaned into the microphone. "The overall winner for the Marine Technology ROV Championship," he said, looking up at the crowd, "goes to Carl Hayden High School of Phoenix, Arizona!"

¶41 Lorenzo threw his arms into the air and looked at Ledge, beaming with pride. Four teenagers from Phoenix did the unthinkable. They beat the team from MIT to win the competition. They beat the brightest minds in the country.

Close Reading

Key Ideas and Details

28. Why does the announcement of the win come as a surprise to the team? Use details in **paragraph 39** to support your answer.

Words and Phrases in Context

29. How does the author feel about the team's achievement? What words and phrases in **paragraph 41** help convey the author's feelings?

Identify Evidence | Analyze Individuals, Events, and Ideas

Reread "La Vida Robot," highlighting the examples that Davis offers to describe what made the Carl Hayden Community High School students an effective team.

- In the Evidence column, record examples from the text that show either the robotics team from Carl Hayden High School working together or an individual student's qualities that make him a good team member. Include examples of descriptions, quotations, and events.
- In the Explanation column, explain how the evidence introduces, illustrates, or elaborates on individuals, events, and ideas.

Evidence	Source	Page	Explanation
1. "[Lorenzo] had grown up rebuilding car engines with his brother and cousin. Now he was ready to build something of his own. The team had found its mechanics man."	Davis	189	Lorenzo is the first member of the team we meet. His expertise with building and mechanics is important because it makes him a valuable member of the robotics team.
2. "We should use glass syntactic flotation foam,' Cristian said excitedly at that first meeting."			
3. "Oscar Vazquez was a born leader."			
4. "[Cristian and Lorenzo] spoke with Luis Aranda . . . The conversation resulted in Luis going to a hardware store to buy PVC pipe."			

Evidence	Source	Page	Explanation
5.			
6.			
7.			

MAGAZINE ARTICLE

Key Ideas and Details

Determining the Central Idea

1. Summarize the key idea of Davis's article. What is the central idea of the text? Use evidence.

2. List three key individuals that Davis introduces in his article. Explain why each individual is important to the central idea.

Individuals	Significance

3. List three important events in the article. Explain why each event is important to the central idea.

Events	Significance

Craft and Structure

Structure of Narrative Nonfiction

Narrative Nonfiction

Narrative nonfiction is a true story about a series of events, told from a particular perspective, that occurred over time.

1. Look back over paragraphs 16-20. What events does the author describe in this section?

Author's Perspective

2. What words and phrases does Davis use to emphasize the obstacles the team faced?

3. From this section, what can you infer about Davis's perspective about the factors necessary to build an effective team?

Academic Vocabulary

from *Steve Jobs* by Walter Isaacson

Rate your understanding of each Target Word. Then read its meaning and write a sample sentence.

Word	Meaning	Example
endeavor (n.) p. 203 ① ② ③ ④	attempt to do something new or difficult	The doctor's endeavor to reduce head injuries paid off when he developed a new helmet.
legend (n.) p. 204 ① ② ③ ④	someone who is famous and admired for being extremely good at something	
replicate (v.) p. 206 ① ② ③ ④		The scientist's job was to try to replicate his coworker's results.
expertise (n.) p. 209 ① ② ③ ④	special skills or knowledge in a particular subject	
fusion (n.) p. 212 ① ② ③ ④	combination of separate qualities or ideas	
dubious (adj.) p. 215 ① ② ③ ④		Sophia was dubious that drinking coconut water would help her read faster.

Rating Scale | ① I don't know the word.   ② I've seen it or heard it.
            ③ I know its meaning.   ④ I know it and use it.

Word Study

Context Clues

Context clues are words in a text that help you figure out the meaning of an unfamiliar word.

Find the context clues to determine the meaning of the bold words in the sentences below.

1. "Wozniak visited the University of Colorado.... He begged his father to go there even though the out-of-state **tuition** was more than the family could easily afford."

2. "Now that they had decided to start a business, they needed a name. ...Finally, Jobs **proposed** Apple Computer."

from

Steve Jobs

by Walter Isaacson

Photo by Albert Watson

¶1 Steve Jobs flowered intellectually during his last two years in [Homestead] high school and found himself at the intersection, as he had begun to see it, of those who were geekily immersed in electronics and those who were into literature and creative **endeavors**. "I started to listen to music a whole lot, and I started to read more outside of just science and technology—Shakespeare, Plato. I loved *King Lear*." His other favorites included *Moby Dick* and the poems of Dylan Thomas.

¶2 "When I was a senior I had this **phenomenal** AP English class. The teacher was this guy who looked like Ernest Hemingway. He took a bunch of us snowshoeing in Yosemite."

¶3 One course that Jobs took would become part of Silicon Valley lore: the electronics class taught by John McCollum, a former Navy pilot who had a showman's flair for exciting his students with such tricks as firing up a Tesla coil. His little stockroom, to which he would lend the key to pet students, was crammed with **transistors** and other components he had scored.

Words to Know

intersection: (*n*.) place where paths cross

phenomenal: (*adj*.) very great or impressive

transistors: (*n*.) small pieces of electrical equipment that control the flow of electricity

---

Close Reading

Words and Phrases in Context

1. In **paragraph 1**, the word "flowered" is an example of figurative language. What does the author mean when he writes, "Steve Jobs flowered intellectually"?

Figurative Language

Figurative language refers to words or phrases whose intended meaning is different from their literal meaning.

Key Ideas and Details

2. What can you infer about the popularity of McCollum's class? What details in **paragraph 3** help you make this inference?

Close Reading

Key Ideas and Details

3. In **paragraph 4** Jobs recalls that "Mr. McCollum felt that electronics class was the new auto shop." What did McCollum mean by this?

Writing

4. Compare and contrast Jobs's upbringing with Wozniak's. How were they alike? How were they different? Use evidence in **paragraphs 6–7** to support your answer.

Jobs and Wozniak both _____.

They were different because _____.

¶4 McCollum's classroom was in a shed-like building on the edge of the campus, next to the parking lot. "This is where it was," Jobs recalled as he peered in the window, "and here, next door, is where the auto shop class used to be." The juxtaposition highlighted the shift from the interests of his father's generation. "Mr. McCollum felt that electronics class was the new auto shop."

¶5 Jobs took McCollum's class for only one year, rather than the three that it was offered. For one of his projects, he made a device with a photocell that would switch on a circuit when exposed to light, something any high school science student could have done. He was far more interested in playing with lasers, something he learned from his father. With a few friends, he created light shows for parties by bouncing lasers off mirrors that were attached to the speakers of his stereo system.

Woz

¶6 While a student in McCollum's class, Jobs became friends with a graduate who was the teacher's all-time favorite and a school **legend** for his <u>wizardry</u> in the class. Stephen Wozniak, whose younger brother had been on a swim team with Jobs, was almost five years older than Jobs and far more knowledgeable about electronics. But emotionally and socially he was still a high school geek.

¶7 Like Jobs, Wozniak learned a lot at his father's knee. But their lessons were different. Paul Jobs was a high school dropout who, when fixing up cars, knew how to turn a tidy profit by striking the right deal on parts. Francis Wozniak, known as Jerry, was a brilliant engineering graduate and former football quarterback from Cal Tech, who became a rocket scientist at <u>Lockheed</u>. He exalted engineering and looked

---

Words to Know

juxtaposition: *(n.)* putting two things that aren't usually together next to each other

wizardry *(n.)* impressive ability at something

<u>**Lockheed:**</u> *(n.)* major U.S. aerospace company that builds planes, rockets, and missiles

down on those in business, marketing, and sales. "I remember him telling me that engineering was the highest level of importance you could reach in the world," Steve Wozniak later recalled. "It takes society to a new level."

¶8 One of Steve Wozniak's first memories was going to his father's workplace on a weekend and being shown electronic parts, with his dad "putting them on a table with me so I got to play with them." He watched with fascination as his father tried to get a waveform line on a video screen to stay flat so he could show that one of his circuit designs was working properly. "I could see that whatever my dad was doing, it was important and good." Woz, as he was known even then, would ask about the resistors and transistors lying around the house, and his father would pull out a blackboard to illustrate what they did. "He would explain what a resistor was by going all the way back to atoms and electrons. He explained how resistors worked when I was in second grade, not by equations but by having me picture it."

¶9 Woz's father taught him something else that became ingrained in his childlike, socially awkward personality: never lie. "My dad believed in honesty. Extreme honesty. That's the biggest thing he taught me. I never lie, even to this day." (The only partial exception was in the service of a good practical joke.) In addition, he imbued his son with an aversion to extreme ambition, which set Woz apart from Jobs. At an Apple product launch event in 2010, forty years after they met, Woz reflected on their differences. "My father told me, 'You always want to be in the middle,'" he said. "I didn't want to be up with the high-level people like Steve. My dad was an engineer, and that's what I wanted to be. I was way too shy ever to be a business leader like Steve."

Words to Know

<u>resistors:</u> (n.) devices used to resist, or prevent the passage of an electric current

<u>ingrained:</u> (adj.) firmly established and therefore difficult to change

<u>imbued:</u> (v.) made someone or something have a quality, idea, or emotion very strongly

<u>aversion:</u> (n.) a strong dislike of something or someone

Close Reading

Key Ideas and Details

5. What anecdote does the author use in **paragraph 8**? What does the anecdote convey about the influence Wozniak's father had on him?

Writing

6. Review **paragraph 9**. In addition to engineering, what lessons does Woz's father teach him? What lessons does Woz does Isaacson communicate through these lessons?

Woz's father also taught him _____ and _____.

These lessons show the reader that Woz will likely grow up to be _____.

Close Reading

Key Ideas and Details

11. What "wonderful offer" does a coworker make Woz? What is the significance of this offer? Use details in **paragraph 14** to answer the questions.

Writing

12. In **paragraph 16**, the author describes the first meeting between Jobs and Wozniak. Why did Wozniak like Jobs upon meeting him? What impressed Jobs about Wozniak?

Woz liked Jobs because _____.

Jobs was impressed by _____.

¶14 After a pleasant year at De Anza, Wozniak took time off to make some money. He found work at a company that made computers for the California Motor Vehicle Department, and a coworker made him a wonderful offer: he would provide some spare chips so Wozniak could make one of the computers he had been sketching on paper. Wozniak decided to use as few chips as possible, both as a personal challenge and because he did not want to take advantage of his colleague's largesse.

¶15 Much of the work was done in the garage of a friend just around the corner, Bill Fernandez, who was still at Homestead High. To lubricate their efforts, they drank large amounts of Cragmont cream soda, riding their bikes to the Sunnyvale Safeway to return the bottles, collect the deposits, and buy more. "That's how we started referring to it as the Cream Soda Computer," Wozniak recalled. It was basically a calculator capable of multiplying numbers entered by a set of switches, and displaying the results in binary code with little lights.

¶16 When it was finished, Fernandez told Wozniak there was someone at Homestead High he should meet. "His name is Steve. He likes to do pranks like you do, and he's also into building electronics like you are." It may have been the most significant meeting in a Silicon Valley garage since Hewlett went into Packard's thirty-two years earlier. "Steve and I just sat on the sidewalk in front of Bill's house for the longest time, just sharing stories—mostly about pranks we'd pulled, and also what kind of electronic designs we'd done," Wozniak recalled. "We had so much in common. Typically, it was really hard for me to explain to people what kind of design stuff I worked on, but Steve got it right away. And I liked him. He was kind of skinny and wiry and full of energy." Jobs was also impressed. "Woz was the first

Words to Know

<u>largesse:</u> *(n.)* generosity

<u>binary code:</u> *(n.)* a coding system using the digits 0 and 1 to represent a letter, digit, or other character in a computer or other electronic device

person I'd met who knew more electronics than I did," he once said, stretching his own **expertise**. "I liked him right away. I was a little more mature than my years, and he was a little less mature than his, so it evened out. Woz was very bright, but emotionally he was my age."

¶17 Jobs had formed a club at Homestead High to put on music-and-light shows and also play pranks. . . It was called the Buck Fry Club, a play on the name of the principal. Even though they had already graduated, Wozniak and his friend Allen Baum joined forces with Jobs.

¶18 One prank involved a pocket device Wozniak built that could emit TV signals. He would take it to a room where a group of people were watching TV, such as in a dorm, and secretly press the button so that the screen would get fuzzy with static. When someone got up and whacked the set, Wozniak would let go of the button and the picture would clear up. Once he had the unsuspecting viewers hopping up and down at his will, he would make things harder. He would keep the picture fuzzy until someone touched the antenna. Eventually he would make people think they had to hold the antenna while standing on one foot or touching the top of the set. Years later, at a keynote presentation where he was having his own trouble getting a video to work, Jobs broke from his script and recounted the fun they had with the device. "Woz would have it in his pocket and we'd go into a dorm . . . where a bunch of folks would be, like, watching *Star Trek*, and he'd screw up the TV, and someone would go up to fix it, and just as they had the foot off the ground he would turn it back on, and as they put their foot back on the ground he'd screw it up again." Contorting himself into a pretzel onstage, Jobs concluded to great laughter, "And within five minutes he would have someone like this."

Close Reading

Key Ideas and Details

13. What anecdote does the author use in **paragraph 18** to illustrate Wozniak's playful personality?

Words and Phrases in Context

14. What figurative words or phrases does the author use in the last sentence of **paragraph 18**? What does he mean by this?

Close Reading

Key Ideas and Details

15. What details in **paragraph 19** does the author use to describe San Francisco and the Santa Clara Valley during the 1960s? What do these details suggest about this time and place?

Words and Phrases in Context

16. According to Stewart Brand, how could technology "be our friend"? Use details in **paragraph 20** to support your answer.

Machines of Loving Grace

¶19 In San Francisco and the Santa Clara Valley during the late 1960s, various cultural currents flowed together. There was the technology <u>revolution</u> that began with the growth of military contractors and soon included electronics firms, microchip makers, video game designers, and computer companies. There was a subculture—filled with wireheads, phreakers, cyberpunks, hobbyists, and just plain geeks—that included engineers who didn't <u>conform</u> to the <u>HP</u> mold and their kids who weren't attuned to the wavelengths of the subdivisions . . . There was the hippie movement, born out of the Bay Area's beat generation, and the rebellious political activists, born out of the Free Speech Movement at Berkeley.

¶20 [Stewart] Brand, [a punkish visionary] ran the Whole Earth Truck Store, which began as a roving truck that sold useful tools and educational materials, and in 1968 he decided to extend its reach with the *Whole Earth Catalog*. On its first cover was the famous picture of Earth taken from space; its subtitle was "Access to Tools." The underlying <u>philosophy</u> was that technology could be our friend. Brand wrote on the first page of the first edition, "A realm of intimate, personal power is developing—power of the individual to conduct his own education, find his own inspiration, shape his own environment, and share his adventure with whoever is interested. Tools that aid this process are sought and promoted by the *Whole Earth Catalog*." Buckminster Fuller followed with a poem that began: "I see God in the instruments and mechanisms that work reliably."

¶21 Jobs became a *Whole Earth* fan. He was particularly taken by the final issue, which came out in 1971, when he was still in high school. He brought it with him to

---

Words to Know

<u>revolution</u>: *(n.)* a complete change in ways of thinking or methods of working

<u>conform</u>: *(v.)* behave the same way everyone else does

HP: *(n.)* an abbreviation for Hewlett-Packard, a leading computer company

<u>philosophy</u>: *(n.)* set of ideas that guide the behavior of a person or organization

college, and then to the All One Farm. "On the back cover of their final issue," Jobs recalled, "was a photograph of an early morning country road, the kind you might find yourself hitchhiking on if you were so adventurous. Beneath it were the words: 'Stay Hungry. Stay Foolish.'" Brand sees Jobs as one of the purest embodiments of the cultural mix that the catalog sought to celebrate. "Steve is right at the <u>nexus</u> of the <u>counterculture</u> and technology," he said. "He got the notion of tools for human use."

¶22 Brand's catalog was published with the help of the Portola Institute, a foundation dedicated to the fledgling field of computer education. The foundation also helped launch the People's Computer Company, which was not a company at all but a newsletter and organization with the motto "Computer power to the people." There were occasional Wednesday-night potluck dinners, and two of the regulars, Gordon French and Fred Moore, decided to create a more formal club where news about personal electronics could be shared.

¶23 They were energized by the arrival of the January 1975 issue of *Popular Mechanics*, which had on its cover the first personal computer kit, the Altair. The Altair wasn't much—just a $495 pile of parts that had to be soldered to a board that would then do little—but for hobbyists . . . it heralded the dawn of a new era. <u>Bill Gates and Paul Allen</u> read the magazine and started working on a version of BASIC, an easy-to-use programming language, for the Altair. It also caught the attention of Jobs and Wozniak. And when an Altair kit arrived at the People's Computer Company, it became the centerpiece for the first meeting of the club that French and Moore had decided to launch.

Words to Know

embodiments: *(n.)* people or things that represent an idea or quality

nexus: *(n.)* the central or most important point or place

counterculture: *(n.)* a way of life and set of attitudes that is different from the social norm

Bill Gates and Paul Allen: *(n.)* the co-founders of Microsoft, the world's largest computer software company

---

Close Reading

Key Ideas and Details

17. Why did Brand consider Jobs "one of the purest embodiments of the cultural mix" in **paragraph 21** to support your answer.

Words and Phrases in Context

18. What is the author's tone when describing the Altair in **paragraph 23**? What words and phrases does he use to help create the tone?

Tone

Tone is the writer's attitude toward his or her characters and the situation.

The Homebrew Computer Club

¶24 The group became known as the Homebrew Computer Club, and it encapsulated the *Whole Earth* fusion between the counterculture and technology. . . . Moore wrote the flyer for the first meeting, held on March 5, 1975, in French's Menlo Park garage: "Are you building your own computer? Terminal, TV, typewriter?" it asked. "If so, you might like to come to a gathering of people with like-minded interests."

¶25 Allen Baum spotted the flyer on the HP bulletin board and called Wozniak, who agreed to go with him. "That night turned out to be one of the most important nights of my life," Wozniak recalled. About thirty other people showed up, spilling out of French's open garage door, and they took turns describing their interests. Wozniak, who later admitted to being extremely nervous, said he liked "video games, pay movies for hotels, scientific calculator design, and TV terminal design," according to the minutes prepared by Moore. There was a demonstration of the new Altair, but more important to Wozniak was seeing the specification sheet for a microprocessor.

¶26 As he thought about the microprocessor—a chip that had an entire central processing unit on it—he had an insight. He had been designing a terminal, with a keyboard and monitor, that would connect to a distant minicomputer. Using a microprocessor, he could put some of the capacity of the minicomputer inside the terminal itself, so it could become a small stand-alone computer on a desktop. It was an enduring idea: keyboard, screen, and computer all in one integrated personal package. "This whole vision of a personal computer just popped into my head," he said. "That night, I started to sketch out on paper what would later become known as the Apple I."

Words to Know

encapsulated: *(v.)* summed up; expressed something in a short way

specification sheet: *(n.)* a piece of paper that explains exactly how a piece of technology works

integrated: *(adj.)* coming together as a whole

Close Reading

Key Ideas and Details

19. What can you infer about the people who would have been interested in the Homebrew Computer Club from the flyer that Moore wrote? Use evidence from **paragraph 24.**

Words and Phrases in Context

20. How does the author define a *microprocessor*? Why does the author define this word in the text?

Writing

21. Why did Wozniak consider the night he attended the Homebrew Computer Club "one of the most important nights" of his life? What "insight" does he later have? Use evidence in **paragraphs 25–26** to support your answer.

Wozniak considers the night he attended the Homebrew Computer Club "one of the most important nights" of his life because _____ .

He later realizes _____ .

¶27 "At first he planned to use the same microprocessor that was in the Altair, an Intel 8080. But each of those "cost almost more than my monthly rent," so he looked for an alternative. He found one in the Motorola 6800, which a friend at HP was able to get for $40 apiece. Then he discovered a chip made by MOS Technologies that was electronically the same but cost only $20. It would make his machine affordable, but it would carry a long-term cost. Intel's chips ended up becoming the industry standard, which would haunt Apple when its computers were incompatible with it.

¶28 After work each day, Wozniak would go home for a TV dinner and then return to [his job at] HP to moonlight on his computer. He spread out the parts in his cubicle, figured out their placement, and soldered them onto his motherboard. Then he began writing the software that would get the microprocessor to display images on the screen. Because he could not afford to pay for computer time, he wrote the code by hand. After a couple of months he was ready to test it. "I typed a few keys on the keyboard and I was shocked! The letters were displayed on the screen." It was Sunday, June 29, 1975, a milestone for the personal computer. "It was the first time in history," Wozniak later said, "anyone had typed a character on a keyboard and seen it show up on their own computer's screen right in front of them."

Words to Know

industry standard (n.) an established norm or requirement in a particular industry

incompatible: (adj.) not able to be used together

moonlight: (v.) work at a second job in addition to your main job

---

Close Reading

Words and Phrases in Context

22. What context clues help you determine the meaning of the word *alternative* in **paragraph 27**?

Text Structure

23. What words and phrases help convey the sequence of events in **paragraph 28**?

Sequence

Sequence is the order of events of a story. Transition words, like first, right now, and years later, can help identify the next event.

Key Ideas and Details

24. In **paragraph 28**, the author states that Wozniak's accomplishment was "a milestone for the personal computer." What evidence does he use to support this statement?

¶29 Jobs was impressed. He peppered Wozniak with questions: could the computer ever be networked? Was it possible to add a disk for memory storage? He also began to help Woz get components. Particularly important were the dynamic random-access memory chips. Jobs made a few calls and was able to score some from Intel for free. "Steve is just that sort of person," said Wozniak. "I mean, he knew how to talk to a sales representative. I could never have done that. I'm too shy."

¶30 Jobs began to accompany Wozniak to Homebrew meetings, carrying the TV monitor and helping to set things up. The meetings now attracted more than one hundred enthusiasts and had been moved to the auditorium of the Stanford Linear Accelerator Center. Presiding with a pointer and a free-form manner was Lee Felsenstein, another embodiment of the merger between the world of computing and the counterculture. He was an engineering school dropout, a participant in the Free Speech Movement, and an antiwar activist. He had written for the alternative newspaper Berkeley Barb and then gone back to being a computer engineer.

¶31 Woz was usually too shy to talk in the meetings, but people would gather around his machine afterward, and he would proudly show off his progress. Moore had tried to instill in the Homebrew an <u>ethos</u> of swapping and sharing rather than <u>commerce</u>. "The theme of the club," Woz said, "was 'Give to help others.'" ..."I designed the Apple I because I wanted to give it away for free to other people," said Wozniak.

¶32 Steve Jobs did not embrace the notion that Wozniak's creations wanted to be free. So he convinced Wozniak to stop giving away copies of his schematics. Most people didn't have time to build it themselves anyway, Jobs argued. "Why don't we build and sell printed circuit boards to them?" It was an example of their <u>symbiosis</u>. "Every time I'd design something great, Steve would find a way to make money for

---

Words to Know

<u>ethos:</u> (n.) a set of ideas and moral attitudes that guides behavior

<u>commerce:</u> (n.) buying and selling of goods and services

<u>symbiosis:</u> (n.) a relationship between two people who work well together

---

Close Reading

Writing

25. What is Jobs's role in creating Apple 1, as described in **paragraph 29**? How was his role different than Wozniak's role, which you read about on page 213?

Jobs's role was to _____.

This was unlike Wozniak's role, which was to _____.

Key Ideas and Details

26. How does Steve Jobs differ from Wozniak and the other members of the Homebrew Computer Club? Use evidence from **paragraphs 31–32.**

Words and Phrases in Context

27. Why would Isaacson use the word *symbiosis* to describe Jobs's and Wozniak's partnership in **paragraph 32**? What can you infer about Isaacson's perspective on their partnership from his use of the word?

us," said Wozniak. Wozniak admitted that he would have never thought of doing that on his own. "It never crossed my mind to sell computers. It was Steve who said, 'Let's hold them in the air and sell a few.'"

¶33 Jobs worked out a plan to pay a guy he knew at Atari to draw the circuit boards and then print up fifty or so. That would cost about $1,000, plus the fee to the designer. They could sell them for $40 apiece and perhaps clear a profit of $700. Wozniak was **dubious** that they could sell them all. "I didn't see how we would make our money back," he recalled. He was already in trouble with his landlord for bouncing checks and now had to pay each month in cash.

¶34 Jobs knew how to appeal to Wozniak. He didn't argue that they were sure to make money, but instead said that they would have a fun adventure. "Even if we lose our money, we'll have a company," said Jobs as they were driving in his Volkswagen bus. "For once in our lives, we'll have a company." This was <u>enticing</u> to Wozniak, even more than any prospect of getting rich. He recalled, "I was excited to think about us like that. To be two best friends starting a company. Wow. I knew right then that I'd do it. How could I not?"

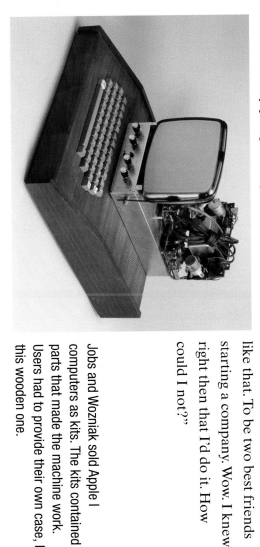

Jobs and Wozniak sold Apple I computers as kits. The kits contained parts that made the machine work. Users had to provide their own case, like this wooden one.

Close Reading

Academic Vocabulary

28. What is Jobs's plan, as described in **paragraph 33**? Why was Wozniak *dubious* about this plan?

Key Ideas and Details

29. How does Jobs convince Wozniak to go along with his plan in **paragraph 34**?

¶35 In order to raise the money they needed, Wozniak sold his HP 65 calculator for $500, though the buyer ended up stiffing him for half of that. For his part, Jobs sold his Volkswagen bus for $1,500. But the person who bought it came to find him two weeks later and said the engine had broken down, and Jobs agreed to pay for half of the repairs. Despite these little setbacks, they now had, with their own small savings thrown in, about $1,300 in <u>working capital</u>, the design for a product, and a plan. They would start their own computer company.

Apple Is Born

¶36 Now that they had decided to start a business, they needed a name. Jobs had gone for another visit to the All One Farm, where he had been pruning the Gravenstein apple trees, and Wozniak picked him up at the airport. On the ride down to Los Altos, they bandied around options. They considered some typical tech words, such as Matrix, and some <u>neologisms</u>, such as Executek, and some straightforward boring names, like Personal Computers Inc. The deadline for deciding was the next day, when Jobs wanted to start filing the papers. Finally, Jobs proposed Apple Computer. "I was on one of my fruitarian diets," he explained. "I had just come back from the apple farm. It sounded fun, spirited, and not intimidating. Apple took the edge off the word 'computer.' Plus, it would get us ahead of Atari in the phone book." He told Wozniak that if a better name did not hit them by the next afternoon, they would just stick with Apple. And they did.

Words to Know

<u>working capital:</u> (*n.*) money that a business can use to invest in new products or make improvements

<u>neologisms:</u> (*n.*) new words or expressions

Close Reading

Text Structure

30. What will the text that appears below the subheading "Apple Is Born" be about? How do you know?

Key Ideas and Details

31. What were Jobs's reasons for suggesting the name "Apple Computer" in **paragraph 36**? What can you infer from his reasons about the type of customers Jobs was trying to appeal to?

¶37 "They were very different, but they made a powerful team," said Ron Wayne, an engineer at Atari. Jobs at times seemed to be driven by demons, while Woz seemed a naïf who was toyed with by angels. Jobs had a <u>bravado</u> that helped him get things done, occasionally by <u>manipulating</u> people. He could be <u>charismatic</u>, even mesmerizing, but also cold and brutal. Wozniak, in contrast, was shy and socially awkward, which made him seem childishly sweet. "Woz is very bright in some areas, but he's almost like a <u>savant</u>, since he was so stunted when it came to dealing with people he didn't know," said Jobs. "We were a good pair." It helped that Jobs was <u>awed</u> by Wozniak's engineering wizardry, and Wozniak was awed by Jobs's business drive.

Words to Know

bravado: (n.) behavior that is deliberately intended to make other people believe you are brave and confident

manipulating (v.) making someone think and behave as you want them to, by skillfully deceiving or influencing them

charismatic: (adj.) having a natural ability to attract and interest other people

savant (n.) someone who has lower intelligence than average but can do one thing very well

awed (v.) felt great respect for

Close Reading

Writing

32. How does the author contrast the personality traits of Steve Jobs and Steve Wozniak in **paragraph 37**? Based on this information, what can you infer about the author's opinion about what makes an effective team?

According to the author,
Steve Jobs _____.
By contrast, Steve Wozniak _____.
I can infer that the author thinks
an effective technology team
consists of _____.

Key Ideas and Details

33. How does the author describe how Jobs and Wozniak felt about each other as teammates in **paragraph 37**? What effect does the author's use of word repetition in this description create?

Identify Evidence | Analyze Individuals, Events and Ideas

Reread **Steve Jobs**, highlighting the moments Isaacson offers that describe what made the partnership between Steve Wozniak and Steve Jobs so successful.

- In the Evidence column, record examples from the text that describe Wozniak and Jobs, as well as how they worked together. Include descriptions and quotations.
- In the Explanation column, explain how the evidence introduces, illustrates, or elaborates on individuals, events, and ideas.

Evidence	Source	Page	Explanation
1. "One course that Jobs took would become part of Silicon Valley lore: the electronics class taught by John McCollum, a former Navy pilot who had a showman's flair for exciting his students with such tricks as firing up a Tesla coil."	Isaacson	203	John McCollum was an electronics teacher who taught a class so great it became legendary. He helped Jobs and Wozniak get interested in electronics.
2. "'I remember him telling me that engineering was the highest level of importance you could reach in the world,' Steve Wozniak later recalled. 'It takes society to a new level.'"			
3. "In eighth grade [Woz] built a calculator that included one hundred transistors, two hundred diodes, and two hundred resistors on ten circuit boards. It won top prize in a local contest run by the Air Force . . ."			

Evidence	Source	Page	Explanation
4.			
5.			
6.			
7.			

Key Ideas and Details

Determining the Central Idea

1. Summarize the key idea of Isaacson's article. What is the central idea of the text? Use evidence.

2. List two key individuals in Isaacson's article. Explain why each individual is important to the central idea.

Individuals	Significance
Steve Jobs	

3. List four key events in Isaacson's article. Explain why each event is important to the central idea.

Events	Significance
Jobs and Wozniak meet for the first time	When the two meet, they have a lot in common, including playing pranks and building electronics. They immediately get along, which is important to a good partnership.

Craft and Structure

Structure of a Biography

1. Biographies contain information about many different aspects of a subject's life. Identify the aspects of Steve Job's life that Isaacson describes in his biography.

Subject of book	
Setting	
Relatives and Friends	
Subject of Major accomplishment in excerpt	

Author's Perspective

2. Reread paragraphs 28–35. Does Isaacson emphasize the similarities or differences between Jobs and Wozniak? Explain.

3. What can you infer from the way Isaacson portrays Jobs and Wozniak about his perspective on building an effective team?

Collaborate and Present

Plan and Deliver a Presentation

Assignment: Unlike Apple I, some products developed by Steve Jobs failed. Using books and Web sites, work with a partner to research one of these products. Generate a list of questions that will help you explore why the product failed. Answer your questions and present your findings to the class. Be sure to include images of the product in your presentation.

Analyze the Content

1. Choose a product to research. Then generate a list of questions that will guide you in your research. Consider using the following question starters:

   - What were the characteristics of _____?
   - Why did _____?
   - What caused _____?
   - How did consumers _____?

2. Record the name of the product, your questions, and answers in the chart below.

Failed product	Questions	Answers

3. As you conduct your research, more questions about the product may arise. Be sure to add them to your chart.

Organize Your Presentation

4. Use the information in your chart as talking points for your presentation.

   - Draft an outline of the presentation to the class.
   - Display or print out images of the product to show to the class.

Present

5. Present your findings to the class.

Seeking Clarification

- So what you are saying is . . . .
- So what you mean is . . .
- In other words, you think . . . .
- If I understand you correctly, you are saying . . .

Reporting Ideas

- _____ pointed out
- _____ indicated that
- _____ emphasized

Presentation

- Be still and have good posture.
- Speak loudly and clearly.
- Make eye contact with your audience.

Presentation Checklist

Use the checklist below to evaluate your collaboration skills, reasoning, and final presentation. Think carefully about your work. If you know you completed an item thoroughly, give yourself a check (✓).

COLLABORATE AND PRESENT CHECKLIST

Comprehension & Collaboration	Evidence and Reasoning	Presentation of Knowledge & Ideas
☐ Engage in group discussions with diverse partners on topics and issues that you read about.	☐ Explain the purpose of the presentation.	☐ Adapt language to a variety of contexts and tasks to demonstrate knowledge of formal English.
☐ Come to discussions prepared, having read and researched material.	☐ State the name of the product I will be discussing.	☐ Include multimedia components (e.g., graphics, images, music, sound) and visual displays.
☐ Refer to evidence to probe and reflect on and contribute to the discussion.	☐ State the questions I used to research my findings.	☐ Express my findings clearly.
☐ Follow rules for discussions and lead by example.	☐ Explain why the product failed using evidence from my research.	☐ Use appropriate volume/tone (clear, not too fast, too slow, or too loud) and avoid using *like* or *ummm*.
☐ Ask and respond to specific questions.		☐ Have strong posture, a confident stance, and make frequent eye contact.
☐ Make informed comments about topics that are being discussed.		☐ Occasionally move from one spot to another, without fidgeting.
☐ Demonstrate understanding of the key ideas presented by classmates by reflection and paraphrasing.		☐ Smile and act relaxed.
Number of ✓ s in this category: ___	**Number of ✓ s in this category:** ___	**Number of ✓ s in this category:** ___

Total # of ✓ s: ___

Add up the total number of checks (✓) in each category. Then use the scoring guide below to calculate your final score.

Scoring Guide

16 to 18 ✓ s	13 to 15 ✓ s	11 to 12 ✓ s	10 or less ✓ s
④ Exemplary	③ Meets Standards	② Needs Work	① Does Not Meet Standards

Read the Model

Writers craft ideas and explore information in different ways. The writer of this informative essay compares and contrasts how two authors approach two similar topics. Read and discuss the model essay below.

Informative Essay

An **informative essay** provides an overview of the key topics and ideas of a text.

The **introduction** states the title and author of the text that the writer will analyze, and includes the thesis statement.

- Describe how the writer introduces the topic.

The two **body paragraphs** express the writer's main points about the text.

- Find two examples of transition words (words or phrases that link ideas, sentences, and paragraphs).
- Find two examples of domain-specific vocabulary.

The **conclusion** sums up or restates the thesis.

- Identify the conclusion.

Analysis of a Team: More Than the Sum of Its Parts
By Ryan Delgado

Joshua Davis, author of "La Vida Robot," and Dava Newman, author of "Building the Future Spacesuit," share some similar views about how to compose the best team. Both writers believe that an effective team consists of members who have unique and complementary skills.

In "La Vida Robot," Davis highlights each student's background and skills to help the reader understand the role that student would play on the team. For example, Davis describes one team member by stating, "Lorenzo . . . had grown up rebuilding car engines with his brother and cousin" (Davis 189). Lorenzo ultimately becomes the team's mechanic. Meanwhile, another team member, Oscar, is described as a "born leader" who knows how to "motivate people." Oscar's skills make him the idea project manager for the team.

Like Davis, Newman emphasizes the importance of a team that has people who have different strengths and think in different ways. The teams become "diverse cooperative communities of engineers, designers, scientists, and artists" (Newman 239). However, Newman also stresses the importance of adapting to each other's skills. "After working together for weeks, the engineers got more comfortable with the idea of sketching solutions and some of the designers added Matlab and its more analytical approach to their repertoires" (Newman 236).

If I were part of a team like those described by the authors, I would hope my unique skills and talents could contribute to the group's success. It's clear from both texts that in teams like these, the individuals' contributions add up to more than the sum of their parts.

Analyze the Model

A compare/contrast essay explains similarities and differences between two texts.

Text Strategy

In a **compare/contrast essay**, a writer describes how two or more topics are alike and how they are different.

The **thesis statement** in the introduction states the subjects that will be compared or contrasted.

- Identify the thesis statement.

Writers of compare/contrast essays may organize their body paragraphs in a **block-by-block** format. In this format, the writer discusses **one topic** in the first body paragraph and the **second topic** in the second body paragraph.

- Identify the topic discussed in each body paragraph.

Relevant evidence, such as examples and quotations from the text, supports each topic.

- Evaluate whether the sentences in each body paragraph support the topic.

The conclusion sums up or **restates** the thesis and **why it matters**.

- Describe how the writer concluded her essay.

Introduction	
Thesis Statement	

Body	
Topic 1 Davis believes the team succeeded because individual members brought complementary skills to the task.	**Relevant Evidence**
Topic 2	**Relevant Evidence**

Conclusion
Restate and why it matters

Step 1 | Gather Evidence

Determine Davis's perspective on the factors necessary for building a strong team. Then write an essay that analyzes his perspective, and either compares or contrasts it with Isaacson's perspective.

What You Need to Know | Examine the evidence you have collected. (See pages 198-99 and 218-19.)

What You Need to Write | Note the key ideas about the authors' perspectives that you have drawn based on your evidence. Select the key ideas you will include in your essay.

"La Vida Robot"

Key Idea:

Evidence:

Page # _____

Key Idea:

Evidence:

Page # _____

Key Idea:

Evidence:

Page # _____

Steve Jobs

Key Idea:

Evidence:

Page # _____

Key Idea:

Evidence:

Page # _____

Key Idea:

Evidence:

Page # _____

Step 2 | Organize Ideas

What You Need to Know | When you compare, you describe similarities. When you contrast, you point out differences.

To develop your topic:

1. Describe Davis's perspective and strategies.
2. Describe Isaacson's perspective and strategies.

What You Need to Write | Determine how the authors' perspectives and strategies are the same and how they are different. Then organize the ideas in a block-by-block format.

Introduction	
Thesis Statement	

Body	
Topic 1	**Relevant Evidence**
Topic 2	**Relevant Evidence**

Conclusion	
Restate and why it matters	

Step 3 | Draft

Write a draft of your essay on the computer or on paper.

Language Study | Organizing a Paragraph

See It | **Good writers organize information within a paragraph in a logical order. They include a topic sentence, either at the beginning or end of a paragraph. They also provide details in supporting sentences to support the topic sentence.**

The following example shows a topic sentence followed by supporting details:

- **Topic Sentence:** Carlton High School currently has the best soccer team in the district.
- **Supporting Sentence:** The team was undefeated this season.
- **Supporting Sentence:** The team won the district championship.

Try It | **Review each set of sentences below. Write a "T" next to each topic sentence. Write an "S" next to each supporting sentence.**

1. ____ The population of orangutans in Borneo has declined by 50 percent in the last 60 years.

   ____ Logging and hunting are two reasons for the decline.

   ____ Orangutans in Borneo are endangered.

2. ____ The Emancipation Proclamation was one of the most important orders ever signed by a U.S. President.

   ____ The order, which was delivered on January 1, 1863, freed millions of slaves.

   ____ It helped bring an end to slavery in the United States.

3. ____ It is visible from the International Space Station.

   ____ The Great Wall of China is one of the most impressive structures ever built.

   ____ The structure spans more than 5,000 miles.

Apply It

Think about the body paragraphs you wrote in your essay. Use the sentence frames below to practice organizing the topic sentence and supporting details within each paragraph.

1. When it comes to building an effective team, _____ believes that _____ is

   (author 1)

   essential. He conveys his perspective in _____ , where he shows _____ .

   (title 1)   (supporting detail)

   Like _____ , _____ feels that feels an effective team _____ .

   (author 1)   (author 2)   (author 2's perspective)

   In _____ , he shows how _____ .

   (title 2)   (supporting detail)

2. In his article, _____ , author _____ demonstrates that _____ .

   (title 1)   (author 1)   (author 1's perspective)

   The author illustrates this by _____ . In addition, the author shows that _____ .

   (supporting detail)   (supporting detail)

   by contrast, _____ believes that _____ . He illustrates this in his article,

   (author 2)   (author 2's perspective)

   _____ where he shows _____ .

   (title 2)   (supporting detail)

Now, go back to your draft and select one body paragraph that you could reorganize.

Conventions Study | Using Verbs for Specific Effects

See It | Writers choose verbs to achieve different effects.

- Verbs in the **active** or **passive voice** emphasize either the action or the actor. In passive voice, a form of *to be* comes before the main verb.

- Verbs in the **conditional mood** express the possibility that something might happen if something else happens. Verbs such as *could, would,* and *might* are used in the conditional mood.

- Verbs in the **subjunctive mood** express uncertainty or describe a condition that does not exist. Helping verbs such as *should, may,* and *were* are typically used to express the subjunctive mood.

Try It | This passage includes an example of each of the uses of verbs described above. Circle and label each example.

If I were part of a team like those described by the authors, I would hope my unique skills and talents could contribute to the group's success. It became clear from both articles that in teams like these, the individual contributions add up to more than the sum of their parts.

Apply It | Now craft your conclusion or a couple of sentences for your body paragraphs. Use verbs in a variety of ways (active or passive voice, conditional and subjunctive mood) to achieve specific effects.

Step 4 | Revise and Edit   Revise your draft with a partner.

Organization and Clarity

State the text titles and author names in the introductory paragraph.	Self	1	2	3	4
	Partner	1	2	3	4
Include a clear, meaningful thesis statement that emphasizes a compare/contrast relationship between each author's perspective on what makes an effective team.	Self	1	2	3	4
	Partner	1	2	3	4
Each body paragraph focuses on only one text and contains information that reflects the topic sentence and supports the thesis statement.	Self	1	2	3	4
	Partner	1	2	3	4
Each body paragraph reflects the purpose of comparing and contrasting the texts.	Self	1	2	3	4
	Partner	1	2	3	4
The conclusion restates the thesis in a new way.	Self	1	2	3	4
	Partner	1	2	3	4

Evidence and Reasoning

Include two or more pieces of evidence to describe each text.	Self	1	2	3	4
	Partner	1	2	3	4
Analyze how each author uses structure, details, and language to convey perspective.	Self	1	2	3	4
	Partner	1	2	3	4

Language and Conventions

Include academic and domain-specific language appropriately in the essay.	Self	1	2	3	4
	Partner	1	2	3	4
Use verbs in passive and active voice for different emphasis.	Self	1	2	3	4
	Partner	1	2	3	4
Use verbs in the conditional and subjunctive moods to express possibility or to make nonfactual statements.	Self	1	2	3	4
	Partner	1	2	3	4
Properly use English conventions of grammar, capitalization, and punctuation.	Self	1	2	3	4
	Partner	1	2	3	4

Step 5 | Publish   Publish your essay either in print or digital form.

Scoring Guide | ① needs improvement   ② average   ③ good   ④ excellent

Publish

Publish your essay either in print or digital form. Use the rubric below to assess your final performance task.

PERFORMANCE TASK RUBRIC

Score Point	Organization and Clarity	Evidence and Reasoning	Language and Conventions
Exemplary ④	<ul><li>introductory paragraph states the **topic clearly** and includes a **strong thesis statement** that compares and/or contrasts</li><li>each body paragraph **focuses on one text** and **effectively explains** each author's strategies and perspective</li><li>includes **well-chosen** text evidence, precise language, and verbs to achieve specific effects</li><li>concluding statement **restates** the focus statement and prompts readers to **consider new ideas**</li></ul>	<ul><li>**effectively compares and contrasts** the structure and language the authors use to express their views on effective technology teams</li><li>includes **several examples of relevant** factual evidence from each text that illustrate each author's perspective</li></ul>	<ul><li>demonstrates a **strong command** of the conventions of standard English grammar and usage, as well as of standard English capitalization, punctuation, and spelling</li><li>vocabulary is **appropriate** to the topic (vocabulary about team-building, accurate terms for referring to text structure and language, vocabulary for making comparisons and contrasts)</li></ul>
Meets Standards ③	<ul><li>introductory paragraph states the **topic clearly** and includes a **thesis statement** identifying points of comparison/contrast</li><li>each body paragraph **focuses on one text** and **explains** each author's strategies and perspective</li><li>includes **some** text evidence, precise language, and verbs to achieve specific effects</li><li>concluding statement **restates** the focus statement</li></ul>	<ul><li>**adequately compares and contrasts** the structure and language the authors use to express their views on effective technology teams</li><li>includes **some** relevant factual evidence from each text that illustrates each author's perspective</li></ul>	<ul><li>demonstrates **a near command** of the conventions of standard English grammar and usage, as well as of standard English capitalization, punctuation, and spelling **with some errors**</li><li>vocabulary is **appropriate** to the topic (vocabulary about team-building, accurate terms for referring to text structure and language, vocabulary for making comparisons and contrasts)</li></ul>

PERFORMANCE TASK RUBRIC

Score Point	Organization and Clarity	Evidence and Reasoning	Language and Conventions
Needs Work ②	• introductory paragraph states the **topic** and includes a **thesis statement** that loosely identifies points of comparison/contrast • body paragraphs are **somewhat organized** by text, and **vaguely explain** each author's strategies and perspective • includes **a limited amount of** text evidence, precise language, and verbs to achieve specific effects • concluding statement **attempts to restate** the focus statement	• **attempts to compare and contrast** the structure and language the authors use to express their views on effective technology teams • includes **some** textual evidence from each text that illustrates each author's perspective	• demonstrates a **marginal command** of the conventions of English grammar and usage, as well as of standard English capitalization, punctuation, and spelling • there **are many errors, however the text is still understandable** • includes only **one or two examples** of vocabulary that is appropriate to the topic (vocabulary about team-building, accurate terms for referring to text structure and language, vocabulary for making comparisons and contrasts)
Does Not Meet Standards ①	• introductory paragraph is **unclear** and does not include a thesis statement • body paragraphs are **not organized logically** and/or **do not explain** each author's strategies and perspective • essay includes **little text evidence** and few verbs to achieve specific effects • concluding statement is **unclear and does not sum up** the ideas in the essay	• response is **partial or inaccurate comparison/contrast** of the structure and language the authors use to express their views on effective technology teams • includes **no textual evidence** from each text	• demonstrates **almost no command** of the conventions of standard English grammar and usage, as well as of standard English capitalization, punctuation, and spelling • there **are many errors that disrupt** the reader's understanding of the text • **does not include** vocabulary that is appropriate to the topic (vocabulary about team-building, accurate terms for referring to text structure and language, vocabulary for making comparisons and contrasts)

Questions

Words and Phrases in Context

1. What does the word *rigidity* mean in **paragraph 3**? Use context clues to determine the meaning.

Text Structure

2. What does the author describe on this page? Why would the author begin an article called "Building the Future Spacesuit" this way?

Building the Future Spacesuit

by Dava Newman from *NASA.gov*

¶1 For the past dozen years, I have been working with colleagues and students here at the Massachusetts Institute of Technology (MIT) and with collaborators in various <u>disciplines</u> from around the world to develop a new kind of spacesuit. My hope is that the astronauts who some day walk on the surface of Mars will be protected by a future version of what we are calling the "BioSuit™."

Beyond the Balloon

¶2 The suits that kept NASA astronauts alive on the moon and those worn by Space Shuttle and International Space Station crew members for extravehicular activities (EVAs), including the Hubble repair missions, are technological marvels; in effect, they are miniature spacecraft that provide the pressure, oxygen, and <u>thermal</u> control that humans need to survive in the vacuum of space.

¶3 The greatest problem with these suits is their rigidity. The air that supplies the necessary pressure to the bodies of wearers turns them into stiff balloons that make movement difficult and tiring. These suits are officially known as EMUs—extravehicular mobility units—but they allow only limited mobility. Astronauts who perform repair work in space find the stiffness of spacesuit gloves especially challenging: imagine manipulating tools and small parts for hours wearing gas-filled gloves that fight against the flexing of your fingers.

¶4 The suppleness of these gloves is improving. Aerospace engineer Peter Homer has won two NASA Centennial Challenge competitions with designs that add an X-shaped bit of fabric to finger joints, creating a kind of hinge that increases <u>dexterity</u>. But that improvement, though significant, has been made within the context of the fundamental limitations of a glove that remains a gas-filled bladder.

Words to Know

<u>disciplines:</u> *(n.)* areas of knowledge or teaching

thermal: *(adj.)* related to heat

<u>dexterity:</u> *(n.)* skill in doing things with the hands

¶5 Future space exploration will be expensive. If we send humans to Mars, we will want to maximize the work effort and science return. One contributor to that efficiency will need to be a new kind of spacesuit that allows our explorer-astronauts to move freely and quickly on the Martian surface. That could be the BioSuit.

A New (and Old) Approach

¶6 The BioSuit is based on the idea that there is another way to apply the necessary pressure to an astronaut's body. In theory at least, a form-fitting suit that presses directly on the skin can accomplish the job. What is needed is an elastic fabric and a structure that can provide about one-third of sea-level atmospheric pressure, or 4.3 psi (approximately the pressure at the top of Mt. Everest). The skintight suit would allow for a degree of mobility impossible in a gas-filled suit. It also would be potentially safer. While an abrasion or micrometeor puncture in a traditional suit would threaten sudden <u>decompression</u> puncturing the balloon and causing a major emergency and immediate <u>termination</u> of the EVA—a small breach in the BioSuit could be readily repaired with a kind of high-tech Ace bandage to cover a small tear.

¶7 The mechanical counter-pressure spacesuit is not a new idea. Physiologist Dr. Paul Webb introduced the concept in the late sixties and developed a prototype in the early seventies. It was a great idea that came before its time, in my opinion; advanced materials that could exert the necessary pressure on the skin were not available then. In addition, the wearer needed help getting Webb's prototype suit on and off (as do astronauts donning and doffing existing spacesuits), which results in expensive downtime for astronauts. A really practical BioSuit would be one the wearer could don and doff herself in, say, less than ten minutes.

¶8 In the late nineties, colleagues and I revived Webb's innovation and began work on second-skin spacesuit designs. Our hypothesis was that new developments in materials (for instance, Spandex and its more sophisticated polymer descendants) plus supportive patterning of the material could make a successful counter-pressure suit feasible.

Words to Know

<u>decompression:</u> (n.) reduction of the pressure of air on something

<u>termination:</u> (n.) act of ending something

<u>prototype:</u> (n.) the first model of something

Questions

Words and Phrases in Context

3. Use a dictionary or a science web site to determine the meaning of *atmospheric pressure*. What can you infer from the details in **paragraph 6** about the importance of atmospheric pressure to the spacesuit design?

Key Idea and Details

4. What were the advantages and disadvantages of Webb's suit? How would the BioSuit improve on Webb's design? Use details in **paragraph 7** to support your answer.

Questions

Key Ideas and Details

5. In **paragraphs 9–11** Newman discusses putting together a team to build the BioSuit. How will each member contribute to the design of the suit? What can you infer from this information about Newman's perspective on what makes a good team?

Key Ideas and Details

6. How does working together influence the way engineers and designers do their jobs? Use details in **paragraph 11** to support your answer.

Learning Together

¶9 Thanks to some funding from the NASA Institute for Advanced Concepts, we were able to gather a team to begin the practical work that would test our hypothesis. Like most research at MIT, the spacesuit work is about teaching as well as practical results. MIT engineers and biomedical engineers are part of the team, as is Jeff Hoffman, a professor who has flown on five shuttle missions, including a Hubble repair. As someone who has worn and worked in current operational spacesuits, he can use his experience to tell us where we may be going wrong in our design.

¶10 Collaborators outside the MIT community include Trotti and Associates, an architectural and industrial design firm in Cambridge, MA; engineers from Draper Laboratories; and Dainese, an Italian manufacturer of motorcycle racing "leathers"—leather and carbon-fiber suits designed to protect racers traveling at up to 200 mph.

¶11 Bringing together designers from Trotti and Associates and students from the Rhode Island School of Design and my MIT engineering students has greatly influenced the way our groups work. In our early sessions together to realize a second-skin spacesuit, my engineering students spent much of their time hunched over their laptops, calculating and analyzing the governing equations, while the designers—visual thinkers— took out sketchbooks and immediately started drawing to attack the problem. After working together for weeks, the engineers got more comfortable with the idea of sketching solutions and some of the designers added Matlab and its more analytical approach to their repertoires. We all ended up better off.

Words to Know

Matlab: (n.) a computer program that performs numerical operations

repertoires: (n.) all the skills that people typically use

¶12 We have "collaborated" with researchers from earlier eras, too. Not only Paul Webb (still active, he is an advisor to our team), but also Dr. Arthur Iberall, a physicist who did important work on mobile spacesuits. He died in 2002, but his daughters—happy to see his work continued—gave me access to his papers. We have expanded his great idea of a pattern of three-dimensional lines on the body that do not extend by deriving the mathematical representation and visualization of what I call a soft exoskeleton and structure for the BioSuit. There is also Dr. Karl Langer, the nineteenth-century Austrian anatomist who experimentally studied and mapped the tension lines in human skin.

¶13 Iberall's and Langer's work informed our thinking about possible patterning designs for our suit, and we've patented our innovations. Elastic fabrics alone cannot provide the essential combination of sufficient pressure and flexibility we need, especially at knees, elbows, and finger joints. (The flexible parts of the body are the biggest challenge, of course.) Laminating our mathematically derived web of less-flexible lines, or the soft exoskeleton pattern, to our elastic compression suit has gotten us closer to the necessary pressure production goals, and we've exceeded our mobility and flexibility performance goals.

¶14 Tremendous challenges remain before we can vacuum test a complete BioSuit, and that will be only one step on the road to an operational system that astronauts could wear in space. So far, we have been testing leg prototypes in a vacuum chamber at MIT. We are within striking distance of our pressure goal. Adding wearable sensors to the suit is another challenge that we are working on currently, and we've designed a new gas-pressured helmet, one that is closer-fitting than current globe-shaped helmets. We would like to give astronauts the ability to turn their heads and look over their shoulders, which means designing a new kind of airtight joint between the helmet and the rest of the BioSuit.

Words to Know

three dimensional: *(adj.)* appearing to have length, depth, and breadth (distance from one side to another)

deriving: *(v.)* developing one thing from something else

laminating: *(v.)* joining together

Questions

Key Ideas and Details

7. How has research from the past helped Newman and her team with their BioSuit design? Use information from **paragraphs 12 and 13** to support your answer.

Words and Phrases in Context

8. Why would the BioSuit need sensors? Use clues in **paragraph 14** to determine the answer.

There is also the question of how to package life support for the suit. The large backpack that supplies oxygen, thermal control, and other necessities to current spacesuits tends to unbalance astronauts working in partial-gravity environments. We have tapped into the professional diving community for help designing a new life-support system for the BioSuit, perhaps a modular one to allow astronauts to carry only what they need and provide quick bottle changes for their extreme exploration assignments.

¶16 Given a full core team of about a dozen people (which we do not have presently because of lack of funding), I think we could have a complete suit ready for testing within three years. But, as with any research and development project, it is important to keep an open mind in this process. We even need to be willing to accept evidence that our idea won't work. (So far, fortunately, we haven't found any deal breakers; our results suggest that the BioSuit is technically feasible and could become a practical reality.) And we have to consider alternatives that may prove more practical than our original concept, though not as elegant—for instance, a hybrid suit that combines mechanical counter-pressure arms and legs with a gas-pressurized trunk.

The Potential

¶17 We started this work with a vision of bio-suited explorers on the surface of Mars. That is still our goal, but for the past five years we have received National Science Foundation funding for applications on Earth that are also exciting.

¶18 We have been working with colleagues at the Children's Hospital in Boston, Harvard's Wyss Institute, Boston University, and Draper Laboratory to see if we can use our technology and engineering designs to help infants with brain damage that affects motor skills, children with cerebral palsy, and stroke victims, who typically lose motor skills on one side of their bodies. The idea is first to use BioSuit "sleeves" with built-in sensors on the legs to measure movements—to understand, for instance, how much motion and kicking by infants is typical, and compare that with the limited

Questions

Text Structure

9. What can you infer from the subheading "The Potential" about the section that follows?

Words and Phrases in Context

10. What context clues in **paragraphs 17 and 18** help you to determine the meaning of *applications*?

kicking and motions of children with cerebral palsy. The next step—a big one—is to add actuators that can enhance and direct movement. In the case of cerebral palsy and stroke victims, that would be a way of giving back some of the lost motion. People with cerebral palsy expend a lot of energy moving and have stiffened muscles; our BioSuit technology and know-how could guide movement and enhance mobility to make it more efficient. And because the brains of newborns are still so plastic, enhancing the natural kicking of infants with potential motor problems from brain damage might actually reshape the motor programs and partly "heal" their brains.

¶19 Like an operational bio-spacesuit, the biomedical applications are in the future, but we are making encouraging progress. In the process, we are learning about materials, science and biomechanics; creating diverse cooperative communities of engineers, designers, scientists, and artists; and training a new generation of creative engineers. The possibilities are endless. How about putting actuators on a skintight spacesuit to give astronauts more-than-normal speed and agility? No one knows how far we can go. Stay tuned.

Questions

Key Ideas and Details

11. How is developing a "biomedical" suit inspiring Newman to think of new features for the BioSuit? Use details in **paragraphs 18 and 19** to support your answer.

Literature Circle Leveled Novels

Eva by Peter Dickinson
After surviving a catastrophic car wreck, Eva wakes up from a coma. She finds out that, in a desperate attempt to save her life, doctors have pulled her brain from the mangled remains of her body and implanted it into the body of a chimpanzee. **Lexile®** measure: 1010L

The Ear, the Eye, and the Arm *by Nancy Farmer*
Tendai and his siblings, the children of a military ruler, live in Zimbabwe in the year 2194. They learn that the world of technological advances they live in exists beside another world, in which people live in slums and work in toxic waste dumps. **Lexile®** measure: 660L

The Hunger Games *by Suzanne Collins*
Katniss is a 16-year-old girl who takes her sister's place in the annual Hunger Games—a nationally televised game where each territory in a post-apocalyptic country is required to sacrifice two players to compete in a fight to the death, like gladiators. **Lexile®** measure: 810L

Fiction, Nonfiction, and Novels

The Giver *by Lois Lowry.* When he begins to train for his job as a Receiver of Memory, Jonas finds out just what humanity has given up and lost in the process of creating a society designed to eliminate pain from everyone's lives. **Lexile®** measure: 760L

Feed *by M.T. Anderson.* Feed is a hybrid of Internet and television fed directly into one's brain. Titus listens to what the feed tells him until he meets Violet, who teaches him to question the feed and look for the truth. **Lexile®** measure: 770L

I, Robot *by Isaac Asimov.* In this collection of interlinked stories, Asimov lays out three laws of robotics, contemplates the evolution of robots in human history and discusses the role they'll play in our future. **Lexile®** measure: 820L

Tomorrowland: Ten Stories About the Future *edited by Michael Cart.* Ten authors share their "visions of times to come." **Lexile®** measure: 840L

Little Brother *by Cory Doctorow.* Marcus finds new technology a frightening means of being tracked and controlled and so begins a revolution to fight its rampant use. **Lexile®** measure: 900L

Ultimate Robot *by Robert Malone.* Learn more about forms and uses of robots, including as artists and art, as surgical aids, as combat tools, and more. **Lexile®** measure: IG1230L

Supercomputers: Charting the Future of Cybernetics *by Charlene W. Billings, et al.* Learn more about the history of these powerful machines and the role they might play in our future.

Where Wizards Stay Up Late *by Katie Hafner, et al.* Track the evolution of the Internet to what we use today, and catch a glimpse of its use in the future.

Films and TV

2001: A Space Odyssey (Warner Home Video, 1968) A space mission is put to the test by a sentient shipboard computer. Compare our reality to Arthur C. Clarke's vision of the future from 1968. (146 min.)

A.I. Artificial Intelligence (Dreamworks Video, 2001) David is a highly advanced robotic boy who wants nothing more than to be accepted and loved as a real boy. (146 min.)

Back to the Future, Part II (Universal Studios, 1989) Marty McFly learns how his choices affect his future and shows us the future as imagined by the creators of the trilogy. (108 min.)

Extreme Engineering (Discovery Channel, 2004) In this series, explore extraordinary engineering feats of the present and future, such as widening the Panama Canal, tunneling under the Alps, and building Hong Kong's airport.

Future Car (Discovery Communications, 2007) What will cars look like and how they will be made in the future? Designers share how they think advancing technology will change cars' shape and function. (172 min.)

Future by Design (Microcinema, 2006) Explore the vision of the future according to Jacque Fresco—a ninety-year-old man who has spent his life inventing new technology. (90 min.)

Smash Lab (Discovery Channel, 2009) A group of engineers and designers looks for new and different ways to use everyday technology to solve problems in this television series.

Wall-E (Walt Disney Video, 2008) A remarkably humanlike robot is designed to take care of Earth in the future, but ends up turning the human world upside down. (98 min.)

Websites

Discovery Channel Under the "Explore by Subject" tab, choose the topic "technology" to explore articles and videos related to the newest advances and what they mean for the future.

National Geographic Navigate to the "Science and Space" page. Choose a specific topic to explore, or browse for information on space technology.

Nova Browse the archives by selecting the topic "Technology." Learn how new technologies are being developed and used.

The History Channel Choose the topic "Science and Technology." Use the playlists to discover how the development of new technology in human history has revolutionized our ability to engineer new structures.

Magazines

Discover: Science, Technology, and the Future Be on the cutting edge of new and future technology and discoveries, and learn what impact they will have on our lives.

The Futurist Read articles by experts in a variety of fields that discuss new developments and make predictions on what the future may hold.

Popular Science Stay up-to-date on technology in a variety of fields, including cars, gears and gadgets, military, aviation, space, the environment, and more.

Scientific American Learn what to expect of future science in such areas as technology, the mind and brain, biology, and more.

SPACE INVADERS

How does science fiction capture society's fears?

WRITING PERFORMANCE TASK

How do these authors portray life on Earth during an alien invasion? Compare and contrast the characters and events in each text and how the authors develop them.

 GRAPHIC SHORT STORY/NOVEL EXCERPT

from *The War of the Worlds*
by H. G. Wells

Language
- Academic Vocabulary
- Word Study:
  Context Clues

Reading a Literary Text
- Identify Evidence
- Key Ideas and Details
- Craft and Structure

 **GRAPHIC SHORT STORY/NOVEL EXCERPT**

adapted from *"Zero Hour"*
by Ray Bradbury

Language
- Academic Vocabulary
- Word Study:
  Using the Dictionary

Reading a Literary Text
- Identify Evidence
- Key Ideas and Details
- Craft and Structure

SPEAKING AND LISTENING

Present a Multi-Media Presentation
- Collaborate and Present

Checklist: Multi-Media Presentation
- Scoring Guide

WRITING

Writing: Literary Analysis
- Read the Model
- Analyze the Model
- Gather Evidence
- Organize Ideas

- Language Study: Combine Sentences
- Conventions Study: Transitions
- Revise, Edit, and Publish
- Performance Task Rubric

EXTENDED READING

Short Story
"The Invasion From Outer Space" by Steven Millhauser

Unit Introduction

In this unit, science fiction authors imagine the consequences of alien invasions on Earth. The plots might seem impossible, but the human responses to this threat ring true. In that way, science fiction stories are often social commentaries.

In one of the genre's earliest extraterrestrial stories, the novel *The War of the Worlds*, written in 1898 by H. G. Wells, tells what happens when armed Martians land near London.

In the short story "Zero Hour," written in the early 1950s by Ray Bradbury, space beings enlist the help of innocent children to invade Earth.

Academic Vocabulary

adapted from "Zero Hour" by Ray Bradbury

Rate your understanding of each word. Then write its meaning and a sample sentence.

Word	Meaning	Example
evoke (v.) p. 245 ① ② ③ ④	call up or produce	Those smells evoke a memory of my mother's cooking.
deceptively (adv.) p. 245 ① ② ③ ④	in a misleading or false way	
disdained (v.) p. 246 ① ② ③ ④	looked down on; disrespected; thought oneself too good for	
invasion (n.) p. 246 ① ② ③ ④		I hope this bug spray stops the ants' invasion of our kitchen!
delight (n.) p. 258 ① ② ③ ④		

Rating Scale | ① I don't know the word.   ② I've seen it or heard it.
                   ③ I know its meaning.   ④ I know it and use it.

Word Study

When you encounter a word you don't know, you can use a dictionary to find the definition. Most words have more than one definition. To make sure you choose the correct definition, look back at the text. Choose the definition that makes the most sense in context.

Use a dictionary to look up the meaning of *fury* in the text below. Use the context to check that you chose the correct definition.

"Such fun, such joy, such tumbling and hearty screaming. It was an interesting fact that this **fury** and bustle occurred only among the younger children."

1. What is one definition of *fury*?

2. What is another definition of *fury*?

3. Which definition fits into the context of the sentence? What context clues helped you choose that definition?

adapted from

ZERO HOUR

by Ray Bradbury

¶1 In 1947, webcams, videoconferencing, and the Internet hadn't been invented. In fact, human beings had yet to walk on the moon. Because people knew so little about space and technology, writers often imagined what the future would look like. It was at this time in history that Ray Bradbury wrote his suspenseful science fiction story "Zero Hour."

¶2 Bradbury's story takes place in a futuristic American neighborhood. People travel in jet-fueled cars, speak to each other over specialized television sets, and order lunch from ultramodern vending machines. Although none of this technology existed when Bradbury wrote the story, some of it actually exists today.

¶3 The world Ray Bradbury created in "Zero Hour" is filled with neat little houses and lawns. Bradbury's setting is meant to **evoke** feelings of peace and happiness. Everything is perfect . . . until one day, when a **deceptively** innocent girl makes a mysterious new friend named Drill.

Words to Know

suspenseful: (adj.) filled with excitement or anxiety as a result of not knowing what will happen next

ultramodern: (adv.) extremely current

Close Reading

Literary Analysis

1. What details do we learn about the setting of "Zero Hour" in this introduction to the story?

2. What does it mean that the protagonist is "deceptively innocent"? What effect can you expect her to have on the peaceful, happy setting?

Writing

The protagonist seems ____, but she really ____. Based on this, I expect her to ____.

Close Reading

Literary Analysis

3. What are the younger children doing at the beginning of "Zero Hour"? How do they feel about this activity?

Academic Vocabulary

4. Why do the older children disdain "Invasion"?

Literary Analysis

5. Consider what you know so far about the game Invasion. What supplies do the children use to play it? What does the name of the game suggest?

Writing

6. Describe the way Mink treats the other kids. What does this tell you about her relationship to them? Based on dialogue and actions, what traits does she have?

Mink _____ the other children and _____.

She seems _____ the leader of the _____.

The author uses _____ to reveal that Mink is _____.

AT LUNCH MINK GULPED HER MILK IN ONE TOSS AND WAS AT THE DOOR.

Hurry, Mom! This is a matter of life and death.

You sit right back down. Hot soup in a minute.

Always life and death. Slow down.

Can't. Drill's waiting for me

Who's Drill? A new boy in the neighborhood?

He's new all right. I got to run if we want to have the invasion!

Who's invading what?

Martians invading Earth. Well not exactly Martians. They're—I don't know. From up.

Drill's a Martian?

No. He's—well —maybe from Jupiter or Saturn or Venus.

Close Reading

Text Structure

7. What does Mrs. Morris think about Invasion? Identify details that reveal her thoughts.

Text Structure

8. What does Mrs. Morris hear through the window? What can you infer from this dialogue?

Literary Analysis

9. Mrs. Morris assumes Mink is using hyperbole when she claims what she's doing is a matter of life and death. Do you think she is correct? Explain.

Foreshadowing

Foreshadowing is when an author hints at what might happen later in the story. It is a way that an author creates interest, or engages the reader.

Literary Analysis

10. According to Mink, what will happen during the Invasion? Does Mrs. Morris take her seriously? Explain.

 Close Reading

Literary Analysis

11. Why couldn't the aliens "figure a way to attack" Earth until now? How have they solved that problem?

Text Structure

12. Look at the word "dimens-shuns" in the first panel on this page. What is this word and why is it spelled that way? What can you infer from Mink's use of the word?

Literary Analysis

13. Why are "guys like Pete Britz and Dale Jerick" the worst, according to Mink?

Writing

14. Why is Mink willing to help attack Earth? Identify her reasons. Why do you think the aliens chose younger children to help them?

Mink is willing to help because the aliens _____. She's also willing because _____. The aliens probably chose younger kids because _____.

Literary Analysis

15. What do we learn about Invasion from this conversation? What does this information imply?

Literary Analysis

16. What does Helen say that makes Mrs. Morris stop to think? Why does this comment make Mrs. Morris pause?

Words and Phrases in Context

17. What does Helen mean when she says "parents learn to shut their ears"? Identify context clues that helped you identify the meaning of this figure of speech.

Text Structure

18. Look at the pictures of the device the women use for talking to each other. What does it tell you about the author's vision of the future?

Can I help?

No thanks. I'll fix it.

Five o'clock—five o'clock. Time's a-wasting. Five o'clock.

Ha! Zero hour.

MOM WENT INSIDE AND SAT IN THE ELECTRIC RELAXING CHAIR.

Children and love and hate, side-by-side. Sometimes children loved you and hated you, all in one second.

TIME PASSED.

A BEETLE CAR HUMMED INTO THE DRIVEWAY, MR. MORRIS.

Hello, Darling.

Hello, Henry.

Close Reading

Literary Analysis

19. What is unusual about Mink's yo-yo? What can you infer about the Invasion from this yo-yo?

Words and Phrases in Context

20. What does Mink mean when she says, "Zero hour's five o'clock"? What can you infer will happen at five?

Text Structure

21. Examine the bottom panel of page 254. What does it reveal about the device the children have been building? Why does Mink refuse her mother's help with the device? Explain how this scene builds suspense.

Writing

22. What evidence in the story suggests the Invasion is just a game? What evidence suggests it is real? What do you conclude?

THE EXPLOSION!

KA-
-KRAKA
FA-
-BOOOOM!

THERE WERE OTHER EXPLOSIONS IN OTHER YARDS ON OTHER STREETS.

Up this way! In the attic! That's where it is!

It's not in the attic! It's outside!

Close Reading

Words and Phrases in Context

23. What is ironic about Mr. Morris's remark in the first panel on page 256?

Text Structure

24. What is Mrs. Morris concerned about when her husband comes home? How has her opinion of the Invasion changed since the beginning of the story? Why has her opinion changed?

Literary Analysis

25. What happens outside just after Mr. Morris arrives home? What causes this event?

Literary Analysis

26. Explain Mary and Henry Morris's reactions to the explosion. Why do they disagree about where it came from?

Close Reading

Academic Vocabulary

27. Why are the children "screaming with delight" outside? What are they delighted about?

Literary Analysis

28. Why does Henry continue to argue and resist as Mary drags him to the attic? Why does she feel he will "think her insane" for running away from a series of explosions?

Words and Phrases in Context

29. Why does Mrs. Morris throw the key "into a far, cluttered, corner"? Why is it important that the corner is cluttered?

Text Structure

30. Who are "they" in Mary's statement that "they'll find us soon enough"? Why does she expect them to find her?

FOOTSTEPS CAME INTO THE HOUSE, HEAVY FOOTSTEPS.

Who's coming in my house? Who's tramping around down there?

Mom? Dad? Where are you?

FZZZZT!

FOOTSTEPS. A LITTLE HUMMING SOUND. THE ATTIC LOCK MELTED.

HEAVY FOOTSTEPS. HEAVY, HEAVY, VERY HEAVY FOOTSTEPS CAME UP THE STAIRS, MINK LEADING THEM.

Who's downstairs? Who's there!

Hush. Oh nonononono! Please, be quiet. They might go away.

Close Reading

Literary Analysis

31. What is the effect of repeating "heavy footsteps, heavy, heavy footsteps" several times on page 260?

Literary Analysis

32. How do Mink and the aliens break into the attic? Why do you think the author describes the sound of this event as a "little humming sound"?

Text Structure

33. Reread the sentence of the text. Why does the story end with Mink saying just one word, "Peekaboo." What rhetorical strategy did the author use in choosing this word?

Writing

34. What happens after the last sentence of the story? Base your response on clues in the text.

> Peekaboo.

Identify Evidence | Analyze Characters, Events, and Ideas

Reread "Zero Hour," highlighting how Bradbury portrays life on Earth during an alien invasion. How does he introduce, describe, and elaborate on individuals, events, and ideas?

- In the Evidence column, record examples from the text that show life on Earth leading up to and during the Invasion. Include examples of descriptions, characters, dialogue, and events.
- In the Explanation column, explain how the evidence introduces, illustrates, or elaborates on individuals, events, and ideas.

Evidence	Source	Page	Explanation
1. Bradbury's setting is meant to evoke feelings of peace and happiness. Everything is perfect.	Introduction	245	As the story begins, life on Earth is pleasant. Nobody is expecting an alien invasion and the violent invasion will provide a sharp contrast to the quiet, pleasant scenes of Mink's neighborhood and house.
2. "It was an interesting fact that this fury and bustle occurred only among the younger children. The older ones disdained the affair and marched off on hikes or played a more dignified version of hide-and-go-seek on their own."	Narrator	246	The younger children are obsessed with a game called "Invasion," while the older kids want to do something more "dignified," or grown-up.
3.			
4.			

	Evidence	Source	Page	Explanation
5.				
6.				
7.				
8.				

Key Ideas and Details

Determining the Central Idea

1. Use the evidence you collected to summarize the central idea of this short story.

2. List three key characters in "Zero Hour." Explain why each is important to the central idea.

Characters	Significance

3. List three important events in the story. Explain why each event is important to the theme.

Events	Significance

Craft and Structure

Structure of the Graphic Short Story

In this graphic adaption of Ray Bradbury's "Zero Hour"—as in any work of graphic fiction or nonfiction—the images support and add to readers' understanding of the text.

1. On pages 246–251, what does the text (including dialogue) tell readers about the game Invasion? What else do you learn about the game from the images?

   Text:

   Images:

2. On page 251, what does Mink's conversation with her mother reveal about the Invasion? What additional information can you infer by examining the images of Mink and her mother?

   Text:

   Images:

3. What does the image on page 257 reveal about the explosion?

4. How does the final image on page 261 add to your knowledge of what's happening and support the inference that the last line is ironic?

Theme

5. Read the definition of theme. What message about humans and life do you think Bradbury wanted to convey through this story of an alien invasion?

Academic Vocabulary

from *The War of the Worlds* by H. G. Wells

Rate your understanding of each word. Then write its meaning and a sample sentence.

Word	Meaning	Example
agony (n.) p. 273 ① ② ③ ④	very severe pain	After burning his hand on the stove, he was in agony.
astonished (v.) p. 268 ① ② ③ ④		We were astonished by the acrobat's tricks.
colossal (adj.) p. 273 ① ② ③ ④		That colossal skyscraper is the world's tallest building.
formidable (adj.) p. 267 ① ② ③ ④		The bully is formidable, but the smaller kids stood up to him.
exultation (n.) p. 271 ① ② ③ ④	triumph; joy about a success or victory	
tumultuous (adj.) p. 272 ① ② ③ ④	full of activity, confusion, or violence	

Rating Scale
① I don't know the word.
② I've seen it or heard it.
③ I know its meaning.
④ I know it and use it.

Words in Context

Context Clues

Context clues are words in a text that help you figure out the meaning of an unfamiliar word. Sometimes words are defined in a text or their meaning is suggested by other nearby words.

The sentences below are from *The War of the Worlds* by H. G. Wells. Use context clues to determine the definitions of the bold words. Underline the context clues.

1. In another moment the huge wave, well-nigh at the boiling point had rushed upon me. I screamed aloud, and **scalded**, half blinded, agonized, I staggered through the leaping, hissing water towards the shore.

2. Thick clouds of steam were pouring off the wreckage, and through tumultuously whirling wisps I could see, intermittently and **vaguely**, the gigantic limbs . . . .

from

THE WAR OF THE WORLDS

by H. G. Wells

¶1 There was a lot of shouting, and one man was even jesting. The idea people seemed to have here was that the Martians were simply **formidable** human beings, who might attack and sack the town, to be certainly destroyed in the end. Every now and then people would glance nervously across the Wey, at the meadows towards Chertsey, but everything over there was still.

Across the **Thames**, except just where the boats landed, everything was quiet, in vivid contrast with the Surrey side. The people who landed there from the boats went tramping off down the lane. The big ferryboat had just made a journey. Three or four soldiers stood on the lawn of the inn, staring and jesting at the **fugitives**, without offering to help. The inn was closed, as it was now within **prohibited** hours.

¶3 "What's that?" cried a boatman, and "Shut up, you fool," said a man near me to a yelping dog. Then the sound came again, this time from the direction of Chertsey, a muffled thud—the sound of a gun.

Words to Know

Thames: (*n.*) a river in England that runs through London and the surrounding towns where this story is set

fugitives: (*n.*) people running away

prohibited: (*adj.*) illegal or not allowed

Close Reading

Writing

1. What does the narrator mean when he says people viewed the Martians as "simply formidable human beings" in **paragraph 1**?

   The narrator means that people expected _____ to fight the way a powerful human army would. Though people knew the town might be _____ they expected the Martians to be _____.

Literary Analysis

2. From what point of view is this story told? Identify a clue that reveals the narrator's point of view.

Close Reading

The fighting was beginning. Almost immediately unseen batteries across the river to our right, unseen because of the trees, took up the chorus, firing heavily one after the other. A woman screamed. Everyone stood arrested by the sudden stir of battle, near us and yet invisible to us. Nothing was to be seen save flat meadows, cows feeding unconcernedly for the most part, and silvery pollard willows motionless in the warm sunlight.

¶5 "The sojers'll stop em," said a woman beside me, doubtfully. A haziness rose over the treetops.

Then suddenly we saw a rush of smoke far away up the river, a puff of smoke that jerked up into the air and hung; and forthwith the ground heaved under foot and a heavy explosion shook the air, smashing two or three windows in the houses near, and leaving us **astonished**.

¶7 "Here they are!" shouted a man in a blue jersey. "Yonder! D'yer see them? Yonder!"

Quickly, one after the other, one, two, three, four of the armored Martians appeared, far away over the little trees, across the flat meadows that stretched towards Chertsey, and striding hurriedly towards the river. Little cowled figures they seemed at first, going with a rolling motion and as fast as flying birds.

Literary Analysis

3. What is happening around the narrator as the fighting begins in **paragraph 4**? Describe the scene and the mood.

Mood

The atmosphere of a story or scene, and the way it makes readers feel.

Text Structure

4. What are "sojers" in **paragraph 5**? How does the word *doubtfully* at the end of the first sentence affect the meaning of the woman's quote?

Academic Vocabulary

5. What leaves the people *astonished*? What can you infer about the battle from their astonishment?

Literary Analysis

6. In **paragraph 8**, the narrator gets his first glimpse of the Martians. Describe what he knows about them.

Words to Know

batteries: *(n.)* several large guns used together

arrested: *(adj.)* motionless; not moving

pollard willows: *(n.)* a type of tree

¶9 Then, advancing obliquely towards us, came a fifth. Their armored bodies glittered in the sun as they swept swiftly forward upon the guns, growing rapidly larger as they drew nearer. One on the extreme left, the remotest that is, flourished a huge case high in the air, and the ghostly, terrible Heat-Ray I had already seen on Friday night <u>smote</u> towards Chertsey, and struck the town.

At sight of these strange, swift, and terrible creatures the crowd near the water's edge seemed to me to be for a moment horror-struck. There was no screaming or shouting, but a silence. Then a hoarse murmur and a movement of feet—a splashing from the water. A man, too frightened to drop the <u>portmanteau</u> he carried on his shoulder, swung round and sent me staggering with a blow from the corner of his burden. A woman thrust at me with her hand and rushed past me. I turned with the rush of the people, but I was not too terrified for thought. The terrible Heat-Ray was in my mind. To get under water! That was it!

¶11 "Get under water!" I shouted, unheeded.

Literary Analysis

7. How does the Martians' Heat-Ray work? Identify clues that illustrate its function. Explain how the narrator knows this.

Writing

8. Describe how people react to the Heat-Ray.

At first, _____. Then they _____.

Close Reading

Words and Phrases in Context

9. What can you infer about the Martian invasion from Wells's use of figurative language? Identify a simile and a analogy that he uses, and explain.

Literary Analysis

10. What happens as the people are diving into the water?

Literary Analysis

11. What is the job of the "Martian machine" the narrator is observing? Why does it raise its case at the end of **paragraph 13**?

I faced about again, and rushed towards the approaching Martian, rushed right down the gravelly beach and headlong into the water. Others did the same. A boatload of people putting back came leaping out as I rushed past. The stones under my feet were muddy and slippery, and the river was so low that I ran perhaps twenty feet scarcely waist-deep. Then, as the Martian towered overhead scarcely a couple of hundred yards away, I flung myself forward under the surface. The splashes of the people in the boats leaping into the river sounded like thunderclaps in my ears. People were landing hastily on both sides of the river. But the Martian machine took no more notice for the moment of the people running this way and that than a man would of the confusion of ants in a nest against which his foot has kicked. When, half suffocated, I raised my head above water, the Martian's hood pointed at the batteries that were still firing across the river, and as it advanced it swung loose what must have been the <u>generator</u> of the Heat-Ray.

¶13 In another moment it was on the bank, and in a stride wading halfway across. The knees of its foremost legs bent at the farther bank, and in another moment it had raised itself to its full height again, close to the village of Shepperton. Forthwith the six guns which, unknown to anyone on the right bank, had been hidden behind the outskirts of that village, fired simultaneously. The sudden near <u>concussion</u>, the last close upon the first, made my heart jump. The monster was already raising the case generating the Heat-Ray as the first shell burst six yards above the hood.

Words to Know

generator: *(n.)* power source

concussion: *(n)* violent, shaking movement, usually caused by an explosion

I gave a cry of **astonishment**. I saw and thought nothing of the other four Martian monsters; my attention was riveted upon the nearer incident. Simultaneously two other shells burst in the air near the body as the hood twisted round in time to receive, but not in time to dodge, the fourth shell.

¶15 The shell burst clean in the face of the Thing. The hood bulged, flashed, was whirled off in a dozen tattered fragments of red flesh and glittering metal.

"Hit!" shouted I, with something between a scream and a cheer.

¶17 I heard answering shouts from the people in the water about me. I could have leaped out of the water with that momentary **exultation**.

The decapitated colossus reeled like a drunken giant; but it did not fall over. It recovered its balance by a miracle, and, no longer heeding its steps and with the camera that fired the Heat-Ray now rigidly upheld, it reeled swiftly upon Shepperton. The living intelligence, the Martian within the hood, was <u>slain</u> and splashed to the four winds of heaven, and the Thing was now but a mere intricate device of metal whirling to destruction. It drove along in a straight line, incapable of guidance. It struck the tower of Shepperton Church, smashing it down as the impact of a battering ram might have done, swerved aside, blundered on and collapsed with tremendous force into the river out of my sight.

Words to Know

momentary: *(adj.)* lasting only a short time

<u>slain</u>: *(v.)* killed

Close Reading

Writing

12. What causes the narrator to feel exultation and shout "Hit!"? Why does he hear "answering shouts" from the "people in the water about" him?

Words and Phrases in Context

13. What is the meaning of the word *colossus*? What clues helped you determine its meaning?

Words and Phrases in Context

14. What happens to the colossus? What is the "living intelligence" and what happens to it?

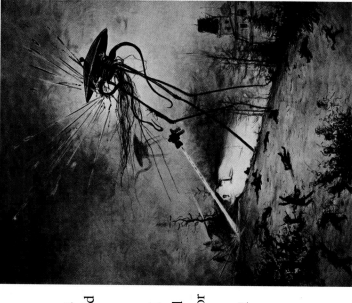

¶19 A violent explosion shook the air, and a spout of water, steam, mud, and shattered metal shot far up into the sky. As the camera of the Heat-Ray hit the water, the latter had immediately flashed into steam. In another moment a huge wave, like a muddy tidal bore but almost scaldingly hot, came sweeping round the bend upstream. I saw people struggling shorewards, and heard their screaming and shouting faintly above the seething and roar of the Martian's collapse.

For a moment I heeded nothing of the heat, forgot the patent need of self-preservation. I splashed through the **tumultuous** water, pushing aside a man in black to do so, until I could see round the bend. Half a dozen deserted boats pitched aimlessly upon the confusion of the waves. The fallen Martian came into sight downstream, lying across the river, and for the most part submerged.

¶21 Thick clouds of steam were pouring off the wreckage, and through the tumultuously whirling wisps I could see, intermittently and vaguely, the gigantic limbs churning the water and flinging a splash and spray of mud and froth into the air. The tentacles swayed and struck like living arms, and, save for the helpless purposelessness of these movements, it was as if some wounded thing were struggling for its life amid the waves. Enormous quantities of a ruddy-brown fluid were spurting up in noisy jets out of the machine.

Words to Know

heeded: (v.) paid attention to

submerged: (adj.) under water

Close Reading

Writing

15. Why does the narrator splash "through the tumultuous water"? What is his main concern at this moment? How is he different from the other people caught up in the battle?

Literary Analysis

16. How does the narrator describe what he sees through the "tumultuously whirling wisps" of steam? What can you infer about the Martians from this description?

Literary Analysis

17. What is the "ruddy-brown fluid"? Why is it "spurting up in noisy jets" out of the machine?

My attention was diverted from this death flurry by a furious yelling, like that of the thing called a siren in our manufacturing towns. A man, knee-deep near the towing path, shouted inaudibly to me and pointed. Looking back, I saw the other Martians advancing with gigantic strides down the riverbank from the direction of Chertsey. The Shepperton guns spoke this time unavailingly.

¶23 At that I ducked at once under water, and, holding my breath until movement was an **agony**, blundered painfully ahead under the surface as long as I could. The water was in a tumult about me, and rapidly growing hotter.

When for a moment I raised my head to take breath and throw the hair and water from my eyes, the steam was rising in a whirling white fog that at first hid the Martians altogether. The noise was deafening. Then I saw them dimly, **colossal** figures of grey, magnified by the mist. They had passed by me, and two were stooping over the frothing, tumultuous ruins of their comrade.

¶25 The third and fourth stood beside him in the water, one perhaps two hundred yards from me, the other towards Laleham. The generators of the Heat-Rays waved high, and the hissing beams smote down this way and that.

Words to Know

unavailingly: (adv.) unsuccessfully

comrade: (n.) friend, especially someone who shares difficult work or danger

Close Reading

Academic Vocabulary

18. What prompts the narrator to hold his breath "until movement was an agony"?

Literary Analysis

19. What imagery does Wells include to describe the scene as the narrator emerges from the water? What do these details tell you about the experience of being in the middle of this alien invasion?

Literary Analysis

20. How do the Martians treat each other? How does their behavior contrast with the narrator's interactions with the people around him?

LITERATURE

Close Reading

Literary Analysis

21. What does the Heat-Ray do to Weybridge? Identify details that describe the effect of the Heat-Ray on the town.

Literary Analysis

22. How does the narrator use personification to describe the Heat-Ray attack on Weybridge?

Personification

Describing an animal, object, or idea as though it were human or had human qualities

---

Literary Analysis

23. What do the narrator's reactions to the "Heat-Ray" in **Paragraph 28** show about his feelings in this situation?

The air was full of sound, a deafening and confusing conflict of noises—the clangorous <u>din</u> of the Martians, the crash of falling houses, the thud of trees, fences, sheds flashing into flame, and the crackling and roaring of fire. Dense black smoke was leaping up to mingle with the steam from the river, and as the Heat-Ray went to and fro over Weybridge its impact was marked by flashes of incandescent white, that gave place at once to a smoky dance of lurid flames. The nearer houses still stood intact, awaiting their fate, shadowy, faint and pallid in the steam, with the fire behind them going to and fro.

¶27 For a moment perhaps I stood there, breast-high in the almost boiling water, dumbfounded at my position, hopeless of escape. Through the <u>reek</u> I could see the people who had been with me in the river scrambling out of the water through the reeds, like little frogs hurrying through grass from the advance of a man, or running to and fro in utter dismay on the towing path.

Then suddenly the white flashes of the Heat-Ray came leaping towards me. The houses caved in as they dissolved at its touch, and darted out flames; the trees changed to fire with a roar. The Ray flickered up and down the towing path, licking off the people who ran this way and that, and came down to the water's edge not fifty yards from where I stood. It swept across the river to Shepperton, and the water in its track rose in a boiling weal crested with steam. I turned shoreward.

¶29 In another moment the huge wave, well-nigh at the boiling point had rushed upon me. I screamed aloud, and **scalded**, half blinded, agonized, I staggered through the leaping, hissing water towards the shore. Had my foot stumbled, it would have been the end. I fell helplessly, in full sight of the Martians, upon the broad, bare gravelly spit that runs down to mark the angle of the Wey and Thames. I expected nothing but death.

Words to Know

<u>din</u>: (*n.*) loud, unpleasant noise that continues for a long time

<u>reek</u>: (*n.*) smoke or vapor

---

274   Common Core Code X

I have a dim memory of the foot of a Martian coming down within a score of yards of my head, driving straight into the loose gravel, whirling it this way and that and lifting again; of a long suspense, and then of the four carrying the <u>debris</u> of their comrade between them, now clear and then presently faint through a veil of smoke, receding <u>interminably</u>; as it seemed to me, across a vast space of river and meadow. And then, very slowly, I realized that by a miracle I had escaped.

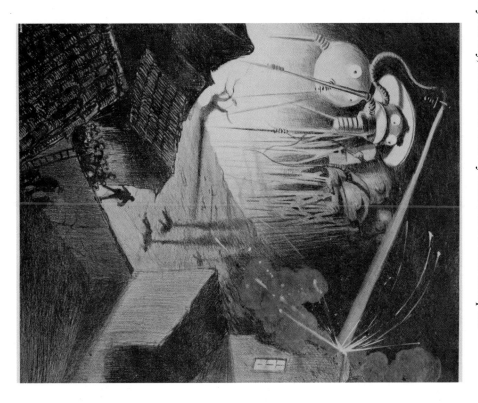

Words to Know

<u>debris</u>: (n.) pieces of something left over after it has been destroyed

<u>interminably</u>: (adj.) forever; endlessly; without ending

Close Reading

Words and Phrases in Context

24. Why does it seem to the narrator that the Martians recede "interminably"?

Writing

25. Why is the narrator's life spared? What does this event tell you about the Martians?

Identify Evidence | Analyze Individuals, Events, and Ideas

Reread the excerpt from *The War of the Worlds*, highlighting how Wells portrays life on Earth during an alien invasion. How does he introduce, describe, and elaborate on individuals, events, and ideas?

- In the Evidence column, record examples from the text that show life on Earth during the "Invasion." Include examples of descriptions, individuals, dialogue, and events.
- In the Explanation column, explain how the evidence introduces, illustrates, or elaborates on individuals, events, and ideas.

Evidence	Source	Page	Explanation
1. "There was a lot of shouting, and one man was even jesting. The idea people seemed to have here was that the Martians were simply formidable human beings, who might attack and sack the town, to be certainly destroyed in the end."	Narrator	267	In the beginning of the invasion, people still thought the battle would be tough, but they would win in the end. The people thought the Martians were just like any other human enemy. So the people are being loud and even joking around.
2. "'The sojers'll stop 'em,' said a woman beside me, doubtfully."			
3. "Their armored bodies glittered in the sun as they swept swiftly forward upon the guns, growing rapidly larger as they drew nearer. One on the extreme left, the remotest that is, flourished a huge case high in the air, and the ghostly, terrible Heat-Ray . . ."			
4. "A man, too frightened to drop the portmanteau he carried on his shoulder, swung round and sent me staggering with a blow from the corner of his burden."			

	Evidence	Source	Page	Explanation
5.				
6.				
7.				

Key Ideas and Details

Determining the Central Idea

1. What is the central idea of the text? Use evidence.

2. List two key characters in *The War of the Worlds*. Explain why each character is important to the theme.

Character	Significance

3. List three important events in the story. Explain why each event is important to the theme.

Event	Significance

Craft and Structure

Structure of the Novel Excerpt

1. Look at paragraph 1. How does Wells present the Martian invasion at the beginning of the short story?

2. What evidence does Wells provide to show that the Martian attack is more serious than people first thought?

3. How does Wells's presentation of the attack change from the beginning of the excerpt to the end?

Author's Purpose

4. All of these details fit together to paint a portrait of life on Earth during an alien attack. How does Wells describe Earth during the attack in *The War of the Worlds*? What lesson does he want readers to take from the story?

5. Compare and contrast Bradbury's portrait of life on Earth during an alien invasion with Wells's. How are they different? How are they similar?

Bradbury	Wells

Collaborate and Present

In 1938, famous director Orson Welles turned *The War of the Worlds* into a radio broadcast. And in 1955, Eva Ashdown adapted "Zero Hour" for an episode of *Suspense Radio*. These broadcasts used various sound effects and other dramatic devices to tell the stories originally told by H. G. Wells and Ray Bradbury.

Plan and Deliver a Multi-Media Presentation

Assignment: Working in groups, search the Internet for recordings of Orson Welles's *The War of the Worlds* or the episode of *Suspense Radio* with "Zero Hour." Listen to the recording, taking notes on the auditory effects used by the production. Then, prepare a presentation comparing the radio broadcasts to the text.

Analyze the Content

1. Listen to the broadcast. Pause often to compare the broadcast to the text and to take notes on the differences.

2. Consider the following questions during your research:
   • What sound effects does the production use?
   • What kind of dialogue does it use?
   • How does the production use silence or pauses?
   • What kind of music does the production use?

3. Create a chart to compare the broadcast you chose to the original text.

Text	Broadcast	Effect of Audio

Create Your Presentation

4. Use details from your chart as talking points for your presentation.
   • Draft the text of your presentation on paper or on the computer.
   • Prepare clips from the broadcast to illustrate the audio elements you will discuss.

Present

5. Deliver your speech.

Seeking Clarification

- What you are saying is . . .
- So what you mean is . . .
- In other words . . .
- If I understand you correctly, you are saying . . .

Reporting Ideas

- _____ pointed out
- _____ indicated that
- _____ emphasized

Presentation

- Stand without fidgeting and have good posture.
- Speak loudly and clearly.
- Make eye contact with your audience.

Multi-Media Presentation Checklist

Use the checklist below to evaluate your collaboration skills, reasoning, and final presentation.
Think carefully about your work. If you know you completed an item thoroughly, give yourself a check (✓).

COLLABORATE AND PRESENT CHECKLIST

Comprehension & Collaboration

- [ ] Come to discussions prepared, having read and studied material.
- [ ] Refer to evidence when contributing to the discussion.
- [ ] Follow rules for discussions and lead by example.
- [ ] Ask and answer specific questions.
- [ ] Make comments that contribute to the topic under discussion.
- [ ] Review the key ideas under discussion and demonstrate understanding of multiple perspectives through reflection and paraphrasing.

▶ **Number of ✓s in this category:** ___

Evidence and Reasoning

- [ ] Explain the purpose of the presentation.
- [ ] Present information relevant to the task.
- [ ] Explain how the broadcast differs from the text.
- [ ] Explain the effects of audio elements in the broadcast.
- [ ] Use at least two examples from the text and two from the broadcast.
- [ ] Synthesize your key ideas with a conclusion.

▶ **Number of ✓s in this category:** ___

Presentation of Knowledge & Ideas

- [ ] Adapt language to a variety of contexts and tasks to demonstrate knowledge of formal English.
- [ ] Include multimedia components (e.g., graphics, images, music, sound) and visual displays.
- [ ] Use appropriate volume/tone (clear, not too fast, too slow, or too loud) and avoid using "like" or "ummm."
- [ ] Have strong posture, a confident stance, and make frequent eye contact.
- [ ] Occasionally move from one spot to another, without fidgeting.
- [ ] Smile and act relaxed.

▶ **Number of ✓s in this category:** ___

Total # of ✓s: ___

Add up the total number of checks (✓) in each category. Then use the scoring guide below to calculate your final score.

Scoring Guide			
16 to 18 ✓s	13 to 15 ✓s	11 to 12 ✓s	10 or fewer ✓s
④ Exemplary	③ Meets Standards	② Needs Work	① Does Not Meet Standards

Read the Model

The writer of this literary analysis compares and contrasts how authors use descriptions of characters and events to develop the theme of life on Earth during an alien invasion. Read and discuss the model essay below.

Informative Essay

A literary analysis is a type of informative essay that examines elements of a text, such as character, theme, plot, or setting.

- The introduction states the title and author of the text that the writer will analyze, and includes the thesis statement.

- The two body paragraphs express the writer's main points about the text.

- The conclusion sums up or restates the thesis. It also explains why the information in the essay matters.

Same Story, Different Invaders   By Myles Green

Both Ray Bradbury in "Zero Hour," and Steven Millhauser in "The Invasion from Outer Space" describe alien invasions on Earth. Through descriptions of characters and events, both authors evoke the fear that many people have of abrupt change. Bradbury was writing in the 1950s, while Millhauser wrote in 2009, but the effect is the same. Both alien invasions portray characters and events that ruin life on Earth and remind readers of one of our greatest fears—change that we cannot control.

Both authors create alien characters who want to change life on Earth. Bradbury's aliens behave like a human army. They have human qualities, like motives and speech. They are people-like invaders who want to take over Earth. In contrast, Millhauser's invader is "animate dust" (Millhauser 295). These invaders look and act differently from Bradbury's aliens, but they have the same motive.

Both authors create suspense leading up to the invasion. In both stories, the characters' failure to react creates more suspense than the invasion itself. In "Zero Hour," the townspeople are unprepared. "Heavy, heavy, very heavy footsteps" catch Bradbury's adults off guard (Bradbury 266). Since the invasion comes via a children's game, people ignore the warning signs. Similarly, Millhauser's townspeople expect "monstrous versions" of themselves, but because the "points of gold . . . like yellow dust" are not the "something grander, something more thrilling" that they expected, "the organisms do not fit easily into our classification scheme." (Millhauser 295).

Both authors trigger fears of change and loss of control. Bradbury describes people-like aliens who take over the Earth by force. In contrast, Millhauser describes "unicellular microorganisms" (295) who cling to everything, like dust. In both stories, people feared and were unprepared for the terrifying and sudden change.

Analyze the Model

Use the outline below to examine how the writer of this literary analysis examines the theme of an alien invasion on Earth.

Point-by-Point Comparison

In this **literary analysis**, the writer establishes the comparison in the introduction. The **thesis statement** tells the focus of the essay.

Introduction

In this literary analysis, what is the purpose of the comparison? Which sentence is the thesis statement of the essay?

Each **body paragraph** has a topic sentence that states a point, and two or more pieces of evidence from each text to support the point.

Body Paragraph 1: Characters

Topic Sentence:

1. **Text Evidence:**
2. **Text Evidence:**

The information in the **body paragraphs** develops the point-by-point comparison. Bradbury is different from Millhauser on point 1, the description of alien characters.

Bradbury is similar to Millhauser on point 2, the suspenseful description of the events leading up to the invasion.

Body Paragraph 2: Events

Topic Sentence:

1. **Text Evidence:**
2. **Text Evidence:**

Transitions, used effectively, allow the writer to show relationships between similar and different ideas.

Conclusion

How does the writer conclude the essay?

The **conclusion** states a characteristic of both texts, ending the essay by restating the comparison.

Step 1 | Gather Evidence

How do these authors portray life on Earth during an alien invasion? Compare and contrast the characters and events in each text and how the authors develop them.

What You Need to Know | Examine the evidence you collected about how each author describes the characters and events during an alien invasion (see pages 264 and 278).

What You Need to Write | Compare and contrast the author's descriptions in each text. Examine how the authors use them to develop the theme.

"Zero Hour"

Evidence: "Who's coming in my house? Who's tramping around down there?" The description of the aliens and Mink coming up the steps is very suspenseful and creepy. The reader is stuck in Mr. and Mrs. Morris's position: they can't see anything, just hear the heavy footsteps.

Page # _____

Evidence:

Page # _____

Evidence:

Page # _____

The War of the Worlds

Evidence:

Page # _____

Evidence:

Page # _____

Evidence:

Page # _____

Step 2 | Organize Ideas

What You Need to Know | When you analyze literature, you interpret the text to understand the author's main message or theme.

To develop your topic:

1. Identify how Bradbury and Wells portray life on Earth during alien invasions.
2. Describe two or three strategies they use to develop the theme.

What You Need to Write | Organize the text evidence about how these authors establish and develop the theme.

Body Paragraph 1: _____

Topic Sentence:

1. Text Evidence:

2. Text Evidence:

Body Paragraph 2: _____

Topic Sentence:

1. Text Evidence:

2. Text Evidence:

Step 3 | Draft

Language Study | Combining and Rewriting Sentences

See It | Writers combine sentences to add interest and variety to their writing style.
Combining sentences with *because* or *since* shows why something is true.
The words *because* and *since* indicate cause-and-effect relationships.

Try It | In the sentences below, choose the combined sentence that shows the correct
cause-and-effect relationship.

1. She was cold. She put on a sweater.
   A. She was cold because she put on a sweater.
   B. Because she was cold, she put on a sweater.

2. It began to rain. We lost the signal on our television.
   A. When it began to rain, we lost the signal on our television.
   B. It began to rain since we lost the signal on our television.

3. He set up his telescope at midnight. He was determined to see a UFO.
   A. He set up his telescope at midnight because he was determined to see a UFO.
   B. Because he set up his telescope at midnight, he was determined to see a UFO.

4. People read science fiction. The genre is highly entertaining.
   A. Because people read science fiction, the genre is highly entertaining.
   B. People read science fiction because the genre is highly entertaining.

5. The astronomer was an expert on extraterrestrial communication. He lectured often at the local college.
   A. Because the astronomer was an expert on extraterrestrial communication, he lectured often at the local college.
   B. The astronomer was an expert on extraterrestrial communication because he lectured often at the local college.

Apply It | Use the frames below to practice combining sentences.

1. The authors _____ because _____.

(identify a writing technique)   (show how the technique presents alien invasion)

2. Because both authors _____, the message in the texts is

    (identify a writing strategy)

_____.

(state how the strategy describes the theme)

3. Since both authors comment on _____, they _____.

    (a theme of the invasion)   (identify a writing strategy)

4. Since _____ shows _____, he _____.

  (author)   (a portrayal of the invasion)   (identify a writing technique)

5. Since _____, _____ _____.

(a portrayal of the invasion)   (author)   (identify a writing technique)

Now, go back to your draft and look for any statements you can combine using *because* or *since* to clarify the relationship between ideas.

_____

_____

_____

_____

Conventions Study | Using Transitions

See It | **Transition words connect ideas and signal changes in writing.**

- Transition words and phrases such as *similarly*, *in addition*, and *also* show similarities, or how things are alike.
- Transition words and phrases such as *however* and *in contrast* show how ideas contrast, or are different.

Try It | Find all the transition words in the model that signal compare and contrast.

Apply It | Now look for transitions that compare and contrast in your draft. Rewrite one of your sentences using a transition word to connect your ideas.

Step 4 | Revise and Edit   Revise your draft with a partner.

Organization and Clarity					
State titles and authors of texts in the introductory paragraph.	Self	1	2	3	4
	Partner	1	2	3	4
Include a thesis statement that emphasizes a compare/contrast relationship between the two texts.	Self	1	2	3	4
	Partner	1	2	3	4
Include topic sentences in the body paragraphs that support the thesis.	Self	1	2	3	4
	Partner	1	2	3	4
Restate the thesis in the conclusion.	Self	1	2	3	4
	Partner	1	2	3	4

Evidence and Reasoning					
Include two or more pieces of specific text evidence in each body paragraph to support the comparison.	Self	1	2	3	4
	Partner	1	2	3	4

Language and Conventions					
Use complex, interesting sentences to show relationships between ideas.	Self	1	2	3	4
	Partner	1	2	3	4
Include formal, academic language appropriate to a literary analysis.	Self	1	2	3	4
	Partner	1	2	3	4
Properly format and punctuate text titles and author names.	Self	1	2	3	4
	Partner	1	2	3	4

Step 5 | Publish   Publish your story either in print or digital form.

Scoring Guide | ① needs improvement   ② average   ③ good   ④ excellent

Publish

Publish your literary analysis either in print or digital form. Use the rubric below to assess your final performance task.

PERFORMANCE TASK RUBRIC

Score Point	Organization and Clarity	Evidence and Reasoning	Language and Conventions
Exemplary (4)	• introductory paragraph **introduces** what the writer will compare and contrast and includes a strong thesis statement • each body paragraph **compares and contrasts one point** and **includes relevant evidence** to **clearly explain** how authors develop theme • includes **well-chosen** text evidence, precise language, and effective transitions • concluding statement **restates** focus statement in a new way	• **effectively compares and contrasts** the writers' portrayals of life on Earth and **analyzes** how the writers use setting, imagery, and events to develop theme • includes **several examples of relevant** factual evidence from the novel or short story that supports the comparison/contrast	• demonstrates a **strong command** of the conventions of standard English grammar and usage, as well as of standard English capitalization, punctuation, and spelling • vocabulary is **appropriate** to the topic (vocabulary about science fiction; accurate terms for discussing setting, imagery, and events; vocabulary for making comparisons or contrasting text)
Meets Standards (3)	• introductory paragraph **introduces** what the writer will compare and contrast and includes a thesis statement • each body paragraph **compares and contrasts one point** and **includes evidence** to **explain** how authors develop theme • includes **some** text evidence, precise language, and effective transitions • concluding statement **restates** the focus statement and compares and contrasts both texts	• **adequately compares and contrasts** the writers' portrayals of life on Earth and **attempts to analyze** how the writers use setting, imagery, and events to develop theme • includes **some relevant** factual evidence from the novel or short story that supports the comparison/contrast	• demonstrates a **near command** of the conventions of standard English grammar and usage, as well as of standard English capitalization, punctuation, and spelling **with some errors** • vocabulary is **appropriate** to the topic (vocabulary about science fiction; accurate terms for discussing setting, imagery, and events; vocabulary for making comparisons or contrasting text)

PERFORMANCE TASK RUBRIC

Score Point	Organization and Clarity	Evidence and Reasoning	Language and Conventions
Needs Work ②	• introductory paragraph **introduces** what the writer will compare and contrast and includes a thesis statement that **loosely identifies** what the essay will be about • body paragraphs **attempt to** compare and contrast points and **explain** how authors develop theme • includes **a limited amount** of text evidence, precise language, and effective transitions • concluding statement attempts to restate the focus statement and includes a **partial** comparison/contrast	• **attempts to compare and contrast** the writers' portrayals of life on Earth and **mentions** the writers' use of setting, imagery, and events • includes **some textual evidence** from the novel or short story that supports the comparison/ contrast	• demonstrates a **marginal command** of the conventions of English grammar and usage, as well as of standard English capitalization, punctuation, and spelling • there **are many errors; however, the text is still understandable** • includes only **one or two examples** of vocabulary that is appropriate to the topic (vocabulary about science fiction; accurate terms for discussing setting, imagery, and events; vocabulary for making comparisons or contrasting text)
Does Not Meet Standards ①	• introductory paragraph is **unclear** and does not include a thesis statement • body paragraphs do **not** compare and contrast points and/or **do not** include evidence and/or explain how authors develop theme • essay includes **little text evidence** and few transitions • concluding statement is **unclear and does not wrap up** the ideas in the essay	• response is **partial or inaccurate explanation** of the writers' portrayals of life on earth • includes **no analyses of textual evidence** from the novel or short story	• demonstrates **almost no command** of the conventions of standard English grammar and usage, as well as of standard English capitalization, punctuation, and spelling • there **are many errors that disrupt** the reader's understanding of the text • **does not include** vocabulary that is appropriate to the topic (vocabulary about science fiction; accurate terms for discussing setting, imagery, and events; vocabulary for making comparisons or contrasting text)

Questions

Literary Analysis

1. Who is telling the story?

Text Structure

2. What is the "it" referred to in the first sentence of **paragraph 1**? What details does the narrator include to signal what "it" is?

"The Invasion From Outer Space"

by Steven Millhauser from *The New Yorker*

¶1   From the beginning we were prepared, we knew just what to do, for hadn't we seen it all a hundred times? — the good people of the town going about their business, the suddenly interrupted TV programs, the faces in the crowd looking up, the little girl pointing in the air, the mouths opening, and there, in the sky, coming closer . . . And so, when it finally happened, because it was bound to happen, we all knew it was only a matter of time, we felt, in the midst of our curiosity and terror, a certain calm, the calm of familiarity, we knew what was expected of us, at such a moment. The story broke a little after ten in the morning. The TV anchors looked exactly the way we knew they'd look, their faces urgent, their hair neat, their shoulders tense, they were filling us with alarm but also assuring us that everything was under control, for they, too, had been prepared for this, in a sense had been waiting for it, already they were looking back at themselves during their great moment. The sighting was indisputable but, at the same time, inconclusive: something from out there had been detected, it appeared to be approaching our atmosphere at great speed, the Pentagon was monitoring the situation closely. We were urged to remain calm, to stay inside, to await further instructions. Some of us left work immediately and hurried home to our families, others stayed close to the TV, the radio, the computer, we were all talking into our cells. Through our windows we could see people at their windows, looking up at the sky. All that morning we followed the news fiercely, like children listening to a thunderstorm in the dark. Whatever was out there was still unknown, scientists had not yet been able to determine its nature, caution was advised but there was no reason for panic, our job was to stay tuned and sit tight and await further developments. And though we were anxious, though quivers of nervousness ran along our bodies like mice, we wanted to see whatever it was, we wanted to be there, since after all it was coming toward us, it was ours to witness, as if we were the ones they'd chosen, out there on the other side of the sky. For already it was being said that our town was the likely landing place, already the TV crews were rolling in. We wondered where it would land: between the duck pond and the seesaws in the public park, or deep in the woods at the north end of town, or maybe in the field out by the mall, where a new excavation was already under way, or maybe it would glide over the old department store on Main Street and crash through the second-floor apartments above Mangione's Pizza and Café, with a great shattering of brick and glass, maybe it would land on the throughway and we'd see eighteen-wheelers turn over, great chunks of pavement rise up at sharp angles, and car after car swerve into the guardrail and roll down the embankment.

Something appeared in the sky shortly before one o'clock. Many of us were still at lunch, others were already outside, standing motionless on the streets and sidewalks, gazing up. There were shouts and cries, arms in the air, a wildness of gesturing, pointing. And, sure enough, something was glittering, up there in the sky, something was shimmering, in the blue air of summer — we saw it clearly, whatever it was. Secretaries in offices rushed to windows, storekeepers abandoned their cash registers and hurried outdoors, road workers in orange hard hats looked up from the asphalt, shaded their eyes. It must have lasted — that faraway glow, that spot of shimmer — some three or four minutes. Then it began to grow larger, until it was the size of a dime, a quarter. Suddenly the entire sky seemed to be filled with points of gold. Then it was coming down on us, like fine pollen, like yellow dust. It lay on our roof slopes, it sifted down onto our sidewalks, covered our shirtsleeves and the tops of our cars. We did not know what to make of it.

¶3 It continued to come down, that yellow dust, for nearly thirteen minutes. During that time we could not see the sky. Then it was over. The sun shone, the sky was blue. Throughout the downpour, we'd been warned to stay inside, to be careful, to avoid touching the substance from outer space, but it had happened so quickly that most of us had streaks of yellow on our clothes and in our hair. Soon after the warnings, we heard cautious reassurances: preliminary tests revealed nothing toxic, though the nature of the yellow dust remained unknown. Animals that had eaten it revealed no symptoms. We were urged to keep out of its way and await further test

Questions

Words and Phrases in Context

3. What descriptive words and phrases contribute to the mood in **paragraph 2**? What is the mood?

Literary Analysis

4. What is the invasion from outer space? What is the narrator's attitude toward it, based on details in the first part of **paragraph 3**?

results. Meanwhile it lay over our lawns and sidewalks and front steps, it coated our maple trees and telephone poles. We were reminded of waking in the morning after the first snow. From our porches we watched the three-wheeled sweepers move slowly along our streets, carrying it off in big hoppers. We hosed down our grass, our front walks, our porch furniture. We looked up at the sky, we waited for more news—already we were hearing reports that the substance was composed of one-celled organisms—and through it all we could sense the swell of our disappointment.

We had wanted, we had wanted—oh, who knew what we'd been looking for? We had wanted blood, crushed bones, howls of agony. We had wanted buildings crumbling onto streets, cars bursting into flame. We had wanted monstrous versions of ourselves with enlarged heads on stalk-like necks, merciless polished robots armed with death rays. We had wanted noble lords of the universe with kind, soft eyes, who would usher in a glorious new era. We had wanted terror and ecstasy—anything but this yellow dust. Had it even been an invasion? Later that afternoon, we learned that scientists all agreed: the dust was a living thing. Samples had been flown to Boston, Chicago, Washington, D.C. The single-celled organisms appeared to be harmless, though we were cautioned not to touch anything, to keep the windows shut, to wash our hands. The cells reproduced by binary fission. They appeared to do nothing but multiply.

¶5   In the morning, we woke to a world covered in yellow dust. It lay on the tops of our fences, on the crossbars of telephone poles. Black tire tracks showed in the yellow streets. Birds, shaking their wings, threw up sprays of yellow powder. Again the street-sweepers came, the hoses splashed on driveways and lawns, making a yellow mist and revealing the black and the green underneath. Within an hour the driveways and lawns resembled yellow fields. Lines of yellow ran along cables and telephone wires.

Questions

Literary Analysis
5. What scientific details does the author include in the second half of **paragraph 3**? What is the effect of including these details? How do the people respond to scientific reports about the dust?

Text Structure
6. How does the purpose of the text shift in **paragraph 4**?

According to the news, the unicellular microorganisms are rod-shaped and nourish themselves by photosynthesis. A single cell, placed in a brightly illuminated test tube, divides at such a rate that the tube will fill in about forty minutes. An entire room, in strong light, will fill in six hours. The organisms do not fit easily into our classification schemes, though in some respects they resemble blue-green algae. There is no evidence that they are harmful to human or animal life.

¶7   We have been invaded by nothing, by emptiness, by animate dust. The invader appears to have no characteristic other than the ability to reproduce rapidly. It doesn't hate us. It doesn't seek our annihilation, our subjection and humiliation. Nor does it desire to protect us from danger, to save us, to teach us the secret of immortal life. What it wishes to do is replicate. It is possible that we will find a way of limiting the spread of this primitive intruder, or of eliminating it altogether; it's also possible that we will fail and that our town will gradually disappear under a fatal accumulation. As we follow the reports from day to day, the feeling grows in us that we deserved something else, something bolder, something grander, something more thrilling, something bristling or fiery or fierce, something that might have represented a revelation or a destiny. We imagine ourselves surrounding the tilted spaceship, waiting for the door to open. We imagine ourselves protecting our children, slashing the tentacles that thrust in through the smashed cellar windows. Instead, we sweep our front walks, hose off our porches, shake out our shoes and sneakers. The invader has entered our homes. Despite our drawn shades and closed curtains, it lies in thick layers on our end tables and windowsills. It lies along the tops of our flat-screen televisions and the narrow edges of our shelved DVDs. Through our windows we can see the yellow dust covering everything, forming gentle undulations. We can almost see it rising slowly, like bread. Here and there it catches the sunlight and reminds us, for a moment, of fields of wheat.

It is really quite peaceful, in its way.

Questions

Words and Phrases in Context

7. How does the author describe the invasion in the last line of the story? Why is his description ironic?

Literature Circle Leveled Novels

The Last Universe *by William Sleator*
Susan and her brother Gary explore the mysterious maze in their garden and discover that they can travel to parallel universes. Can they find a universe in which Gary is cured of his devastating illness? **Lexile®** measure: 690L

Laika *by Nick Abadzis*
A stray dog named Laika becomes part of the Russian space program and must undergo rigorous training and testing before she can be the first creature sent into space. **Lexile®** measure: GN370L

Ender's Game *by Orson Scott Card*
After being attacked by aliens, the government begins breeding child geniuses to defend Earth. Ender Wiggins is drafted to be a soldier, but can he handle the loneliness and demands of Battle School? **Lexile®** measure: 780L

Fiction, Nonfiction, Poetry, and Novels

Some of the Kinder Planets *by Tim Wynne-Jones.* Choose from nine short short stories that tell tales of ghosts, aliens, and historical figures. **Lexile®** measure: 720L

Bruce Coville's Book of Aliens: Tales to Warp Your Mind *by Bruce Coville.* Read ten scary stories about the adventures and exploits of aliens from space. **Lexile®** measure: 730L

Space Station Science: Life in Free Fall *by Marianne J. Dyson.* Explore what it is like to live and work in space, including how to eat and sleep. **Lexile®** measure: 910L

On the Wing: American Poems of Air and Space Flight *edited by Karen Yelena Olsen.* Find poems on the amazing feat of space flight in the "Space Odysseys" section of this collection of poems. **Lexile®** measure: NP

50 Years in Space: What We Thought Then . . . What We Know Now *by Patrick Moore.* See our understanding of space and the technology used to explore it evolve through the spectacular art created by David Hardy.

Astronomy and Space: From the Big Bang to the Big Crunch *edited by Phillis Engelbert.* A comprehensive overview of astronomy and space exploration. Learn about space objects, piloted space missions, and famous astronomers and astronauts.

Into That Silent Sea: Trailblazers of the Space Era, 1961–1965 *by Francis French.* Learn about the first astronauts and cosmonauts to be launched into space.

What If . . . ?: Amazing Stories *selected by Monica Hughes.* Find out what happens when you ask a group of science fiction writers "What if?" in this collection of short stories.

Films and TV

2001: A Space Odyssey (Warner Home Video, 1968; G) Compare our current reality to Arthur C. Clarke's vision of the future in the year 2001, when a space mission is put to the test by a sentient shipboard computer. (148 min.)

Apollo 13 (Universal Studios, 1995; PG) An explosion seriously damages a moon-bound spacecraft in 1970, and astronauts Lovell, Swigert, and Haise must find a way home. (140 min.)

Contact (Warner Home Video, 1997; PG) Ellie Arroway travels farther into space than any human after receiving a radio message that provides information about how to travel to deep space. (153 min.)

Explorers (Paramount, 1985; PG) Three young boys build their own spaceship and travel into the galaxy for a strange journey full of adventure. (109 min.)

Mission to Mars (Walt Disney Video, 2000, PG) In the year 2020, astronauts set off on the first manned mission to Mars, a journey that leads to a mysterious disaster and a recovery mission. (114 min.)

The Planets (New Video Group, 1999) Explore the beauty and mystery of space, including the technology that has allowed humans to travel in space, and catch a glimpse of the universe beyond our reach. (400 min.)

The Right Stuff (Warner Home Video, 1983; PG) Follow the story of the first astronauts who went into orbit at the inception of the American space program. (193 min.)

Star Wars (1977; PG) Imagine what it might be like to travel the galaxies and meet creatures from other planets in this exciting tale of outer space adventure. (121 min.)

Websites

How to Become an Astronaut 101 On this page of the NASA Web site, Lt. Col. Catherine G. "Cady" Coleman discusses what it's like to be an astronaut, and how she became one.

Mars Exploration Program Learn more about NASA's program to explore Mars, and search for more information about the planet.

SETI Institute The SETI Institute seeks to explore the origin and nature of life in the universe.

Smithsonian National Air and Space Museum Search for information about current space-related exhibits and collections at the museum.

Magazines

Discover: Science, Technology, and the Future Be on the cutting edge of new technology, including advancements in the technology of space exploration, and examine the impact it will have on our lives.

Popular Science Stay up-to-date with the latest news in a variety of fields, including space exploration and technology.

Scientific American Learn about existing science and predictions about future discoveries.

Smithsonian: Air and Space Find articles related to technology and space exploration, including current space missions.

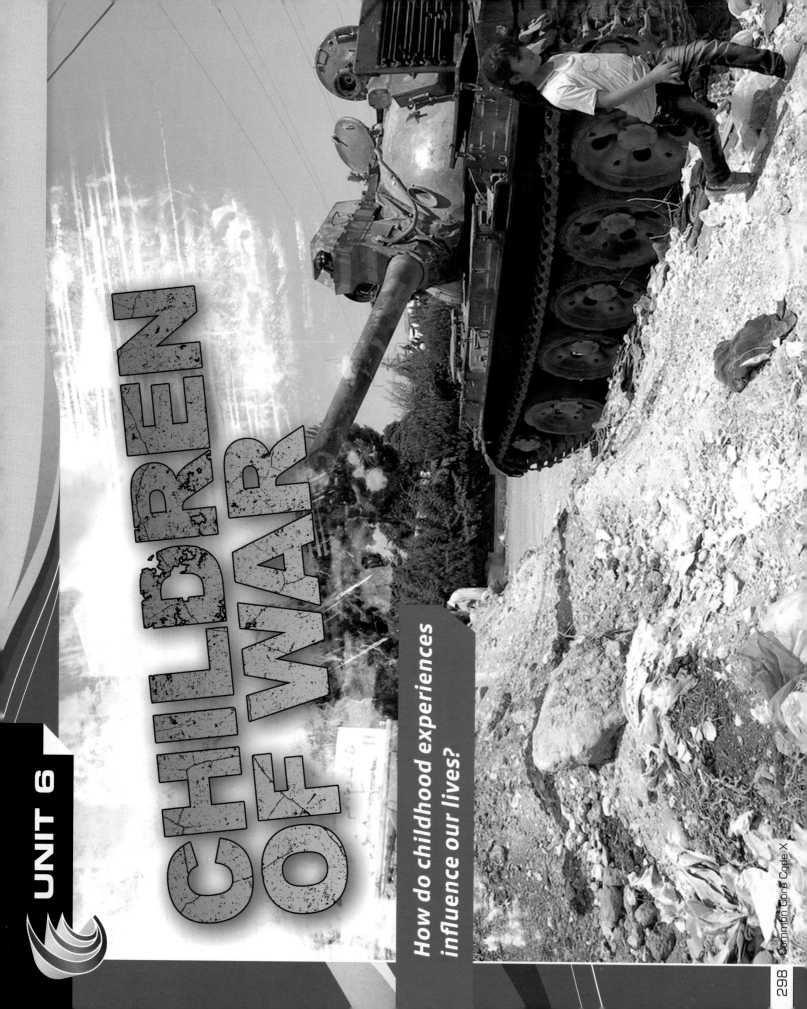

CHILDREN OF WAR

How do childhood experiences influence our lives?

Unit Introduction

In these two informational text selections, you will discover how two modern-day children lost their childhoods to war, fighting, and government constraints.

"Babes in Arms," by William Boyd, is a review of *A Long Way Gone*, Ishmael Beah's memoir of his two years as a child soldier in the Sierra Leone Army. Loung Ung shares her story of the terror and violence inflicted by the Khmer Rouge on her family and other citizens of Cambodia at a work camp in the excerpt from her memoir *First They Killed My Father*.

WRITING PERFORMANCE TASK

Analyze in detail how childhood wartime experiences had an impact on Beah's or Ung's life. Consider how the author introduces, illustrates, and elaborates upon the events.

📖 BOOK REVIEW/MEMOIR EXCERPT

from **"Babes in Arms"**
by William Boyd, from *The New York Times Book Review*

Language
- Academic Vocabulary
- Word Study:
  References: Dictionary

Reading a Book Review
- Identify Evidence
- Key Ideas and Details
- Craft and Structure and Writing Assignment

🔊 SPEAKING AND LISTENING

Present a Speech
- Collaborate and Present

✍ WRITING

Writing: Informative Essay
- Read the Model
- Analyze the Model
- Gather Evidence
- Organize Ideas

📖 EXTENDED READINGS

Memoir Excerpt
from *A Long Way Gone*
by Ishmael Beah

---

from *First They Killed My Father*
by Loung Ung

Language
- Academic Vocabulary
- Word Study:
  References: Thesaurus

Reading a Memoir Excerpt
- Identify Evidence
- Key Ideas and Details
- Craft and Structure and Writing Assignment

Checklist: Speech
- Scoring Guide

- Language Study:
  Describing Sequence of Events
- Conventions Study:
  Precise Language and Domain-Specific Vocabulary
- Revise, Edit, and Publish
- Performance Task Rubric

Academic Vocabulary

from "Babes in Arms" by William Boyd

Rate your understanding of each word. Then read its meaning and write an example sentence. If the example is given, write the meaning.

Word	Meaning	Example
contemporary (adj.) p. 301 ① ② ③ ④	modern; of the present time	
consciousness (n.) p. 301 ① ② ③ ④		The thought that the team might lose did not enter the fans' consciousness.
distinguish (v.) p. 303 ① ② ③ ④	to tell apart; to recognize as different	
credence (n.) p. 303 ① ② ③ ④		I can't give credence to his excuses for being late anymore.
unpremeditated (adj.) p. 305 ① ② ③ ④		The police say that the crime was unpremeditated.
unrelenting (adj.) p. 305 ① ② ③ ④	not stopping, slowing down, or becoming less severe	

Rating Scale ① I don't know the word. ② I've seen it or heard it.
③ I know its meaning. ④ I know it and use it.

Word Study

References

References are sources that tell the meaning of a word and other information about the word. They include dictionaries, glossaries, and thesauruses in both print and digital form.

Use the dictionary entry for the word *contemporary* to answer the questions below:

contemporary (kən•tem•pə•rer•ee) *adj.* modern: of the present time. *The museum displays both contemporary and ancient art.*

1. Is the first *r* in *contemporary* pronounced in the third or fourth syllable?

2. What part of speech is the word *contemporary*?

3. How does the example sentence help you understand the meaning of the word *contemporary*?

from Babes in ARMS

by William Boyd from *The New York Times Book Review*

¶1 What is it about African wars that is so disturbing? Why do they unsettle us so? We in the civilized West know all about bestial and mindless cruelty, as the events of 1939–45 graphically prove. And yet as we read about Darfur and Mogadishu today and recall Rwanda and Sierra Leone not long ago, or Biafra and Congo further back, we realize that these vicious, bitter African conflicts have left their trace on **contemporary consciousness**, in ways somehow different from the usual squalid reckoning that modern warfare encourages.

¶2 The great benefit of Ishmael Beah's memoir, *A Long Way Gone*, is that it may help us arrive at an understanding of this situation. Beah's autobiography is almost unique, as far as I can determine—perhaps the first time that a child soldier has been able to give literary voice to one of the most distressing phenomena of the late 20th century: the rise of the pubescent (or even prepubescent) warrior-killer.

Words to Know

bestial: *(adj.)* animal-like

the events of 1939–45: the author is referring to World War II, during which Adolf Hitler and the German Nazi army killed six million Jews and other people from minority groups

---

Close Reading

Text Structure

1. What rhetorical device does the reviewer use to begin his book review? What is the effect of beginning the text this way?

Key Ideas and Details

2. Based on details on this page, identify the topic and perspective of the book that Boyd is reviewing.

Book Review

A **book review** is a description and an evaluation of a book. An author of a book review describes and evaluates the book in a way that allows readers to determine if they would like to read the book.

Close Reading

Key Ideas and Details

3. What was the change in status Sierra Leone underwent that was marked by the difficult "rites of passage" that Boyd describes in **paragraph 3?** How did this change affect Beah's life?

Academic Vocabulary

4. Discuss why the reviewer explains in **paragraph 4** that "a 12-year-old is conscious only of immediate circumstances."

Writing

5. What details does Boyd include in **paragraph 4** to help the reader understand why Beah was susceptible to being recruited as a boy soldier into the Sierra Leone Army?

¶3 Beah was 12 years old when the civil war in Sierra Leone entered his life, in 1993. Sierra Leone, a former British colony in West Africa, sandwiched between Guinea and Liberia, suffered the usual post-independence <u>rites of passage</u> of corruption, unrest, military coups and <u>gerrymandered elections</u>. In the '90s, civil strife in Liberia prompted the rise of the R.U.F. (the Revolutionary United Front), a ragtag liberation army headed by a former corporal, Foday Sankoh, who took over the diamond mines in eastern Sierra Leone and whose brutal militia moved on toward the country's capital, Freetown. There is a historical chronology at the back of the book, but you will gain little idea of the internecine political struggle from Beah's account.

¶4 In a sense, however, this is beside the point. A 12-year-old is conscious only of immediate circumstances, and in Beah's case the arrival of the rebels in his small town meant sudden separation from his parents and months of indeterminate flight from danger with a handful of other boys. These terrified youngsters wandered aimlessly along jungle tracks, starving and desperate, harassed and suspected as they scrounged for food and tried to make sense of what was going on. Finally they reached the Atlantic Ocean, but, once again, fearful villagers sent them packing, and they were eventually recruited into the Sierra Leone Army as boy soldiers.

Words to Know

<u>rites of passage:</u> (*n.*) events that mark a transition, or change, from one status, or place or stage, to another

<u>gerrymandered elections:</u> (*n.*) elections made unfair by the way voting districts were set up

¶15 Given rudimentary training, Beah seems then to have gone on a two-year mind-bending killing spree, until he was rescued by some UNICEF fieldworkers and sent to a rehabilitation center in Freetown. There, with counseling, care and attention, and the psychological ministrations of a kindly nurse named Esther, Beah's slow return to normality began, further augmented when he was sent to the <u>United Nations</u> with the task of explaining the lot of the child soldier to a baffled and concerned international community. He came to live in the United States, graduating from high school and Oberlin College. *A Long Way Gone* is his first, remarkable book.

¶16 It is interesting to try to comprehend what act of remembering is going on here. Who of us in our 20s could accurately summon up our day-by-day lives as preteens? As you read *A Long Way Gone*, the details allow you to **distinguish** precise recall from autobiographical blur. Beah can remember the logo on the sneakers he is issued by the army. When he is captured by hostile villagers, he is released because he has a few rap cassettes on him and can mime the songs and dance to them. All this has the idiosyncratic ring of precisely remembered truth. But with lines like these, the effect is quite different: "We walked around the village and killed everyone who came out of the houses and huts." If these and similar passages are to be given **credence**, his personal body count must total dozens. Such knowledge is shocking, but it's the reader's imagination that delivers the cold sanguinary shudder, not the author's boilerplate prose. It is a vision of hell that Beah gives us, one worthy of Hieronymus Bosch, but as though depicted in primary colors by a <u>naïve artist</u>.

Words to Know

United Nations: (*n.*) an international group that works for goals like world peace and human rights

naïve artist: (*n.*) an artist who paints in a simple style and may have little formal training

---

Close Reading

Words and Phrases in Context

6. Determine the meaning of the word *lot* in "the lot of the child soldier" in **paragraph 5**. Identify clues that helped you determine its meaning.

Key Ideas and Details

7. Identify the rhetorical question the reviewer asks in **paragraph 6**. Discuss the point he is making by asking this question.

Writing

8. Identify what Boyd claims in **paragraph 6** that Beah recalls precisely and what he is vague about in his autobiography. What is Boyd's attitude toward Beah's "autobiographical blur"?

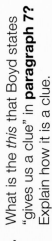

Close Reading

Text Structure

9. What is the *this* that Boyd states "gives us a clue" in **paragraph 7?** Explain how it is a clue.

Key Ideas and Details

10. Cite evidence from the text to explain why Boyd includes an experience from his own life in his review of Beah's book.

Words and Phrases in Context

11. Use context clues to determine the meaning of *anarchy*. What is the effect of describing the moment as "pure potential anarchy" in **paragraph 7?**

¶7   However, perhaps this gives us a clue to the nature and effect of these terrifying African conflicts. I have been close to only one, in Nigeria from 1968 to 1970, during that country's civil war, known as the Biafran war. I was in my teens too, not much older than Beah, and far from the actual fighting. But at dusk one night with my father, our car was stopped at a roadblock on a back road in the <u>bush</u> by a unit of Nigerian soldiers. They were young, aggressive, bored and ostensibly looking for <u>currency</u> smugglers. They waved their Kalashnikovs at us and angrily ordered us out of the car. We were roughly searched, the trunk was opened, and then my father cracked a joke and everybody laughed. But for a few moments I was profoundly aware that anything might have happened to us: there was no control, no "rules of engagement," no chain of command. We were powerless; they had all the power. Night was falling, and there were no witnesses. It was a moment of pure potential anarchy that could have gone any way.

Words to Know

<u>bush</u>: *(n.)* area with lots of trees and bushes; not the city or the suburbs

<u>currency</u>: *(n.)* money

¶18 Beah's book confirms this feeling. The unbelievable violence and dread, the blood and death, seem—if this does not appear too awful an oxymoron—somehow **guileless** and innocent, random, **unpremeditated**. Is that what fundamentally disturbs us about these African conflicts?

¶19 Beah's memoir joins an elite class of writing: Africans witnessing African wars. I think of "Sozaboy," Ken Saro-Wiwa's masterly novel about a young soldier during the Biafran war, or "Machete Season," Jean Hatzfeld's book of blood-chilling interviews with Rwandan killers. A *Long Way Gone* makes you wonder how anyone comes through such **unrelenting** ghastliness and horror with his humanity and sanity intact. Unusually, the smiling, open face of the author on the book jacket provides welcome and timely reassurance. Ishmael Beah seems to prove it can happen.

Beah has created a happier life for himself in the United States.

Words to Know

oxymoron: *(n.)* a figure of speech in which the words or concepts seem to contradict each other; e.g., "innocent violence"

guileless: *(adj.)* honest; without cunning or trickery

Close Reading

Academic Vocabulary

12. Describe the "unpremeditated" nature of the violence and death in Sierra Leone as presented by Boyd in the review. Discuss why this is perhaps what "fundamentally disturbs" him about African conflicts.

Key Ideas and Details

13. Explain why Beah's face on the book jacket reassures the reviewer, as he discusses in **paragraph 9.**

Writing

14. Express whether Boyd feels that people should read Beah's autobiography. List three details that helped you come to a conclusion about Boyd's opinion of Beah's book.

Identify Evidence | Analyze Individuals, Events, and Ideas

In his book review **"Babes in Arms,"** William Boyd claims the "great benefit" of Ishmael Beah's memoir is the light it sheds on the experiences of child soldiers. Reread "Babes in Arms" and highlight evidence that supports Boyd's claim. How does he introduce, illustrate, and elaborate on people, events, and ideas?

• As you read, use the Evidence column to record examples from the text that show how Beah's memoir helps illuminate the phenomenon of the "pubescent (or even prepubescent) warrior-killer."

• In the Explanation column, explain how Boyd uses the evidence to introduce, illustrate, or elaborate on Beah and his experiences, as well as his own ideas about them.

Evidence	Source	Page	Explanation
1. "A 12-year-old is conscious only of immediate circumstances, and in Beah's case the arrival of the rebels in his small town meant sudden separation from his parents and months of indeterminate flight from danger with a handful of other boys."	Boyd	302	This detail introduces how Beah and the other boys who became his fellow child-soldiers had no real understanding of the conflict they were recruited to fight in beyond how it affected them personally.
2. "These terrified youngsters wandered aimlessly along jungle tracks, starving and desperate, harassed and suspected . . . they were eventually recruited into the Sierra Leone Army as boy soldiers."	Boyd	302	
3. "Given rudimentary training, Beah seems then to have gone on a two-year mind-bending killing spree."	Boyd	303	

Evidence	Source	Page	Explanation

Key Ideas and Details

Determining the Central Idea

1. Use the evidence you collected to summarize the key idea of this book review by William Boyd.

2. List three key events from Beah's memoir that Boyd discusses in his review. Explain why each is important to the central idea of Boyd's book review.

Event	Significance

Craft and Structure

Structure of the Book Review

1. What words and phrases does Boyd use to reveal his opinion of Beah's book? What idea about the book does he convey through these choice of words?

Opinion Words and Phrases	Idea About the Book

Author's Purpose

2. What is Boyd's message for readers about Beah's book? Does he think others should read the book? Why or why not? Explain using examples from the text.

Author's Perspective

3. How do Boyd's own experiences, as described in the review, inform his perspective on Beah's book? Explain.

Academic Vocabulary

from *First They Killed My Father* by Loung Ung

Rate your understanding of each word. Then read its meaning and write an example sentence. If the example is given, write the meaning.

Word	Meaning	Example
capitalists (n.) p. 312 ① ② ③ ④	people who practice capitalism, a system in which individuals—not the government—own most of the money and property	
revolution (n.) p. 313 ① ② ③ ④		The government officials left the country when the revolution began.
abolished (v.) p. 313 ① ② ③ ④	done away with; put to an end; ended	
regulations (n.) p. 315 ① ② ③ ④		City regulations say that you cannot park your car on this street.
comprises (v.) p. 318 ① ② ③ ④	includes; consists of	
allegiance (n.) p. 319 ① ② ③ ④		The soldiers pledged allegiance to the king and promised to defend him from invaders.

Rating Scale
① I don't know the word.
② I've seen it or heard it.
③ I know its meaning.
④ I know it and use it.

Word Study

Thesaurus

A thesaurus is a book that contains lists of synonyms. Some thesauruses also include antonyms.

Use the dictionary entry and the thesaurus entry for the word "allegiance" to answer the questions below.

Dictionary Entry

allegiance: (ah•lee•jens) *noun.* allegiances; loyalty or devotion to a country, leader, or cause. *The soccer players had great allegiance to their coach, who had guided them to the championship.*

Thesaurus Entry

allegiance: *noun.* loyalty. *synonyms:* dedication, faithfulness. *antonyms:* disloyalty, treason

1. What definition does the dictionary provide for the word *allegiance*?

2. What definition does the thesaurus provide for the word *allegiance*?

3. Which definition is more precise?

from

FIRST They Killed MY FATHER

by Loung Ung

**November 1975.
Cambodia, Southeast Asia.**

¶1 *General Pol Pot and his Khmer Rouge army took over the capital city seven months ago. The Khmer Rouge soldiers terrorize the cities and countryside, forcing people out of their homes and into work camps. By the end of their brutal reign, nearly two million will be dead of <u>execution</u>, starvation, <u>forced labor</u>, or disease.*

¶2 The town square is situated forty feet from the road and consists of nothing more than a dried up piece of land and a few trees. The town square is a place where people gather to hear announcements, instructions, work assignments, or, in our case, wait for the village chief. Behind the town square, villagers live in the same kind of thatched-roof huts that sit on raised stilts, all lined up in neat rows about fifty feet from each other at the edge of the forest.

Words to Know

execution: (*n.*) murder; putting to death as punishment

forced labor: (*n.*) work—often harsh, brutal work—that people are made to do against their will

Close Reading

Text Structure
1. Explain how **paragraph 1** differs from **paragraph 2.**

Key Ideas and Details
2. Identify the word in **paragraph 2** that helps signal that this text is a memoir.

Memoir

A memoir is a text about the author's own experiences. A memoir is similar to an autobiography, in that they both tell about the author's life. However, a memoir focuses on a single event or experience or a shorter period of time in the author's life.

Close Reading

Key Ideas and Details

3. How does the author describe how the villagers are dressed in **paragraph 3?** Identify a likely reason for their attire in the text. What can you infer about the Khmer Rouge from the way the villagers are dressed?

Writing

4. Explain what you can infer from the use of "capitalists" as an insult against the new arrivals in **paragraph 4.** What other details in the text support your inference?

Words and Phrases in Context

5. Define *cower.* What context clues helped you determine its meaning? What does the use of this word help you visualize when you read **paragraph 4?**

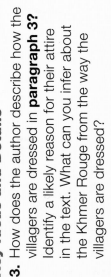

¶3   The truck driver orders the new arrivals to get out and wait for instructions from the village chief. My family quickly jumps off the truck, leaving me behind. Standing at the edge of the truck, I fight the impulse to run and hide in the far corner. All around the truck, villagers have gathered to take their first look at us new people. These villagers are all dressed in the familiar loose-fitting black pajama pants and shirts with a red-and-white checkered scarf wrapped across their shoulders or around their head. They look like an older version of the Khmer Rouge soldiers that stormed into our city, except they do not carry guns.

¶4   "**Capitalists** should be shot and killed," someone yells from the crowd, glaring at us. Another villager walks over and spits at Pa's feet. Pa's shoulders droop low as he holds his palms together in a gesture of greeting. I cower at the edge of the truck, my heart beating wildly, afraid to get off. Fearing that they might spit at me, I avoid their eyes.

¶5   They look very mean, like hungry tigers ready to pounce on us. Their black eyes stare at me, full of **contempt**. I don't understand why they are looking at me as if I am a strange animal, when in reality, we look very much the same.

¶6   "Come, you have to get off the truck," Pa says gently to me. As Pa lifts me in his arms, I whisper in his ear, "Pa, what are capitalists and why should they be killed?" Saying nothing, Pa puts me down.

Words to Know

<u>arrivals:</u> *(n.)* people or things that have recently arrived somewhere

<u>contempt:</u> *(n.)* disrespect

¶17 There are five hundred base people already living in Ro Leap. They are called "base people" because they have lived in the village since before the **revolution.** Most of them are illiterate farmers and peasants who supported the revolution. The Angkar says they are model citizens because many have never ventured out of their village and have not been corrupted by the West. We are the new people, those who have migrated from the city.

¶18 Peasants who have lived in the countryside since before the revolution are rewarded by being allowed to stay in their villages. All others are forced to pick up and move when the soldiers say so. The base people will train us to be hard workers and teach us to have pride in our country. Only then will we be worthy to call ourselves Khmer. I cannot comprehend why they hate me or why capitalists must be killed, but this will have to wait. I walk over and take hold of [my older sister] Chou's hand, and together we follow Ma to the gathering at the town square.

¶19 When I ask my ten-year-old brother, Kim, what a capitalist is, he tells me it is someone who is from the city. He says the Khmer Rouge government views science, technology, and anything mechanical as evil and therefore it must be destroyed. The Angkar says the ownership of cars and electronics such as watches, clocks, and televisions created a deep class division between the rich and the poor. This allowed the urban rich to flaunt their wealth while the rural poor struggled to feed and clothe their families. These devices have been imported from foreign countries and thus are **contaminated.** Imports are defined as evil because they allowed foreign countries a way to invade Cambodia, not just physically but also culturally. So now these goods are **abolished.** Only trucks are allowed to operate, to relocate people and carry weapons to silence any voices of dissent against the Angkar.

Words to Know

Angkar: *(n.)* the government of Cambodia under the Khmer Rouge

contaminated: *(adj.)* dirty or toxic

Close Reading

Key Ideas and Details

6. Describe the Angkar's value system based on details in **paragraphs 7–9.** Whom does it approve of? Whom and what does the Angkar disapprove of? What is the Angkar's plan for spreading its value system throughout Cambodia?

Text Structure

7. Name the tense the author used to write this text. What effect does this choice create?

Close Reading

Key Ideas and Details

8. Explain what the author signals about the chief by mentioning his "gray hair" in **paragraph 10.**

Words and Phrases in Context

9. Define the word *casual* as used in **paragraph 10.** What context clues helped you determine its meaning? How does this word reflect the power of the Khmer Rouge?

¶10 Shuddering at Kim's explanation, I nestle closer to Chou and lean my head on her shoulder. While we wait for the chief, other trucks full of migrants continue to arrive. By the end of the day, approximately sixty families, about five hundred new people, now fill the town square. As the sun lowers itself behind the tree line, the chief finally makes his appearance to the crowd of new people. He is as tall as Pa, with an <u>angular</u> body and cropped gray hair that sits straight on his head like dense jungle bushes. Where his eyes should be are two dark pieces of coal separated by a sharp, thin nose, below which are thin lips that spit out saliva. The chief walks in a slow, casual stride, hands and legs moving precisely, deliberately. The black pajama pants hang looser on his body than those on the two soldiers who follow behind him. There is nothing remarkable about him, except that he is able to command the two men who wear rifles <u>slung</u> across their backs.

Ung and her family were sent to a work camp like the one shown in this photograph.

Words to Know

<u>angular</u>: *(adj.)* lean and bony

<u>slung</u>: *(v.)* placed; hung

¶11 "In this village, we live by strict rules and **regulations** set for us by the Angkar. We expect you to follow every rule. One of our rules applies to how we dress. As you see, we wear the same clothes. Everyone wears his or her hair in the same style. By wearing the same thing, we rid ourselves of the corrupt Western creation of vanity." He speaks in the heavy accent of the jungle people, which is hard for me to understand.

¶12 With a flick of the chief's wrist, one soldier walks up to a family. He reaches out and takes a bag from a woman. She lowers her eyes as the bag slides off her shoulder. He rummages through the bag and looks in disgust at the colorful clothes inside. He dumps the contents of the bag in the middle of the circle of people. One by one this is repeated. Bags upon bags of clothes belonging to all the families in the square are dumped into a pile. Lying on top of the pile is a pink silk shirt, a blue jean jacket, and brown corduroy pants—all <u>remnants</u> of past lives to be destroyed.

¶13 Before the soldier even approaches, Ma has gathered all our bags and put them in a small pile in front of our family. The soldier picks up our bags and begins to throw our clothes onto the pile. His hand reaches into one bag and pulls out something red—my breath quickens. A little girl's dress. He scowls as if the sight of such a thing turns his stomach, then balls up the dress in his hand and throws it on top of the pile. I follow the dress with my eyes, focusing all my energy on it, wanting desperately to rescue it from the pile. My first red dress, the one Ma made for me for the New Year's celebration. I remember Ma taking my <u>measurements</u>, holding the soft chiffon cloth against my body, and asking me if I liked it. "The color looks so pretty on you," she said, "and the chiffon material will keep you cool." Ma made three identical dresses for Chou, Geak, and me. All had puffy sleeves and skirts that flared above the knee.

Words to Know

<u>remnants:</u> *(n.)* leftovers; remaining pieces or parts

<u>measurements:</u> *(n.)* height, waist size, etc.

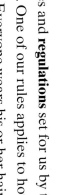

Close Reading

Key Ideas and Details

10. Synthesize what you learn about the chief in **paragraph 11** with what you learned about him in **paragraph 10.**

Literary Analysis

11. Discuss what the clothing in the pile in **paragraph 12** symbolizes. Why does the author mention the colors of the clothes? What do the colors symbolize?

Symbolism

Symbolism is the use of symbols or anything concrete that is meant to be taken both literally and as a representation of a higher and more complex or abstract significance.

Writing

12. Explain why the soldier scowls at the red dress "as if the sight of such a thing turns his stomach" in **paragraph 13.** Cite evidence from the text to support your ideas.

¶14 I do not know when the soldier finishes dumping all the clothes on to the pile. I cannot take my eyes off of my dress. I stand there, with Ma and Pa on either side of me. My insides are tied up in knots, a scream claws its way up my throat but I push it all down. "No! Not my dress. What have I done to you?" I scream in my head, tears welling up in my eyes. "Please help me! I don't know if I can handle it anymore! I don't understand why you hate me so much!" I grind my teeth so hard the pain in my throat moves up to my <u>temples</u>. My hands clench in fists; I continue to stare at my dress. I do not see the soldier's hand reach into his pocket and retrieve from it a box of matches. I do not hear his fingers strike a match against the side of the box. The next thing I know the pile of clothes bursts into flames and my red dress melts like plastic in the fire.

¶15 "Wearing colorful clothes is forbidden. You will take off the clothes you have on and burn those as well. Bright colors only serve to corrupt your mind. You are no different from anyone else here and from now on will dress in black pants and shirts. A new set will be issued to you once a month." To drive his point home, the chief paces around, looking the new people in the eye, pointing his long index finger at them.

¶16 "In Democratic Kampuchea," the chief continues, "we are all equal and do not have to cower to anyone. When the foreigners took over Kampuchea, they brought with them bad habits and fancy titles. The Angkar has <u>expelled</u> all foreigners so we no longer have to refer to each other using fancy titles. From now on, you will address everyone as 'Met!' For example, he is Met Rune, she is Met Srei. No more Mr., Mrs., Sir, Lord, or His Excellency."

Words to Know

<u>temples</u>: (n.) the flat areas on either side of the forehead

<u>expelled</u>: (v.) kicked out

Close Reading

Literary Analysis

13. Identify what the author explains through personification in **paragraph 14.** Why does she "push it all down" and scream only in her head?

Personification

Personification is the attribution of human qualities to nonhuman or inanimate objects. Ideas and abstractions can also be personified.

Key Ideas and Details

14. Compare and contrast the reality of the situation at the work camp to the ideal the chief claims exists under the Khmer Rouge when he states that "we are all equal and do not have to cower to anyone" in **paragraph 16.**

Words and Phrases in Context

15. Elaborate on the meaning of *Met* as used in **paragraph 16.** What can you infer about what it signifies? Cite evidence from the text.

¶17 "Yes, comrade," we reply collectively.

¶18 "The children will change what they call their parents. Father is now 'Poh' and not Daddy, Pa, or any other term. Mother is 'Meh.'" I hold on to Pa's finger even tighter as the chief rants off other new words. The new Khmer have better words for eating, sleeping, working, stranger; all designed to make us equal.

¶19 "In this village, as in the whole of our new and pure society, we all live in a communal system and share everything. There is no private ownership of animals, land, gardens, or even houses. Everything belongs to the Angkar. If the Angkar suspects you of being a <u>traitor</u>, we will come into your home and go through whatever we like.

¶20 "The Angkar will provide you with everything you need. You new people will eat your meals together. Meals will be served from 12 to 2 p.m., and from 6 to 7 p.m. If you come late, you will get nothing. Your meal will be <u>rationed</u> to you; the harder you work, the more you'll eat. After dinner each night, I will let you know whether or not there will be meetings. The base people and our comrade soldiers will patrol your work area. If they see you neglecting your duties and report that you are lazy, you will get nothing to eat." My eyes follow the chief as he paces around the circle of people. I pray that I will remember all he has said.

Words to Know

<u>traitor</u>: (*n.*) someone who betrays, or is disloyal to, someone else

<u>rationed</u>: (*v.*) given in fixed, limited amounts

Close Reading

Literary Analysis

16. Explain the effect of the author's verb choice when she writes that the chief "rants off" the new words in **paragraph 18.** How are the new words supposed to make everyone equal?

Words and Phrases in Context

17. Define *communal.* Identify clues in **paragraph 19** that indicate its meaning. Based on what the chief says, what is not *communal* in the village?

Writing

18. Explain why the author prays in **paragraph 20** that she "will remember all [the chief] has said."

Close Reading

Words and Phrases in Context

19. Define *comrade*. Identify the context clues that help you determine its meaning? What irony about village life does the repetitive use of "Yes, comrade" emphasize?

Writing

20. Explain the Angkar's plan for children as discussed by the author in **paragraph 25**. What details in the previous paragraphs help you understand why the Angkar would forbid schooling?

¶21 "You must follow all the rules set for you by the Angkar. This way, we will never have to deal with the crimes and corruption of the city people."

¶22 "Yes, comrade," the new people echo in <u>unison</u>.

¶23 "Each family will be assigned a house in the village. Those who do not get a house today will be built one tomorrow. Your first work assignment is to build houses for each other!"

¶24 "Yes, comrade."

¶25 "Children in our society will not attend school just to have their brains <u>cluttered</u> with useless information. They will have sharp minds and fast bodies if we give them hard work. The Angkar cannot tolerate laziness. Hard work is good for everyone. Any kind of schooling carried out by anyone without the government's approval is strictly forbidden."

¶26 "Yes, comrade."

¶27 Though we are all supposed to be equal, there are nonetheless three levels of citizenship in the village. The first-class citizenry **comprises** the chief, who has authority over the whole village, his aides, and the Khmer Rouge soldiers. They have the power to teach, police, judge, and execute. They make all decisions: work details, food rations per family, severity of punishment. They are the eyes and ears of the Angkar at the local level. They report all activities to the Angkar and have full power to enforce the Angkar's law.

Words to Know

unison: *(n.)* at the same time

cluttered: *(adj.)* made messy or disorganized; filled with junk

¶28 Then there are the base people. If the first-class citizens are the all-powerful brutal teachers, the base people are the bullies who work closely with them.

¶29 The new people are <u>considered</u> the lowest in the village structure. They have no freedom of speech and must obey the other classes. The new people are those who lived in cities and have been forced out to the villages. They cannot farm like the rural people. They are suspected of having no **allegiance** to the Angkar and must be kept under an ever-watchful eye for signs of rebellion. They have led corrupt lives and must be trained to be productive workers. To <u>instill</u> a sense of loyalty to the Angkar and break what the Khmer Rouge views as an inadequate urban work ethic, the new people are given the hardest work and the longest hours.

¶30 After the chief issues us our meal bowls and spoons and assigns us our hut, we have only minutes to settle down before the 6 p.m. bell rings, signaling mealtime. Gripping my wooden bowl and spoon, I run with my family to the communal kitchen. The kitchen is nothing but a long table, with no chairs or benches, and under a thatched roof with no walls. In the middle of the open hall, there are a few brick ovens and one long table but no chairs or benches. On the long table sit two pots, one full of rice and the other salted grilled fish. There are six or seven base women stirring and scooping food from the pots. A long line of new people has already formed around the table. Like us, they have all changed from their city clothing into their black pajama pants and shirts, the only clothes we will wear from now on.

Words to Know

<u>considered</u>: (*v.*) thought to be

<u>instill</u>: (*v.*) to put an idea slowly into people's mind or feelings, until it becomes their own

---

Close Reading

Key Ideas and Details

21. Explain the three levels of citizenship in the village that the author discusses in **paragraphs 27–29.** Describe each level and whom it comprises.

Academic Vocabulary

22. Use text evidence to explain why the new people "have no allegiance to the Angkar," as the author states in **paragraph 29.** Does the Khmer Rouge strategy for instilling loyalty seem likely to work?

Literary Analysis

23. Identify the words the author uses to create the mood surrounding the meal time in **paragraph 30.** What is the mood?

> **Mood**
>
> The **mood** is the overall atmosphere the author creates. It is the feeling a reader gets from reading. Authors create a mood through word choices, descriptive details, dialogue, and sensory language.

Close Reading

Key Ideas and Details

24. Discuss how the author and her mother feel as they wait for and receive their food in **paragraphs 31–32.** Identify the details the author includes to convey how they feel.

Words and Phrases in Context

25. Define *blankly* as used in **paragraph 31.** Identify the context clues that help you determine its meaning. What does the use of this word suggest about the power of the Khmer Rouge?

Writing

26. Explain how the author conveys the lack of equality in the village in **paragraph 33.**

¶31 My heart <u>lurches</u> as I see the long line in front of me. Eyeing the many black pots filled with steamy food on the ground, I tell my stomach to be calm. The line moves quickly and silently. Under my breath I count the heads before me, eliminating them one by one, anxiously waiting for my turn. Finally, it is Ma's turn. She puts Geak down and holds up two bowls. She bends her head and shoulders so she is lower than the cook, and quietly says, "Please comrade, one for me and one for my three-year-old daughter." The woman looks down blankly at Geak, who barely reaches Ma's thigh and puts two scoops of rice and two fish into Ma's bowl and one of each in Geak's bowl. Ma lowers her head and thanks the woman and walks away with her food, Geak trailing behind her.

¶32 My stomach growls loudly as I step up to the table. I cannot see into the pot and my mouth <u>salivates</u> at the smell of the rice and fish. I raise my bowl to my eye level to make it easier for the comrade to serve me. I dare not look up at her, afraid she might become angry with me for staring and not give me my food. Eyes focused on my bowl, I see her hand dump some rice in my bowl and drop a whole fish on top of it. Somehow, I manage to whisper, "Thank you, comrade" and walk away, praying that I won't fall and spill my food.

¶33 Sitting in the shade underneath a tree, our family eats the food together. Though it is the most food we have eaten in a long time, before nightfall we are all hungry again. Realizing we have to find a way to get more food, Pa somehow arranges for Kim to work at the chief's house as his errand boy. The next night, Kim comes home with leftovers.

* * *

Words to Know

<u>lurches:</u> (*v.*) moves suddenly

<u>salivates:</u> (*v.*) fills with spit, in preparation for eating

¶34 Day after day we work, seven days a week. Some months, if we have been very <u>productive</u> workers, we are given half a day to rest. In those hours, Ma and us girls wash our clothes in a nearby stream, but without <u>detergent</u> they are not very clean. I look forward to those hours off as our special time together. Of the five hundred or so new people in our village, there are only two or three babies among the families. Although I cannot fully understand her words, I overhear Ma say women are so overworked, underfed, and filled with fear that most cannot become pregnant anymore. Even when they do, many suffer miscarriages. Most newborn babies do not survive more than a couple of days. Pa says there will be a generation of children completely missing from our country. Shaking his head, he looks at Geak. "The first victims are always the children."

¶35 Pa says Geak will not become the Khmer Rouge's next victim because the chief likes him. The chief allows Kim to bring extra food home, and he knows that things are easier for us because of that. Pa works harder and longer than anyone else in the village. Because of his humble upbringing, Pa has many skills and can do anything the chief asks of him. He is a skilled carpenter, builder, and farmer. Pa is always quiet and even seems enthusiastic about the work—a trait which proves to the chief that Pa is an uncorrupted man. He picks Pa to be the leader of the new people, a position that comes with a raise in the food ration.

¶36 Though the Angkar says we are all equal in Democratic Kampuchea, we are not. We live and are treated like slaves. In our garden, the Angkar provides us with seeds and we may plant anything we choose, but everything we grow belongs not to us but to the community. The base people eat the berries and vegetables from the community gardens, but the new people are punished if they do. During harvest season the crops from the fields are turned over to the village chief, who then rations the food to the fifty families.

Words to Know

<u>productive</u>: *(adj.)* producing a lot; getting a lot of work done

<u>detergent</u>: *(n.)* soap for washing laundry or dishes

Close Reading

Writing

27. Summarize what the author's life is like in the village. What can you infer about how her new life is different from her old life?

Words and Phrases in Context

28. Define *enthusiastic*. Identify the context clues that help you determine its meaning. What does the use of this word in **paragraph 35** convey about how Pa has adapted to life in the work camp?

Key Ideas and Details

29. Identify a detail in **paragraph 36** that helps explain why the "base people" are willing to be "bullies" and enforce the rules of the Khmer Rouge. What could happen to the "base people" if they fail to enforce the rules?

¶37 As always, no matter how plentiful the crops, there is never enough food for the new people. Stealing food is viewed as a <u>heinous</u> crime and, if caught, offenders risk either getting their fingers cut off in the public square or being forced to grow a vegetable garden in an area near identified minefields. The Khmer Rouge soldiers planted these land mines to protect the provinces they took over from the Lon Nol army during the revolution. Since the Khmer Rouge planted so many land mines and drew no maps of where these mines are, now many people are injured or killed traversing these areas. People who work in these areas do not come back to the village. If people step on one and their arms or legs are blown off, they are no longer of any value to the Angkar. The soldiers then shoot them to finish the job. In the new pure <u>agrarian</u> society, there is no place for disabled people.

¶38 The Khmer Rouge government also bans the practice of religion. Kim says the Angkar do not want people worshipping any gods or goddesses that might take away devotion to the Angkar. To ensure that this rule is enforced, the soldiers destroyed Buddhist temples and worshipping sites throughout the country with major destruction done to the area known as Angkor Wat, an ancient religious site important in Kampuchean history.

¶39 Covering more than twenty-five miles of temples, Angkor Wat was built by powerful Khmer kings as monuments of self-glorification in the ninth century and completed three hundred years later. In the fifteenth century, Angkor Wat was abandoned to the jungles after an invasion by Siam and forgotten about until French explorers rediscovered it in the nineteenth century. Since then, the battle-scarred temples with their beautiful statues, stone sculptures, and multilayered towers remain one of the seven man-made wonders of the world.

Words to Know

<u>heinous:</u> *(adj.)* extremely bad or shocking

<u>agrarian:</u> *(adj.)* dependent on farming

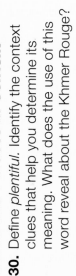

Close Reading

Words and Phrases in Context

30. Define *plentiful*. Identify the context clues that help you determine its meaning. What does the use of this word reveal about the Khmer Rouge?

Key Ideas and Details

31. Discuss why people are punished by forcing them to farm in minefields. What does the author mean by "finish the job" in **paragraph 37?** Why do the soldiers shoot people who have been disabled by land mines? What does this say about equality under the Angkar government?

Writing

32. Explain why the Angkar bans religion and did "major destruction . . . to the area known as Angkor Wat" and other religious sites, as described in **paragraphs 38–39.** What does this reveal about the Angkar's view of itself?

¶40 I remember clutching tightly to Pa's finger as we walked along wide crumbling corridors. The temple walls are decorated with magnificent detailed carvings of people, cows, wagons, daily life, and battle scenes from long ago. Guarding the ancient steps are giant granite lions, tigers, eight-headed snakes, and elephants. Next to them, sandstone gods with eight hands who sit cross-legged on lotus flowers watch over the temple ponds. On the walls beneath the jungle vines, thousands of beautiful apsara goddesses wearing only short wraparound skirts smile at visitors.

¶41 Pa led me to a temple area where the trees were so tall that they seemed to reach the heavens. Their twisted trunks, roots, and vines wrapped themselves around the ruins like gigantic boa constrictors, crushing and swallowing the overturned stones. He lifted me over the wobbly steps to the dark mouth of the temple cave. "This is where the gods live," he said quietly, "and if you call out to them, they will answer." Anxiously, I wet my lips and yelled, *"Chump leap sursdei, dthai pda!"* ("Hello, gods!") Then wrapped my arms around Pa's leg when the gods answered me: *"Dthai pda! Dthai pda! Dthai pda!"*

¶42 At the temples in this area, my sixteen-year-old brother, Khouy, says the soldiers mutilated its animal guards, and either knocked or shot off the stone heads of the gods, riddling the sacred bodies with bullets. After they destroyed the temples, the soldiers roamed the country searching for monks and forced them to convert to the Angkar. Those monks who refused were murdered or made to work in minefields. To escape extermination, many monks grew their hair and went into hiding in the jungle. Although these monks maintained and took care of the temples, now they are left to the jungle once again. I wonder where the gods go now that their homes have been destroyed.

Words to Know

<u>corridors:</u> *(n.)* hallways or passageways

<u>mutilated:</u> *(v.)* damaged severely

Close Reading

Literary Analysis

33. Explain the purpose the flashback in **paragraphs 40 and 41** serves. What is the mood of the scene in the flashback?

Flashback

A flashback is a scene that takes place before the present time in the story. Authors often use a flashback to either provide background information for the present-time scene or as a way to comment on the present-time scene.

Text Structure

34. Discuss how **paragraph 42** is different from the previous two paragraphs. What purpose does this paragraph serve?

Identify Evidence | Analyze Individuals, Events, and Ideas

In this excerpt from *First They Killed My Father*, author Luong Ung writes about the drastic changes that occurred in her life when the Khmer Rouge took over Cambodia and relocated her family to a rural village. Reread the excerpt, highlighting examples and evidence that reveal what life was like for Ung and her fellow "new people" under the rule of the Angkar. How does she introduce, illustrate, and elaborate on individuals, events, and ideas?

• As you read, use the Evidence column to record examples from the text that show what life was like in the rural village where Ung and her family were forced to live and work.

• In the Explanation column, explain how the evidence introduces, illustrates, or elaborates on ideas.

Evidence	Source	Page	Explanation
1. "Capitalists should be shot and killed,' someone yells from the crowd, glaring at us. Another villager walks over and spits at Pa's feet."	Ung	312	With this detail, the author introduces the hostile attitude of the villagers toward the new arrivals, including the author and her family.
2. "In this village, we live by strict rules and regulations set for us by the Angkar. We expect you to follow every rule.'"	Ung	315	
3. "I cannot take my eyes off of my dress. . . . My insides are tied up in knots, a scream claws its way up my throat but I push it all down."	Ung	316	
4. "In this village . . . we all live in a communal system and share everything. There is no private ownership . . . Everything belongs to the Angkar.'"	Ung	317	

Evidence	Source	Page	Explanation

Read the Model

Writers use many strategies to analyze a topic and share information about it. The writer of this informative essay uses relevant evidence to convey his ideas about how Beah's childhood wartime experiences had an impact on his life. Read and discuss the model essay below.

Life After War   By Cameron Prindle

In *A Long Way Gone*, Ishmael Beah describes his life as a child soldier during the civil war in Sierra Leone, and then explains his return to "normal society." Based on the details Beah includes in his memoir, it is evident that his childhood wartime experiences had an impact on his post-war life in three incredibly painful ways.

Nearly a year after escaping the Sierra Leone Army, Beah was still haunted by his experiences. Night after night, as he lay awake in his bed, he questioned, "Why have I survived the war?" (340). Furthermore, in the midst of a joke-filled conversation with his cousin at a dance, his mind filled with a flashback from his time as a child soldier. He saw "the blood cover the dance floor" (345) from one of his attacks.

In addition to being haunted by questions and flashbacks, Beah also had difficulty connecting with people in the "normal" world. At the dance, rather than dancing with the crowd, he danced by himself in a corner. Even after he had "adjusted to being around people who were happy all the time" (343), Beah still could not sustain a relationship with a girlfriend for more than a few weeks because he could not bear to talk about his past. He claimed, instead, that he liked "being alone" (345).

Though Beah was not alone, because his sadness was his constant companion. Prior to being reunited with his uncle, Beah worried about how he would hide his sadness (340). Later, he reflects on a time before his childhood wartime years when he "was truly happy" (343), indicating that he was no longer happy.

Beah clearly wants to adapt to life in "normal society." He spends time with his family, he goes to dances, and he attempts to date. However, despite Beah's efforts to live the life of a normal young person, it is clear that he will fight the demons from his childhood for his entire life.

Informative Essay

An **informative essay** conveys information and ideas about a topic.

The **introduction** states the topic that the writer will discuss, and includes a thesis statement that previews the writer's ideas about the topic.

- Identify the topic and how the writer previews his ideas about the topic

The three **body paragraphs** express the writer's main ideas about the topic. The ideas are grouped logically and are supported by relevant evidence.

- Explain the main idea of the first body paragraph.

- Find one piece of relevant evidence.

The **conclusion** sums up or restates the thesis, and adds a final thought.

- Identify the final thought.

Analyze the Model

Use the outline below to analyze the model essay. Your notes can be written using shorthand and phrases.

Introduction		
Thesis Statement		
Body		
Topic Sentence	**Relevant Evidence**	
Topic Sentence	**Relevant Evidence**	
Topic Sentence	**Relevant Evidence**	
Conclusion		

Text Structure

- The **thesis statement** presents a clear plan for the essay.

- The **topic sentence** of each body paragraph clearly states the main idea of that paragraph. It is the leading or controlling sentence of the paragraph. All the topic sentences support the thesis statement.

- The body paragraphs also contain **supporting sentences** that build on the idea stated in the topic sentence.

- Supporting sentences include logical reasoning and **relevant evidence**, such as direct quotations from the text, that support the writer's ideas.

- The conclusion should **restate** the thesis and say **why** the **information matters.**

Step 1 | Gather Evidence

[**Analyze in detail how childhood wartime experiences had an impact on Beah's or Ung's life. Consider how the author introduces, illustrates, and elaborates upon the events.**]

What You Need to Know | Examine the evidence you have collected. (See pages 306 and 324).

What You Need to Write | Pick one text to analyze. Then note the key ideas you have drawn for your analysis based on your evidence.

Evidence	Page #	Wartime Impact on Author

Step 2 | Organize Ideas

What You Need to Know | In order to write a successful informative essay, you need to group your ideas logically and support them with relevant evidence.

To develop your analysis:

1. Craft two or three topic sentences that encompass the impact childhood wartime experiences had on Beah or Ung.

2. Identify relevant evidence for each of your ideas.

What You Need to Write | Analyze the impact of the wartime experiences on Beah or Ung.

Introduction	
Thesis Statement	

Body	
Topic Sentence	Relevant Evidence
Topic Sentence	Relevant Evidence
Topic Sentence	Relevant Evidence

Conclusion
Restate thesis and why it matters

Step 3 | Draft

Write a draft of your essay on the computer or on paper.

Language Study | Describing a Sequence of Events

See It | Good writers identify sequence clearly with sequence signal words.

Though Beah was not alone, because his sadness was his constant companion. Prior to being reunited with his uncle, Beah worried about how he would hide his sadness (340). Later, he reflects on a time before his childhood wartime years when "he was truly happy" (343), indicating that he was no longer happy.

Try It | The sentences below tell about a soccer match. Add sequence signal words to the sentences to make the order of events clear to the reader. Use sequence signal words from the word bank, or ones that you think of yourself. Be prepared to discuss your choice of sequence signal words.

There was just one minute left in the match. ____, Nina saw she had a shot and kicked the ball. It went into the net. Nina's team won the match. ____, a player from the other team congratulated Nina. ____, Nina felt very proud of herself. She had a big smile on her face at school ____.

Sequence Signal Word Bank

- Soon
- Finally
- Just then
- That night
- Afterwards
- The next day

Apply It | Think about the topic you wrote about in your essay. Use the sentence frames below to practice writing about your topic using sequence words.

1. _____ Beah/Ung was _____.
   (sequence word)   (an event from the text)

2. Beah/Ung _____ _____.
              (sequence word)   (a detail related to the event)

3. _____ Beah/Ung felt _____.
   (sequence word)   (an analysis of the impact the event had)

Now, **go back to your draft** and select at least two sentences that you could make clearer through the use of sequence signal words.

_____

_____

_____

Conventions Study | Using Precise Language

See It

Precise language conveys exactly what you mean. Domain-specific vocabulary words relate to a specific subject. Using precise language and domain-specific vocabulary makes your writing clear.

Clear	Unclear
After the Khmer Rouge took control of Cambodia, Ung often lived in fear. She suppressed a scream when her dress was thrown into the pile and burned.	After the group took over the country, Ung often lived in fear. She didn't scream when her dress was put into the pile and burned.

Try It

Circle the precise language or domain-specific vocabulary in each set. Then write a sentence using the word you circled

1. left/escaped

_____

2. Sierra Leone Army/group of soldiers

_____

3. repatriated/sent back

_____

4. war/civil war

_____

Apply It

Now revise one of your body paragraphs. Use precise language and domain-specific vocabulary to clearly convey your ideas about the topic.

Step 4 | Revise and Edit   Revise your draft with a partner.

Organization and Clarity					
State the title and author of the text in the introductory paragraph.	Self	1	2	3	4
	Partner	1	2	3	4
Provide a thesis statement in the introduction that clearly sets up the analysis of the impact of childhood wartime experiences on either Beah or Ung.	Self	1	2	3	4
	Partner	1	2	3	4
Include topic sentences in the body paragraphs that present the general reasons that support the analysis.	Self	1	2	3	4
	Partner	1	2	3	4
Conclude by summarizing the key ideas and restating the analysis.	Self	1	2	3	4
	Partner	1	2	3	4
Evidence and Reasoning					
Include two or more pieces of specific and relevant text evidence in each body paragraph.	Self	1	2	3	4
	Partner	1	2	3	4
Provide an analysis of the evidence and how it supports the ideas about how childhood wartime experiences had an impact on Beah or Ung.	Self	1	2	3	4
	Partner	1	2	3	4
Language and Conventions					
Signal sequence by using sequence words and phrases.	Self	1	2	3	4
	Partner	1	2	3	4
Use precise language and domain-specific vocabulary as appropriate.	Self	1	2	3	4
	Partner	1	2	3	4
Spell all words correctly. Use standard capitalization and effective punctuation.	Self	1	2	3	4
	Partner	1	2	3	4

Step 5 | Publish   Publish your essay either in print or digital form.

Scoring Guide | ① needs improvement   ② average   ③ good   ④ excellent

Publish

Publish your essay either in print or digital form. Use the rubric below to assess your final performance task.

PERFORMANCE TASK RUBRIC

Score Point	Organization and Clarity	Evidence and Reasoning	Language and Conventions
Exemplary ④	• introductory paragraph **identifies** the topic clearly and **previews** points for analysis • each body paragraph **focuses on one point** and **includes relevant evidence** that supports the thesis statement • includes **well-chosen** text evidence, details, and precise and concise language • concluding statement **restates** the thesis statement and **summarizes** the techniques the writer used to illustrate the impact of war on his or her life	• **accurately explains and convincingly analyzes** how the writers' wartime experiences impacted his or her life • includes **several examples of relevant** text evidence from the review or memoir that **supports** the analysis	• demonstrates a **strong command** of the conventions of standard English grammar and usage, as well as of standard English capitalization, punctuation, and spelling • vocabulary is **appropriate** to the topic (vocabulary about wartime; accurate terms for discussing techniques for developing ideas; vocabulary for analyzing cause and effect)
Meets Standards ③	• introductory paragraph **identifies** the topic clearly • each body paragraph **addresses one point** and **includes evidence** that supports the thesis statement • includes **some** text evidence, details, and precise and concise language • concluding statement **restates** the thesis statement and **summarizes** the techniques the writer used to illustrate the impact of war on his or her life	• **accurately explains and generally analyzes** how the writers' wartime experiences impacted his or her life • includes **relevant** text evidence from the review or memoir that **supports** the analysis	• demonstrates **a near command** of the conventions of standard English grammar and usage, as well as of standard English capitalization, punctuation, and spelling **with some errors** • vocabulary is **appropriate** to the topic (vocabulary about wartime; accurate terms for discussing techniques for developing ideas; vocabulary for analyzing cause and effect)

PERFORMANCE TASK RUBRIC

Score Point	Organization and Clarity	Evidence and Reasoning	Language and Conventions
Needs Work ②	• introductory paragraph **identifies** the topic • body paragraphs **address one point** that may or may not be valid and/or includes weak evidence • includes **a limited amount** of text evidence, details, and precise and concise language • concluding statement **attempts to restate** the focus statement and attempts to summarize the techniques the writer used to illustrate the impact of war on his or her life	• **accurately explains** how the writers' wartime experiences impacted his or her life with **limited analysis** • includes **some** text evidence from the review or memoir that **supports** the analysis	• demonstrates a **marginal command** of the conventions of English grammar and usage, as well as of standard English capitalization, punctuation, and spelling • there **are many errors; however, the text is still understandable** • includes only **one or two examples** of vocabulary that is appropriate to the topic (vocabulary about wartime; accurate terms for discussing techniques for developing ideas; vocabulary for analyzing cause and effect)
Does Not Meet Standards ①	• introductory paragraph is **unclear** and does not include a thesis statement • body paragraphs do **not** address valid points and/or **do not** include evidence that supports the focus statement • essay includes **little text evidence** and concise language • concluding statement is **unclear and does not wrap up** the ideas in the essay	• response is **partial or inaccurate explanation** of how the writers' wartime experiences impacted his or her life • includes **no analyses of textual evidence** from the review or memoir	• demonstrates **almost no command** of the conventions of standard English grammar and usage, as well as of standard English capitalization, punctuation, and spelling • there **are many errors that disrupt** the reader's understanding of the text • **does not include** vocabulary that is appropriate to the topic (vocabulary about wartime; accurate terms for discussing ideas; techniques for developing ideas; vocabulary for analyzing cause and effect)

Questions

Text Structure

1. Identify the pronoun in **paragraph 1** that helps you understand the point of view of this text. What is the point of view? Based on the point of view, the title, and the byline, what is the text type? What do you already know about the author and his book?

Words and Phrases in Context

2. What is the meaning of *repatriated*? What does the use of quotation marks around the word in **paragraph 1** signal about Beah's use of the word and the group he fought for?

---

from *A Long Way Gone*

by Ishmael Beah

¶1 … I was to be "repatriated" and reinstated into normal society. I was to live with my uncle. Those two weeks felt longer than the eight months I had spent at Benin Home. I was worried about living with a family. I had been on my own for years and had taken care of myself without any guidance from anyone. I was afraid that I might look ungrateful to my uncle, who didn't have to take me in, if I distanced myself from the family unit. I was worried about what to do when my nightmares and migraines took hold of me. How was I going to explain my sadness, which I am unable to hide as it takes over my face, to my new family, especially the children? I didn't have answers to these questions. …

¶2 I lay in my bed night after night staring at the ceiling and thinking, Why have I survived the war? Why was I the last person in my immediate family to be alive? I didn't know … what life was going to be like after the center.

¶3 When the day of my repatriation finally came, I packed my few belongings in a plastic bag. I had a pair of sneakers, four T-shirts, three shorts, toothpaste, a toothbrush, a bottle of Vaseline lotion, a Walkman and some cassettes, two long-sleeved shirts, two pairs of pants and a tie. … I waited, my heart beating faster, the way it had when my mother dropped me off for the first time at a boarding school. The van was heard galloping on the gravel road, making its way to the center. Picking up my plastic bag, I walked to the hospital building where I was to wait. [My friends,] Mohamed, Alhaji, and Mambu were sitting on the front steps, and Esther emerged, smiling. The van made a turn and halted at the side of the road. It was late afternoon, the sky was still blue, but the sun was dull, hiding behind the only cloud. …

Words to Know

reinstated: *(v.)* put back into place or use

ungrateful: *(adj.)* not thankful

¶4 "I have to go," I said to everyone, my voice shaking. I extended my hand to Mohamed, but instead of shaking it, he leapt up and hugged me. Mambu embraced me while Mohamed was still holding me. He squeezed me hard, as if he knew it was goodbye forever. (After I left the center, Mambu went back to the front lines, because his family refused to take him in.) At the end of the hug, Alhaji shook hands with me. We squeezed each other's hand and stared into each other's eyes, remembering all that we had been through. I tapped him on the shoulder and he smiled, as he understood that I was saying we were going to be fine. I never saw him again, since he continually moved from one foster home to another. At the end of our handshake, Alhaji stepped back, saluted me, and whispered, "Goodbye, squad leader." I tapped him on the shoulder again; I couldn't salute him in return. Esther stepped forward, her eyes watery. She hugged me tighter than she ever had. I didn't return her hug very well, as I was busy trying to hold back my tears. After she let go, she gave me a piece of paper . . .

¶5 My uncle picked me up in his arms as soon as I got off the van and carried me onto the verandah. "I welcome you today like a chief. Your feet may touch the ground when you lose your chieftaincy, which begins now," my uncle said, laughing, as he set me down. I smiled but was nervous. My four cousins—Allie and the three girls, Matilda, Kona, and Sombo—took turns hugging me, their faces bright with smiles.

¶6 "You must be hungry; I cooked you a welcome home *sackie thomboi*," my aunt said. She had made cassava leaves with chicken just to welcome me. To have chicken prepared for anyone was a rarity, and it was considered an honor. People ate chicken only on holidays like Christmas or New Year's. Auntie Sallay held my hand and made me sit on a bench next to my uncle. She brought the food out, and my uncle and I ate together from the same plate with our hands. It was a good meal and, I licked my fingers, enjoying the rich palm oil. My uncle looked at me, laughing, and said to his wife, "Sallay, you have done it again. This one is here to stay."

Words to Know

the front lines: (*n.*) the boundary between warring areas where much fighting takes place.

Questions

Key Ideas and Details

3. What can you infer about Ishmael's friends, Mohamed, Alhaji, and Mambu, from the details in **paragraph 4?** How does Ishamael's current situation compare to that of the other boys'?

Key Ideas and Details

4. Identify details that convey how Beah's uncle and his uncle's family feel about having Beah move into their home. What was Beah feeling before joining them? What can you infer about him from this?

¶7 After we washed our hands, my cousin Allie, twenty-one years old, was called to the verandah and asked to show me where I was to sleep. I took my plastic bag and followed him to another house that was behind the one with my uncle's bedroom. The passageway between the houses was like a pathway with stones carefully placed on each side of the walkway.

¶8 Allie held the door for me as I entered the clean, organized room. The bed was made, the clothes that hung on a post were ironed, the shoes were properly lined on a rack, and the brown tile floor was shiny. He pulled a mattress from under the bed and explained to me that I would sleep on the floor, as he and his roommate shared the bed. I was to fold the mattress and put it back under the bed every morning. After he was done explaining how I could contribute to keeping the room clean and in order, I went back to the <u>verandah</u> and sat with my uncle. He put his arm around me and pulled on my nose.

¶9 "Are you familiar with the city?" Uncle asked.

¶10 "Not really."

¶11 "Allie will take you around sometime, if you like. Or you can venture out, there yourself, get lost, and find your way. It will be a good way to get to know the city." He chuckled. We heard a call for prayer that echoed throughout the city.

¶12 "I have to go for prayers. If you need anything, ask your cousins," he said taking a kettle from the stoop and beginning to perform <u>ablution</u>. After he was done, he walked down the hill to a nearby mosque. My aunt came out of the room, tying her head with a cloth, and followed my uncle.

Words to Know

verandah: (n.) a roofed deck that runs along the side of a house or building

ablution: (n.) the washing of one's body as part of a religious ritual

Questions

Key Ideas and Details

5. Identify details in **paragraphs 7–8** that show that Ishmael will have some independence in his uncle's home.

Key Idea and Details

6. What does the conversation between the uncle and Ishmael in **paragraphs 9–12** indicate about Ishmael's new living situation? How does this conversation help to develop the relationship between Ishmael and his uncle?

¶13 I sighed, sitting alone on the verandah. I was no longer nervous, but I missed Benin Home. Later that night, when my uncle and aunt returned from prayers, all my new family gathered around a cassette player on the verandah to listen to stories. My uncle rubbed his hands, pressed the play button, and a famous storyteller named Leleh Gbomba began telling a story about a man who had forgotten his heart at home when he went traveling around the world. I had heard the story in my grandmother's village when I was younger. My new family laughed throughout the telling of the story. I only smiled and was very quiet that night, as I was to be for a while more. But gradually I adjusted to being around people who were happy all the time.

¶14 A day or two after I had started living with my uncle, Allie gave me my first pair of dress shoes, a dress belt, and a stylish shirt.

¶15 "If you want to be a gentleman, you have to dress like one." He laughed. I was about to ask him why he had given me these things when he began to explain: "This is a secret. I want to take you to a dance tonight so you can enjoy yourself. We will leave after Uncle goes to bed." That night we snuck out and went dancing . . . As Allie and I walked, I remembered when I used to go dancing back in secondary school with friends. It seemed so long ago, but I still recalled the different names of the dance nights: "Back to School," "Pens Down," "Bob Marley Night," and many more. We would dance until cockcrow, then take off our sweaty shirts, enjoying the cool morning breeze as we walked back to our dorms. I was truly happy back then.

Words to Know

gradually: (adj.) slowly

cockcrow: (n.) slang for "morning," when the rooster crows

Questions

Key Ideas and Details

7. Why is Ishmael "no longer nervous," as he describes in **paragraph 13?** Why must he adjust "to being around people who were happy all the time"?

Text Structure

8. What does Beah describe in a memory in **paragraph 15?** What can you infer about him based on this?

¶16 "We are here," Allie said, shaking my hand and snapping his fingers. There were lots of young people waiting in line to get into the pub. The boys were well dressed, their pants ironed and shirts tucked in. The girls wore beautiful flowered dresses and high heels that made them taller than some of the boys they were with. Their lips were also painted with bright colors. Allie was excited and he chatted with the people in front of us. I was quiet, looking at the different colored lights that hung at the entrance. There was one big blue light that made people's white shirts especially beautiful. We finally made it to the entrance and Allie paid for the two of us. The music was extremely loud inside, but then again, I had not been to a pub for many years. I followed Allie to the bar area, where we found a table and sat on two high stools.

¶17 "I am going to the dance floor," Allie announced, screaming so that I could hear him. He disappeared into the crowd. I sat for a while scoping out the place, and slowly began dancing by myself in the corner of the dance floor. Suddenly an extremely dark girl whose smile illuminated the dance floor pulled me and led me to the middle of the floor before I could <u>resist</u>. She started dancing close to me. I looked back at Allie, who was standing at the bar. He gave me a thumbs-up, and I began to move slowly until the rhythm took over. I danced one *raggamorphy* song with the girl, and then there was a slow jam . . . She tried to catch my eyes, but I looked away. In the middle of the song, some older boy pulled her away from me. She waved as she was being <u>escorted</u> through the crowd and toward the door.

¶18 "You are smooth, man. I saw that." Allie was now standing next to me. He began walking toward the bar, and I followed him. We leaned against the counter, facing the dance floor. He was still smiling.

Questions

Key Ideas and Details

9. Identify a contrast in how Allie and Beah behave upon arriving at the dance in **paragraph 16.** What can you infer about Beah based on his behavior?

Words and Phrases in Context

10. What does Ishmael mean when he writes in **paragraph 17** that the girl's "smile illuminated the dance floor"? What type of figurative language is this? What is its effect?

Words to Know

<u>resist</u>: *(v.)* to stop oneself from taking part in

<u>escorted</u>: *(v.)* led or guided

¶19 "I really didn't do anything. She just wanted to dance with me and I couldn't say no," I said.

¶20 "Exactly, you say nothing and the women come to you," he teased. I didn't want to talk anymore. A memory of a town we had attacked during a school dance had been triggered. I could hear the terrified cries of teachers and students, could see the blood cover the dance floor. Allie tapped me on the shoulder and brought me back to the present. I smiled at him, but I was deeply sad for the rest of our stay. We danced all night and returned before Uncle woke up.

¶21 A few nights later, I returned to the dance club alone and saw the same girl. She told me her name was Zainab.

¶22 "Sorry about last time," she said. "My brother wanted to go home and I had to go with him, otherwise my parents would have gotten worried."

¶23 Like me, she was alone this night.

¶24 I dated her for three weeks, but then she began to ask too many questions. Where was I from? What was it like growing up *upline*? *Upline* is a Krio word mostly used in Freetown to refer to the backwardness of the inner country, its <u>inhabitants</u>, and their <u>mannerisms</u>. I was unwilling to tell her anything, so she broke it off. That was the story of my relationship with girls in Freetown. They wanted to know about me, and I wasn't ready to tell them. It was okay. I liked being alone.

Words to Know

<u>inhabitants:</u> *(n.)* people who live in a place

<u>mannerisms:</u> *(n.)* the way people walk, gesture, and behave

Questions

Key Ideas and Details

11. Compare and contrast the memory in **paragraph 20** to the one in **paragraph 15**. What can you infer about Beah from his differing memories?

Key Ideas and Details

12. What details help you understand why Beah liked being alone, as he claims in **paragraph 20**. What details suggest that he might not really feel this way?

Literature Circle Leveled Novels

The False Prince *by Jennifer Nielsen*
An orphan boy competes to be chosen to impersonate the king's long-lost son, and must win the competition or face death. **Lexile**® measure: 710L

Maus I: A Survivor's Tale: My Father Bleeds History *by Art Spiegelman*
The author uses graphic art to tell the story of his parents, Vladek and Anna, who survived the horrors of the Holocaust, but continue to struggle with its effects years later. **Lexile**® measure: NP

In the Time of the Butterflies *by Julia Alvarez*
In the Dominican Republic, three sisters risk their lives to help overthrow the Trujillo dictatorship of the 1960s. Can they succeed? **Lexile**® measure: 910L

Nonfiction

Night *by Elie Wiesel.* The Nobel laureate remembers the horror of life in a concentration camp during the Holocaust and confronts his complicated feelings about having survived. **Lexile**® measure: 590L

Red Scarf Girl: A Memoir of the Cultural Revolution *by Ji-li Jiang.* The author recalls her teenage years during the violent times of the Chinese Cultural Revolution. **Lexile**® measure: 780L

The Story of My Life: An Afghan Girl on the Other Side of the Sky *by Farah Ahmedi* with Tamim Ansary. A young woman tells her story of loss and hope after surviving a land mine and fleeing Afghanistan. **Lexile**® measure: 850L

A Long Way Gone: Memoirs of a Boy Soldier *by Ishmael Beah.* A young man recalls being forced to fight with rebel forces in Sierra Leone's civil war, and describes his later rehabilitation and advocacy for children's rights. **Lexile**® measure: 920L

Farewell to Manzanar: A True Story of Japanese American Experience During and After the World War II Internment *by Jeanne Wakatsuki Houston and James D. Houston.* Read about the experiences of a Japanese-American girl who faced detention in her own country. **Lexile**® measure: 1040L

Kaffir Boy: The True Story of a Black Youth's Coming of Age in Apartheid South Africa *by Mark Mathabane.* Read the inspiring true story of one man's struggle to overcome the segregation and oppression of apartheid. **Lexile**® measure: 1040L

Only the Names Remain: The Cherokee and the Trail of Tears *by Alex W. Bealer.* Learn about the grueling forced relocation of the Cherokee Nation from their ancestral lands and the tragic consequences for the Cherokee people. **Lexile**® measure: 1050L

The Wall: Growing Up Behind the Iron Curtain *by Peter Sís.* Artwork, journal entries, and photography tell the author's story of growing up in Communist Eastern Europe during the Cold War.

Films and TV

Heroes of the Holocaust (A&E Home Video, 2008) This documentary series presents the inspiring stories of people who, in very different ways, resisted victimization and instead acted as heroes to others. (300 min.)

Schindler's List (Universal Studios, 1993; R) Experience the powerful story of Oskar Schindler, who saved the lives of more than 1,000 Jews during the Holocaust. (195 min.)

Sophie Scholl: The Final Days (Zeitgeist Films, 2005) Learn about the resistance work and subsequent arrest, trial, and execution of Sophie Scholl, a German anti-Nazi activist. (117 min.)

S21: The Khmer Rouge Killing Machine (First Run Features, 2002) Learn about the history of the Khmer Rouge genocidal campaign in Cambodia, and hear firsthand accounts from survivors. (101 min.)

Time of Fear (PBS Home Video, 2005) Watch interviews to learn more about the experiences of the thousands of Japanese Americans forced into relocation camps during World War II. (60 min.)

We Shall Remain: Trail of Tears (PBS, 2009) Learn about the experience of thousands of Cherokee as they were driven from their homes and forced on a deadly march. (420 min.)

Websites

The Authentic History Center Explore this Web site to find audio, visual, and textual primary sources from many periods of American history.

EyeWitness to History Follow links to read firsthand accounts from witnesses to different events throughout world history, and view photos, video footage, and artifacts.

In the First Person Search this online index to find letters, diaries, oral histories, and personal narratives of individuals from all over the world.

Library of Congress: American Memory Browse the collections at the Library of Congress to find written accounts, sound recordings, moving images, prints, and maps that document the American experience.

Magazines

American Heritage Find primary and secondary sources—such as articles, artwork, photographs, diary entries, and biographical excerpts—from American history.

History Today Read articles and features about topics ranging from prehistory to current events.

The New York Times Upfront Read about important issues in today's world, and consider how people react to world events.

Scholastic News Stay up-to-date with today's news, and read firsthand accounts about events that will become part of history.

DO THE RIGHT THING

What does a difficult situation reveal about character?

WRITING PERFORMANCE TASK

Many events of the Little Rock Nine tested the strength of people to be brave, do the right thing, heal, and forgive. Write a historical fiction narrative about one such event. Describe the event using narrative technique, such as dialogue, description, and reflection.

BOOK EXCERPTS

from **The Little Rock Nine: Struggle for Integration**
by Stephanie Fitzgerald

Language
- Academic Vocabulary
- Word Study: Roots and Affixes

Reading a Book Excerpt
- Identify Evidence
- Key Ideas and Details
- Craft and Structure and Writing Assignment

SPEAKING AND LISTENING
- Hold a Debate
- Collaborate and Present

Checklist: Debate
- Scoring Guide

WRITING

Writing: Historical Fiction
- Read the Model
- Analyze the Model
- Gather Evidence
- Organize Ideas

EXTENDED READING

Memoir Excerpt
from **Warriors Don't Cry**
by Melba Pattillo Beals

from **Elizabeth and Hazel: Two Women of Little Rock**
by David Margolick

Language
- Academic Vocabulary
- Word Study: Context Clues

Reading a Book Excerpt
- Identify Evidence
- Key Ideas and Details
- Craft and Structure and Writing Assignment

- Language Study: Narrating Events With Variety
- Conventions Study: Using Transition Words and Phrases
- Revise, Edit, and Publish
- Performance Task Rubric

Interview Excerpt
from **"Minnijean Brown Trickey Looks Back"**
conducted by Veronica Majerol

Unit Introduction

The two book excerpts featured in this unit describe how two very different women found their strength of character tested and shaped by an important event in the civil rights movement.

In *The Little Rock Nine: Struggle for Integration*, Stephanie Fitzgerald describes how Elizabeth Eckford, an African American student, is blocked from integrating an all-white school by an angry mob of white people.

In *Elizabeth and Hazel: Two Women of Little Rock*, David Margolick tells about the attempt at a friendship by Elizabeth and Hazel, a member of that angry mob, forty years later.

Academic Vocabulary

from *The Little Rock Nine* by Stephanie Fitzgerald

Rate your understanding of each word. Then read its meaning and write an example sentence. If the example is given, write the meaning.

Word	Meaning	Example
occasion (n.) p. 351 ① ② ③ ④		Jeremy wore a suit and tie to mark the occasion of his birthday.
determined (adj.) p. 351 ① ② ③ ④	having a strong desire to do something	
furious (adj.) p. 353 ① ② ③ ④		Melissa was furious that her brother had used her music player without asking her.
mission (n.) p. 355 ① ② ③ ④		Bella made it her mission to get her family to eat healthy food.
segregation (n) p. 355 ① ② ③ ④	the practice of separating people of different races, sexes, or religions	
courageously (adv.) p. 355 ① ② ③ ④	bravely; confidently dealing with a dangerous or painful situation	

Rating Scale
① I don't know the word.
② I've seen it or heard it.
③ I know its meaning.
④ I know it and use it.

Word Study

Roots and Affixes

A **root** is a word part to which affixes may be added. A **prefix** is an affix added to the beginning of a root to change its meaning. A **suffix** is an affix added to the end of a root to change its meaning. You can use these word parts to determine the meaning of a word.

miss is a Latin root that means:
- "to send"

-ion is a Latin suffix that means:
- "the action or condition of"

Use a dictionary to look up the meanings of the prefixes *ad-*, *com-*, and *sub-*. Then use roots and affixes as clues to determine the meaning of the words below. Confirm your definitions with a dictionary.

1. admission _____

2. commission _____

3. submission _____

Close Reading

Writing

1. Identify what the author compares in the metaphor in **paragraph 2**. What is the effect of this metaphor?

Key Ideas and Details

2. Explain how not having a telephone affected Elizabeth's experience that morning. Cite evidence from the text.

---

from

The Little Rock Nine
Struggle for Integration

☆ ★ ☆ ★ ☆ ★ ☆ ★ ☆

by Stephanie Fitzgerald

¶1 On the morning of September 4, 1957, 15-year-old Elizabeth Eckford said a prayer and got ready for school. She was wearing a new dress that she had made for the **occasion**, because this was not any <u>ordinary</u> school day. Today, Elizabeth and nine other black students would be <u>enrolling</u> at Central High School in Little Rock, Arkansas. They would be the first black students ever to attend the school, and many white people did not want them there.

¶2 As she neared the school, Elizabeth tried not to be afraid even though she had much to fear. A crowd of angry white people had already gathered in front of the school. They were **determined** not to let in the 10 black pupils. Elizabeth did not see any of the other black students in front of the school. She was quite alone—and surrounded by a sea of angry white faces.

¶3 Elizabeth did not know that the other black students had made a plan the night before to meet in the morning and walk into the school together. They had not been able to talk to Elizabeth because her family did not own a telephone.

¶4 Suddenly, Elizabeth heard someone in the crowd yell out:

¶5 "Here she comes, get ready!"

Words to Know

<u>ordinary</u>: *(adj.)* common or usual; of no remarkable value

<u>enrolling</u>: *(v.)* officially signing up to join a school

¶6 As if this had been their cue, everyone else in the mob started to shout insults at the teenager. Later in the day, Elizabeth explained how she felt at that moment:

¶7 "My knees started to shake all of a sudden, and I wondered whether I could make it to the center entrance a block away. It was the longest block I ever walked in my whole life."

¶8 From where she stood, Elizabeth could see members of the Arkansas National Guard standing at the school entrance. She thought they were there to make sure that she and the nine other black students made it safely into the school. But when she got closer, a soldier blocked the entrance and waved her away. Elizabeth turned to another soldier. He did not speak to her. He and the other soldiers who joined him just raised their bayonet-tipped rifles and blocked her path. It was clear that Elizabeth was not going to be allowed into the school. She had no choice but to turn around and walk back through the angry mob that filled the street.

An angry mob surrounded Elizabeth as she attempted to make her way to Central High School.

Words to Know

National Guard: (n.) a branch of the US Armed Forces whose members serve locally or nationally, rather than internationally, on a part-time basis

bayonet-tipped rifles: (n.) long guns with sword-like extensions at the end of the barrels

---

Close Reading

Words and Phrases in Context
3. Define *cue* as used in **paragraph 6**. What context clues helped you determine its meaning? What does the use of this word convey about the crowd?

Literary Analysis
4. Explain the use of hyperbole in **paragraph 7**. What does this use of hyperbole help communicate?

Hyperbole
Hyperbole is a deliberate exaggeration in order to create humor or for emphasis.

Key Ideas and Details
5. Identify the evidence the author includes to support her claim that "it was clear that Elizabeth was not going to be allowed into the school" in **paragraph 8**.

Claim
A claim is an arguable statement or position. Most authors include evidence to support the claims they make.

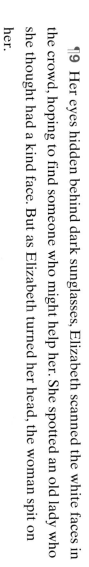

¶9 Her eyes hidden behind dark sunglasses, Elizabeth scanned the white faces in the crowd, hoping to find someone who might help her. She spotted an old lady who she thought had a kind face. But as Elizabeth turned her head, the woman spit on her.

¶10 Elizabeth kept walking. Nearly 500 angry adults surrounded her and walked along with her, calling her ugly names. Elizabeth fought to control her tears as news photographers took pictures. Elizabeth spotted a bus stop in the distance. She felt that if she could just make it to that bench, she would be safe. As she soon found out, it was not the bus stop that would save her.

¶11 Elizabeth sat down on the bench with her head bowed as people continued to jeer.

¶12 Benjamin Fine, an education reporter, was covering the story for *The New York Times*. He sat down next to Elizabeth, put his arm around her, and whispered:

¶13 "Don't let them see you cry."

¶14 At the same time, a white woman named Grace Lorch struggled through the mob toward Elizabeth. She was **furious**, screaming at the crowd:

¶15 "Leave this child alone! Why are you tormenting her? Six months from now, you will hang your heads in shame."

¶16 The crowd was **enraged** that two white people would take the side of a black girl. They turned their hatred on Lorch and Fine and started calling them horrible names.

Words to Know

jeer: (v.) to shout at someone in order to frighten or insult them

enraged: (adj.) very angry

Close Reading

Literary Analysis

6. Explain what the author foreshadows in **paragraph 10**.

Academic Vocabulary

7. Identify the evidence the author includes in **paragraphs 14–15** to support the idea that Grace Lorch was *furious*.

Writing

8. Compare and contrast Benjamin Fine and Grace Lorch with the other people in the crowd surrounding Elizabeth.

Close Reading

¶17 When the bus finally came, Lorch helped Elizabeth on board and watched as it pulled away. Elizabeth took the bus to the Negro School for the Deaf and Blind, where her mother worked in the laundry room. Elizabeth ran to find her mother, with whom she could finally find comfort.

¶18 Elizabeth did not realize that news of what had happened at the school had been spreading through the town. False reports that Elizabeth had been physically injured when she tried to enter school had reached her parents. Elizabeth's father left work to search for her. Her mother waited and prayed.

¶19 When Elizabeth found her mother, she was standing at a window with her head bowed. As Elizabeth entered the room, her mother turned—it was clear she had been crying. Elizabeth later recalled:

¶20 "I wanted to tell her I was all right. But I couldn't speak. She put her arms around me and I cried."

Key Ideas and Details

9. Identify what Lorch does after the bus finally arrived in **paragraph 17**. What can you infer about her based on this action?

Words and Phrases in Context

10. Define *comfort*. What context clues in **paragraph 17** helped you determine its meaning? What contrast does the use of this word help emphasize?

Key Ideas and Details

11. Discuss the significance of Elizabeth crying when her mother hugged her, as described in **paragraph 20.**

Text Structure

12. How is **paragraph 20** different from the previous paragraph?

Words to Know

<u>false</u>: *(adj.)* untrue

Close Reading

Words and Phrases in Context

13. Explain what the author means when she writes "splashed across" in **paragraph 21**. What context clues helped you understand what she meant? What can you infer about the newspapers, based on the use of this phrase?

Text Structure

14. Describe how **paragraphs 21–23** are different from the previous paragraphs.

Writing

15. Explain how the author supports her claim that the Little Rock Nine were "inspiring."

¶21 Newspapers across the country covered the scene at Central High School. The word spread very quickly about how Elizabeth—and the other black students who had tried to enter the school at another door—had been treated that day. Pictures of white people yelling at the teenagers were splashed across newspapers. Many people—both black and white—were shocked at how the children had been treated. They could not imagine how the students could bear to try to enter Central High School again. In fact, one of the 10 would never return to Central at all. The other nine would not return right away.

¶22 The group that came to be known as the Little Rock Nine refused to give up. They knew the importance of their **mission**. They understood that by standing up to hatred and racism, by challenging the system of **segregation**, they were changing the world for the better.

¶23 By quietly and **courageously** standing up for their rights, the Little Rock Nine made progress for all Americans. They helped change the education system in America and brought worldwide attention to their inspiring example.

Words to Know

inspiring: (*adj.*) giving people a feeling of excitement and hope that they can do something great

Identify Evidence | Analyze Individuals, Events, and Ideas

In this excerpt from *The Little Rock Nine*, author Stephanie Fitzgerald depicts the harrowing events of the morning Elizabeth Eckford tried to help integrate Central High School. Reread the excerpt, highlighting the evidence Fitzgerald offers to convey Elizabeth's experiences. How does she introduce, describe, and elaborate on individuals, events, and ideas?

- In the Evidence column, record examples from the text of quotations, descriptions, reflections, and other details that tell about Elizabeth's day and convey how her strength was tested.

- In the Explanation column, explain how the evidence introduces, illustrates, or elaborates on individuals, events, and ideas.

Evidence	Source	Page	Explanation
1. "As she neared the school, Elizabeth tried not to be afraid even though she had much to fear."	Fitzgerald	351	This description shows that Elizabeth was afraid because she knew the people in front of the school didn't want her to be there. She tried to be brave even though the people were "determined not to let" her in.
2. "'Here she comes, get ready!'"			
3. "'My knees started to shake all of a sudden, and I wondered whether I could make it to the center entrance a block away.'"			
4. "She spotted an old lady who she thought had a kind face. But as Elizabeth turned her head, the woman spit on her."			

	Evidence	Source	Page	Explanation
5.				
6.				
7.				

Key Ideas and Details

Determining the Central Idea

1. Use the evidence you collected to summarize the key idea of this excerpt from Fitzgerald's nonfiction book.

2. List three key individuals or groups of people that Fitzgerald introduces in this article. Explain why each individual or group is important to the central idea.

Individuals or Groups	Significance

3. List three key quotations that Fitzgerald includes in this excerpt. Explain why each piece of dialogue is important to the central idea.

Quotation	Significance

Craft and Structure

Structure of the Nonfiction Book

1. The author presents Elizabeth's experiences in chronological order. Use the chart below to describe Elizabeth's experiences with people outside of the school in the order that they happened.

Paragraph #	Interaction
8	
9	
12–13	
14–16	

Author's Perspective

2. List details that help you understand the author's perspective toward the angry mob and toward Elizabeth.

Angry Mob	Elizabeth

3. What is the author's perspective on integrating Central High School in Little Rock?

Academic Vocabulary

from *Elizabeth and Hazel: Two Women of Little Rock* by David Margolick

Rate your understanding of each word. Then read its meaning and write an example sentence. If the example is given, write the meaning.

Word	Meaning	Example
commemoration (n.) p. 361 ① ② ③ ④	act of remembering and respecting an important person or event in the past	
reconciliation (n.) p. 363 ① ② ③ ④		The teacher helped Michael and Richard find reconciliation after they fought on the playground.
bitter (adj.) p. 364 ① ② ③ ④	jealous and upset because you feel you have been treated unfairly	
rapprochement (n.) p. 364 ① ② ③ ④		The people of both countries hoped for a rapprochement and an end to the war.
inconsistencies (n.) p. 365 ① ② ③ ④		The review board found several inconsistencies in the scientist's paper and refused to publish it until he corrected them.
incredulously (adv.) p. 365 ① ② ③ ④	being unable or unwilling to believe something	

Rating Scale
① I don't know the word.
② I've seen it or heard it.
③ I know its meaning.
④ I know it and use it.

Word Study

Context Clues

Context clues are words in a text that help you figure out the meaning of an unfamiliar word. Sometimes words are defined in the text or meaning is suggested.

The sentences below are from Margolick's book excerpt. Find the context clues to determine the meaning of the bold words.

1. Elizabeth had to be **coaxed** into participating in the 40th anniversary celebrations [of the historic integration of the Little Rock High School] in 1997, even though they promised to be the most glorious yet: President Bill Clinton would **preside.**

2. Having pondered Hazel's face for decades, Jacoway had been expecting an uneducated **hick** and was surprised by how **articulate** and **remorseful** she was.

from
Elizabeth and Hazel
Two Women of Little Rock

by David Margolick

DAVID MARGOLICK

ELIZABETH AND HAZEL
TWO WOMEN OF LITTLE ROCK

¶1 Elizabeth had to be coaxed into participating in the 40th anniversary celebrations [of the historic integration of Little Rock High School] in 1997, even though they promised to be the most glorious yet: President Bill Clinton would preside. Elizabeth gradually became involved, meeting planners of the visitor centre the National Park Service planned to open in the old Mobil station near the school.

¶2 Also involved in the **commemorations** was Elizabeth Jacoway of the University of Arkansas at Little Rock, who was writing a history of the school's crisis. Jacoway had interviewed dozens of participants, including Elizabeth (in 1994) and Hazel (in 1996). Having pondered Hazel's face for decades, Jacoway had been expecting an uneducated hick and was surprised by how articulate and remorseful she was.

¶3 In the years after Little Rock, Hazel had become increasingly political, branching out into peace activism and social work. One program focused on self-esteem for teenagers. She took black teenagers who rarely had left Little Rock on field trips, climbing Pinnacle Mountain and picking strawberries. And, putting her course work in child psychology to use, she counseled young unwed mothers, many of them black, on parenting skills.

Words to Know

pondered: (v.) thought about carefully

psychology: (n.) the scientific study of the human mind and behavior

Close Reading

Text Structure

1. Identify details in **paragraphs 1–3** that signal the topic of this book excerpt. What do these first three paragraphs indicate about how the author structures his text and the perspectives he includes?

Writing

2. Look at the photograph on page 349. What details in **paragraph 3** present a different image of Hazel from how she appears in that photograph?

Close Reading

Words and Phrases in Context

3. Define *atoning* as used in **paragraph 4**. What context clues helped you determine its meaning? What can you infer about Hazel from the author's use of this word?

Writing

4. Explain what photograph the author is referring to in the first sentence of **paragraph 5**. How is it the opposite of the photograph Jacoway and Counts want to display?

Literary Analysis

5. Identify the details the author chooses to include to create mood in **paragraph 7**. What mood does he create?

¶4   All this do-gooding with blacks, her husband Antoine, joked, was really her way of atoning for the picture. And maybe he was right. Her whole outlook towards black people had changed. At the Barnes & Noble in Little Rock, she perused the sections on black history. She read David Shipler's study of black-white relations in America, *A Country of Strangers*, a book Elizabeth herself had helped inspire.

¶5   Someone had suggested that an entire wall of the new visitor center be devoted to the photograph. But Jacoway had another idea: subordinating the original photograph to a contemporary picture of Elizabeth and Hazel together—one symbolizing the racial progress Little Rock had made. Will Counts was thinking similar thoughts. Newly retired from a professorship at Indiana University, the photographer had returned to Arkansas to chronicle the changes at Central since 1957.

¶6   When Elizabeth cut the ribbon at the dedication of the new visitor center on September 20, Counts looked on. Afterward, Jacoway gave him Hazel's number. Later that day, he spoke to both women. They agreed to meet.

¶7   For a moment, the two women faced one another. Still imagining Hazel as a blonde, Elizabeth was taken a bit aback to behold a brunette. "Hi, I've always wanted to meet you," Elizabeth told her. "You're mighty brave to face the cameras again," she told Hazel as the three visitors entered the house. Hazel found the remark puzzling: Elizabeth seemed to be warning her of risks she couldn't foresee.

Words to Know

subordinating: (*v.*) making less important than

cut the ribbon: (*v.*) to show that a new business or public building has officially opened, someone may cut a ribbon stretched across the front door

¶8 Counts had already <u>scouted</u> possible locations to shoot the pair. He was thinking not so much about making great art, but about making a point, about the power of human beings to grow, and to forgive. And these two women actually looked comfortable with each other; they weren't just putting on a show. Watching it was, for him, a near-religious experience, one of the most thrilling moments in his life.

¶9 When the anniversary commemorations ended in late September of 1997, Elizabeth and Hazel prepared to go their very separate ways. But, as time passed, Hazel realized that she wasn't quite ready to let go.

¶10 In mid-November, Hazel invited Elizabeth and two of her sister Anna's grandchildren to her house. Then, later that month, came the poster signing.

¶11 A large crowd showed up. As for the poster itself, Hazel thought the original picture was too small: as much as she hated it, she believed it couldn't and shouldn't be hidden. Elizabeth had a different problem with it: she thought the title— **"Reconciliation"**—<u>overstated</u>; there was a big difference between that and forgiveness.

Elizabeth and Hazel met for the first time forty years after the infamous photo of Hazel snarling at Elizabeth had first been published.

Words to Know

<u>scouted</u>: (v.) searched for

<u>overstated</u>: (adj.) made something seem better or more important than it is

---

BOOK EXCERPT

Close Reading

Key Ideas and Details

6. Explain how Counts reacts to the meeting between Hazel and Elizabeth in **paragraph 8**. How is his reaction different from Elizabeth's and Hazel's reaction to meeting each other? What is the effect of including his reaction?

Words and Phrases in Context

7. Discuss what the author means when he writes in **paragraph 9** that Elizabeth and Hazel "prepared to go their very separate ways." What do the words "very separate ways" tell you about the two women's lives?

Academic Vocabulary

8. Describe what author means when he states in **paragraph 11** that Elizabeth thought that the title "Reconciliation" was "overstated." What is the difference between reconciliation and forgiveness?

¶12 Their encounters gradually became more frequent, almost routine. Over the next several months, they went to a home and garden show, and bought daylilies and irises together. They shopped for fabrics together. They heard Maya Angelou read poetry together.

¶13 The two enrolled in a seminar on racial healing offered by Little Rock's racial and cultural diversity commission. Discussing race relations in a group of 20 every Monday night for 12 weeks was a revelation to each: Elizabeth had never realized how paralyzed by anger and hate she had been, and hoped to leech some of that rage. It seemed to work, and she came to look forward to each session.

¶14 As for Hazel, she was naïve about how **bitter** some blacks were; here was a problem one couldn't simply wish away, or eliminate with soothing words. She was also amazed by how little race history she knew: after one class, Elizabeth mentioned *Strange Fruit*, the anti-lynching song Billie Holiday had made famous, and, much to Elizabeth's astonishment, Hazel knew nothing about either the song or the subject. The picture itself was never discussed. But their classmates were tickled to be sitting alongside two such famous antagonists and, week by week, watching them bond.

¶15 Quietly, though, some considered the **rapprochement**, however lovely in principle, a triumph of <u>sentimentality</u>, wishful thinking, and marketing over reality. They wondered how deep it went and how long it could last. In some segments of her own community, Elizabeth stood accused of whitewashing reality. "I have been surprised by the vitriol that some young blacks approach me with," she told the BBC. "They feel like I'm saying that what happened, it's all over with and there are no repercussions. They feel like I'm wiping away the past."

Words to Know

<u>naïve</u>: *(adj.)* lacking experience, information, or judgment

<u>sentimentality</u>: *(n)* an act or feeling based on emotion rather than reason, often related to nostalgia for the past

---

Close Reading

Words and Phrases in Context

9. Define *revelation*. What context clues help you determine its meaning? What does the use of this word in **paragraph 13** emphasize about Elizabeth and Hazel?

Literary Analysis

10. Identify the use of figurative language in **paragraph 13**. What does the author convey about Elizabeth through this use of figurative language?

Writing

11. Explain what the author means when he writes in **paragraph 15** that some people thought Elizabeth's and Hazel's friendship was "a triumph of sentimentality, wishful thinking, and marketing over reality."

¶16 Almost from the outset, Hazel encountered hostility from whites. Some doubted her sincerity; more resented it. Soon, and most seriously, tensions developed with Elizabeth. Novelty and companionability, excitement and relief had propelled them along for a time.

¶17 But strains soon surfaced. The source was Elizabeth, and it was predictable, for she had always been the harder sell. Her usual wariness, <u>vigilance</u>, and perfectionism could be kept at bay only so long. As the two shared more time and platforms, Elizabeth spotted what she perceived to be discrepancies, **inconsistencies** and evasions, in Hazel's story.

¶18 The <u>fissure</u> was painfully apparent that March, 18 months into their relationship, when they met Linda Monk, a lawyer turned writer who hoped to write a book about the women. She recorded some of their sessions, and those taped conversations captured how Elizabeth's mood had changed.

¶19 "After you saw [Counts's] pictures in the paper, *you don't remember how you felt or what people close to you talked about?*" she asked Hazel **incredulously** at one point. "There wasn't much conversation about it, really," replied Hazel. What she'd done that morning had been so banal—"just hamming up and being recognized—getting attention"—that it hadn't been worth remembering, she insisted. Maybe she had a block. But Elizabeth wasn't buying it.

Words to Know

<u>vigilance</u>: (*n.*) careful attention given to what is happening in order to spot danger

<u>fissure</u>: (*n.*) crack, tear, or break

Close Reading

Key Ideas and Details

12. Describe how the reaction Elizabeth received from people in her community about her friendship with Hazel was similar to what Hazel faced as presented in **paragraphs 15 and 16**. How was it different? What ideas presented earlier in the text do the references to the reactions from the two groups support?

Words and Phrases in Context

13. Define *evasions*. What is the connotation of the word as used in **paragraph 17**?

Connotation

Connotation is the feeling or emotion associated with a word or phrase.

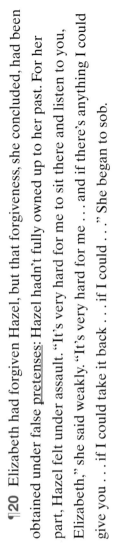

Close Reading

Writing

14. Explain what Hazel means when she says in **paragraph 21**, "The honeymoon is over and now we're getting to take out the garbage."

Key Ideas and Details

15. Discuss what the author is referring to when he writes "Hazel had had enough" in **paragraph 22**.

¶20 Elizabeth had forgiven Hazel, but that forgiveness, she concluded, had been obtained under false <u>pretenses</u>: Hazel hadn't fully owned up to her past. For her part, Hazel felt under assault. "It's very hard for me to sit there and listen to you, Elizabeth," she said weakly. "It's very hard for me . . . and if there's anything I could give you . . . if I could take it back . . . if I could . . ." She began to sob.

¶21 In the spring of 1999 I traveled to Little Rock and arranged to meet Elizabeth and Hazel at a barbecue. Afterwards we went to Hazel's house and talked some more. It was, I thought, a friendly chat. Elizabeth did not let on that she and Hazel were having problems; the two of them were "very close," she said. They talked a lot, she went on, maybe once a week. Hazel was more forthright about where things stood between them, but still oblique. "I think she still . . . at times we have a little . . . well, the honeymoon is over and now we're getting to take out the garbage," she said.

¶22 Early in 2000 Cathy Collins, the sociologist who had conducted the racial healing seminar Elizabeth and Hazel had attended, invited them for catfish at a local restaurant. Collins planned to write her <u>dissertation</u> on the two of them, and wanted to discuss the project. She had picked up no bad vibes that evening, but Elizabeth had: Hazel seemed very much on edge. Her instincts were sound. Hazel had had enough. They would no longer see each other. Quietly, unceremoniously, their great experiment in racial rapprochement was over.

Words to Know

pretenses: *(n.)* way of behaving that is meant to make people believe something that isn't true

<u>dissertation</u>: *(n.)* a paper researched and written by a student working to earn a doctoral degree

¶23 The "reconciliation" poster was popular enough to warrant another printing. Elizabeth let them go ahead; it was her way of supporting the place. Now, though, she insisted that it carry a caveat, one she devised herself. Soon, a small sticker, resembling the surgeon general's warning on cigarette packs, appeared in the upper right hand corner. It was gold, and relatively inconspicuous, particularly against Central's ochre bricks: "True reconciliation can occur only when we honestly acknowledge our painful, but shared, past." —Elizabeth Eckford.

¶24 The message puzzled Hazel, who had not been consulted about either the reprinting or the disclaimer. As far as she was concerned, "acknowledging the painful but shared past" was just what she had been trying to do. She'd have liked to have had her own sticker, one that said, "True reconciliation can occur only when we honestly let go of resentment and hatred, and move forward." The poster continued to hang in the office of Central's principal, Nancy Rousseau, though more as an ideal than a reflection of reality.

¶25 "I just had hoped that I could show this picture and say, 'This happened, and that happened, and now . . .' and there is no 'now,'" she said. "And that makes me sad. It makes me sad for them, it makes me sad for the future students at our school, and for the history books, because I'd like a happy ending. And we don't have that."

Words to Know

caveat: (*n.*) warning

resentment: (*n.*) bitterness; feeling of anger because something you think is unfair happened to you

---

Close Reading

Literary Analysis

16. Identify the device the author uses to compare Elizabeth and Hazel in **paragraphs 23–24.** What does the comparison reveal about each of them and their friendship?

Words and Phrases in Context

17. Define *reflection*, as used in **paragraph 24.** What context clues helped you determine its meaning?

Text Structure

18. Explain from whose perspective the author ends this section of the book excerpt. What is the effect of ending the section this way?

Identify Evidence | Analyze Individuals, Events, and Ideas

In this excerpt from *Elizabeth and Hazel: Two Women of Little Rock,* author David Margolick recounts the first meeting and attempted friendship between Elizabeth Eckford and Hazel Massery. Reread the excerpt, highlighting the techniques Margolick uses to present the interaction between the two women. How does he introduce, describe, and elaborate on individuals, events, and ideas?

- In the Evidence column, record evidence from the text that conveys the interaction between Elizabeth and Hazel. Include examples of quotations, descriptions, and reflections on events, as well as other details.
- In the Explanation column, explain how the evidence introduces, illustrates, or elaborates on individuals, events, and ideas.

Evidence	Source	Page	Explanation
1. "Still imagining Hazel as a blonde, Elizabeth was taken a bit aback to behold a brunette."	Margolick	362	This description shows that Elizabeth still thought of Hazel as the teenager in the original picture; Elizabeth is surprised because Hazel looks so different.
2. "'You're mighty brave to face the cameras again,' she told Hazel as the three visitors entered the house."			
3. "But, as time passed, Hazel realized that she wasn't quite ready to let go."			
4. "Elizabeth had never realized how paralyzed by anger and hate she had been, and hoped to leech some of that rage."			

	Evidence	Source	Page	Explanation
5.				
6.				
7.				

Key Ideas and Details

Determining the Central Idea

1. Use the evidence you collected to summarize the key idea of this excerpt from Margolick's book.

2. List three key individuals that Margolick introduces in this article. Explain why each individual is important to the central idea.

Individuals	Significance

3. List three key events that Margolick describes in this article. Explain why each event is important to the central idea.

Events	Significance

Craft and Structure

Structure of the Nonfiction Book

1. Record Elizabeth's and Hazel's quotations in the chart.

Elizabeth Eckford	Hazel Bryan

Author's Perspective

2. What is Margolick's perspective on the women's relationship?

3. Compare and contrast Fitzgerald's and Margolick's perspectives on the events surrounding the integration of Central High School in Little Rock, Arkansas.

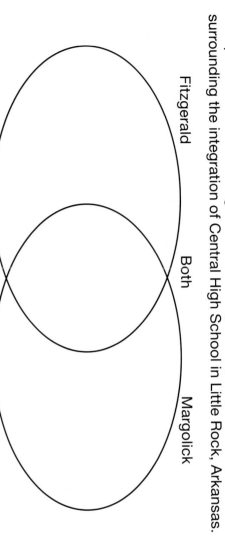

Fitzgerald   Both   Margolick

Collaborate and Present

Plan and Hold a Debate

After some discussion, the contemporary photograph of Elizabeth and Hazel was given prominence at the visitor center. Was this the best decision? Or should the photograph from 1957 be displayed more prominently?

Assignment: With a partner, gather evidence supporting your assigned stance on the issue of which photograph should be displayed the most prominently at the visitor center. Then debate a team who has been assigned the opposing stance.

Analyze the Content

1. Consider the following questions:

Seeking Clarification

- Is it accurate to say that you are claiming . . . .
- Can you elaborate on your point about . . . .
- If I understand you correctly, you are saying . . .

   • What is the purpose of the visitor center? Which photograph best complements its purpose?

   • Who visits the visitor center? What kind of information are they seeking?

2. Write down the strongest evidence, the claim you feel this evidence supports, and a potential counterclaim. Discuss why you think your evidence is strong.

Reporting Ideas

- _____ claimed that
- _____ argued that
- _____ countered with

Evidence	Claim	Counterclaim

3. Write down your claims, counterclaims and evidence on your debate cards to refer to during the debate.

Presentation

- Face your audience as you present.
- Emphasize certain words or pause for effect.
- Listen with respect and do not interrupt as your opposing team makes their argument.

Prepare Your Debate Points

4. Work with your partner to practice your debate points. Then argue the opposing view to prepare for countering your opponents' claim in the official debate.

Debate

5. Participate in the debate.

Debate Checklist

Use the checklist below to evaluate your collaboration skills, reasoning, and final presentation. Think carefully about your work. If you know you completed an item thoroughly, give yourself a check (✓).

COLLABORATE AND PRESENT CHECKLIST

Comprehension & Collaboration

☐ Come to discussions prepared, having read and studied material.

☐ Refer to evidence when contributing to the debate.

☐ Follow rules for debate and lead by example.

☐ Ask and answer specific questions.

☐ Make comments that contribute to the topic under debate.

☐ Review the key ideas under debate and demonstrate understanding of multiple perspectives through reflection and paraphrasing.

Number of ✓s in this category: ___

Evidence and Reasoning

☐ Explain the purpose of the debate.

☐ Present information relevant to the task.

☐ Explain which photograph should be displayed.

☐ Support claims with clear reasons and relevant evidence from unit texts and analysis of the photographs.

☐ Respond to opposing claims with clear reasons and relevant evidence.

☐ Synthesize the key ideas from your debate with a conclusion.

Number of ✓s in this category: ___

Presentation of Knowledge & Ideas

☐ Adapt language to a variety of contexts and tasks to demonstrate knowledge of formal English.

☐ Include multimedia components (e.g., graphics, images, music, sound) and visual displays.

☐ Use appropriate volume/tone (clear, not too fast, too slow, or too loud) and avoid using "like" or "ummm."

☐ Have strong posture, a confident stance, and make frequent eye contact.

☐ Occasionally move from one spot to another without fidgeting.

☐ Smile and act relaxed.

Number of ✓s in this category: ___

Total # of ✓s: ___

Add up the total number of checks (✓) in each category. Then use the scoring guide below to calculate your final score.

Scoring Guide

16 to 18 ✓s	13 to 15 ✓s	11 to 12 ✓s	10 or fewer ✓s
④ Exemplary	③ Meets Standards	② Needs Work	① Does Not Meet Standards

Read the Model

Writers of historical fiction use many techniques to craft stories set in the past, about real or imagined experiences or events. The writer of this historical fiction short story uses dialogue, description, and reflection to convey how an experience tested the strength of the fictional narrator. Read and discuss the model historical fiction short story below.

Finding Strength   By Liza Reyes

That poor child. That's all I could think as I watched her try to be brave on her first day of school. But how could she? Thousands of people screamed insults as she and nine other students tried to integrate Central High School. National Guard troops, clutching rifles, refused to intercede. I took a few steps toward the girl, and then stopped. At that moment, I was too afraid to help her. I lowered my head in shame. Soon, helicopters hovered overhead. Reporters shoved cameras in the girl's face. The mob got larger. The girl walked away from the school, and I got lost in the crowd.

The brave child was sitting alone at a bus stop when I saw her again. With her bravery in mind, I sat down on the bench next to her, and she flinched. Up close, I could see that her hair was neatly styled, and her clothes looking freshly starched and ironed, even in the September heat. I patted her hand as we sat there together. "It'll be okay," I told her. I wasn't sure I believed my own words, as a hoard of angry white faces began to circle us. After she got on the bus, I ran home, fearful of the mob—and unsure that I had the strength to help someone in that situation again.

That night, I told Albert about the girl. "Betty! Whatever possessed you to get involved!" he demanded, as I dished out the mashed potatoes and gravy.

"Can you imagine how scared she must have felt?" I asked Albert, incredulously. I didn't say much through the rest of dinner that night, but my blood was boiling with anger. I suspected that if Albert put himself in the place of somebody who couldn't just walk into any store or drink from any water fountain in town, he might have wanted to get involved, too. However, I didn't push the point with Albert, not that night in 1957, anyway. But as the anger flushed my cheeks, I felt a sense of calm come over me. I'd done the right thing, and at that moment, I knew I'd do it again.

Historical Fiction

Historical fiction tells a story set in the past about real or imagined experiences or events.

The **introduction** engages the reader and establishes the setting and introduces the narrator and/or characters.

- Find the clues that describe the narrator's point of view.

The **body paragraphs** use descriptions and dialogue to develop characters, events, and settings.

- Find one description that develops a setting as set in the past.

- Find one example of dialogue that develops a character.

The **conclusion** follows from narrated events and contains the resolution.

- Describe the resolution of this story.

Analyze the Model

A historical fiction narrative includes characters, setting, plot events, a problem or conflict that a character faces, a climax, and the resolution to the problem.

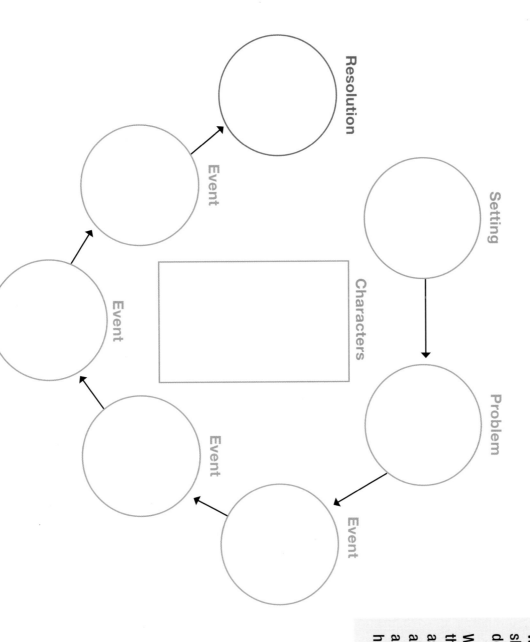

Setting

Characters

Problem

Event

Event

Event

Event

Resolution

Character Development

Writers develop characters by showing what they think, say, and do over the course of the story.

Writers can show what a character thinks in a specific moment, as well as what that character thinks later about that same moment, or a reflection on the moment, to show how the character has grown.

Step 1 | Generate Ideas

Many events related to the Little Rock Nine tested the strength of people to be brave, do the right thing, heal, and forgive. Write a historical fiction narrative about one such event. Describe the event using narrative technique, such as dialogue, description, and reflection.

What You Need to Know | Examine the evidence you collected from *The Little Rock Nine* and *Elizabeth and Hazel: Two Women of Little Rock*, including dialogue, descriptions, and reflections (see pages 356 and 368).

What You Need to Write | Select narrative techniques used in the texts to incorporate into your historical fiction narrative.

excerpts from *The Little Rock Nine* and *Elizabeth and Hazel*

Dialogue

Example: *"You're mighty brave to face the cameras again," Elizabeth told her.*

Effect: *It helps the reader understand Elizabeth's perspective and moves the story forward by making Hazel feel defensive.*

Page # ___362___

Descriptive Details

Example:

Effect:

Page # _____

Reflection

Example:

Effect:

Page # _____

My Historical Fiction Narrative

Dialogue

Example:

Effect:

Page # _____

Descriptive Details

Example:

Effect:

Page # _____

Reflection

Example:

Effect:

Page # _____

Step 2 | Organize Ideas and Write

What You Need to Know | The big ideas about how a character's strength was tested in an event related to the Little Rock Nine.

To develop your historical fiction narrative:

1. Describe the characters your narrative will feature and the setting in which it will take place.

2. Establish the problem/challenge that the main character will face.

What You Need to Write | Develop a sequence of events that lead to the resolution of the problem.

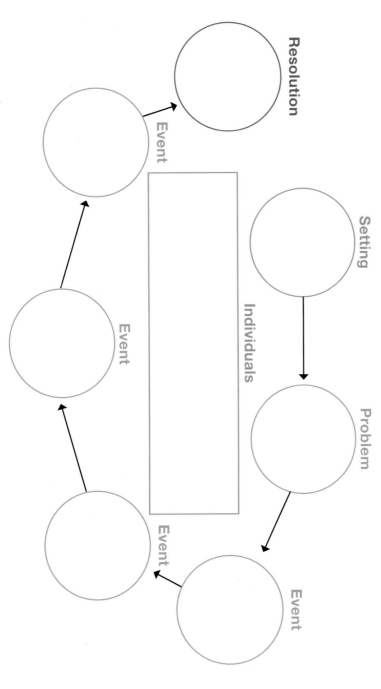

Resolution

Event

Event

Individuals

Setting

Problem

Event

Event

Step 3 | Draft

Write a draft of your historical fiction narrative on the computer or on paper.

Language Study | Narrate Events with Variety

See It | Good writers vary their sentence patterns to connect experiences and events in interesting ways.

Without Variety	With Variety
First, Elisa tried to walk around the puddle near the school entrance. Then, a group of students blocked her way. Next, she tried to jump over the puddle. Then, she tripped. She got all muddy. After that, the students laughed and teased Elisa. Last, a girl Elisa knew helped her stand up and gave her a tissue to wipe her muddy hands.	A group of students blocked Elisa's way as she tried to navigate around the puddle near the school entrance. Her legs got tangled in midair when she tried to jump over the puddle. The students laughed and teased Elisa while she lay there in the mud puddle. After an eternity, a girl Elisa knew came to her rescue, helping her stand and giving her a tissue to wipe her muddy hands.

Try It | Read each set of sentences below. Identify which set of sentences reflect variety. Explain why.

1. Every Sunday night, my grandparents host a big family dinner. After arriving, we all help set the table. While we work, the house fills with the aroma of broiled meats and roasted vegetables. At the end of the meal, we are all stuffed. Even so, we can't wait to meet again the following Sunday.

2. My grandparents host a big family dinner every Sunday night. Their house fills with the aroma of broiled meats and roasted vegetables as we all help set the huge table. At the end of the meal, we are all stuffed, yet we can't wait to meet again the following Sunday.

Apply It

Follow the steps and use the questions below to help you narrate events with variety.

1. Reread your introductory paragraph. *What characters, events, or experiences do you set up?*

2. Determine which sentences you can begin differently, in order to create variety. *Which sentences should you start with a transition word? Which sentences can you start with dialogue or a description?*

3. Select transition words that you can replace to add variety. *Why have you selected these transition words to replace? Are they vague? Do they follow the same pattern?*

4. Identify whether you use mostly simple, compound, or complex sentences, and decide which sentences to revise for variety. *Which sentences should you keep simple for effect? Which ones can you combine to improve the flow of the text?*

5. Rewrite your introductory paragraph. *Think about the purpose of the paragraph that you identified before rewriting it. Are the ideas you want to set up still clear in your revision?*

Now, go back to your draft and repeat the process for each body paragraph and your conclusion.

Writing Tip

Try to use at least two different sentence types in each paragraph.

- **A simple sentence** has a subject and a verb: *We left the cafeteria.*

- **A compound sentence** has two independent clauses joined by a coordinating conjunction: *We left the cafeteria, and Joe went to math class.*

- **A complex sentence** has an independent clause and two or more dependent clauses: *After Joe finished eating, we left the cafeteria.*

Conventions Study | Using Transition Words and Phrases

See It | Writers use transitional words and phrases to create cohesion and clarify the relationships among events, settings, and individuals.

Transitions to Connect Events	Transitions to Connect Settings	Transitions to Connect Reasons or Purposes and Results
before long	between	as a consequence of
as	outside	as a result
meanwhile	beyond	consequently
afterward	up close	for the purpose of
when suddenly	alongside	otherwise
as soon as	wherever	because the, because of
instantly	in the middle of	with this in mind

Try It | Find the transition words or phrases that the writer used in the excerpt below from the model. How do they show connections between events and experiences?

The poor thing was sitting alone at a bus stop when I saw her again. With her bravery in mind, I sat down on the bench next to her, and she flinched. Up close, I could see that her hair was neatly styled, and her clothes looked freshly starched and ironed, even in the September heat.

Apply It | Now revise one of your narrative paragraphs. Use transition words and phrases to connect settings, events, and reasons and help the reader follow your narrative.

Step 4 | Revise and Edit Revise your draft with a partner.

Organization and Clarity					
Establish the narrator and setting at the beginning of the story.	Self	1	2	3	4
	Partner	1	2	3	4
Establish the problem that tests the strength of the narrator/main character at the beginning of the story.	Self	1	2	3	4
	Partner	1	2	3	4
Organize the events of the story in a clear and logical order.	Self	1	2	3	4
	Partner	1	2	3	4
Provide an ending that comes naturally after the events/experiences of the story and resolves the narrator's/main character's problem.	Self	1	2	3	4
	Partner	1	2	3	4

Evidence and Reasoning					
Introduce and develop an event related to the Little Rock Nine, as discussed in the Unit texts.	Self	1	2	3	4
	Partner	1	2	3	4
Develop characters and events with narrative techniques such as dialogue, description, and reflection.	Self	1	2	3	4
	Partner	1	2	3	4

Language and Conventions					
Include a variety of sentence patterns.	Self	1	2	3	4
	Partner	1	2	3	4
Use transition words and phrases to connect events, settings, and ideas.	Self	1	2	3	4
	Partner	1	2	3	4
Correctly spell all words and use punctuation and capitalization correctly.	Self	1	2	3	4
	Partner	1	2	3	4

Scoring Guide | ① needs improvement   ② average   ③ good   ④ excellent

Step 5 | Publish Publish your story either in print or digital form.

Publish

Publish your story either in print or digital form. Use the rubric below to consider the success of your final performance task.

PERFORMANCE TASK RUBRIC

Score Point	Organization and Clarity	Evidence and Reasoning	Language and Conventions
Exemplary ④	• beginning of narrative **effectively** introduces the main character(s) and describes the setting • includes a **well-placed and logical** conflict • includes **well-chosen** transition words and phrases that connect events in a **well-structured** sequence • ending of narrative **expertly describes** the resolution or attempts at resolution, and **thoughtfully explains** the character's insights	• **clearly establishes** a point of view and maintains that point of view throughout the narrative • develops the conflict and its resolution by **flawlessly describing** events and the actions of key characters • events and characters **accurately reflect** factual evidence from the texts • **meaningfully** uses narrative strategies such as dialogue, description, and reflection to describe events and develop characters	• **demonstrates a strong command** of the conventions of standard English grammar and usage, as well as of standard English capitalization, punctuation, and spelling • vocabulary is **appropriate** to the narrative (vocabulary about the civil rights movement; vocabulary to narrate events, including effective transitions; sensory language)
Meets Standards ③	• beginning of narrative **effectively** introduces the main character(s) and setting • includes a **well-placed or logical** conflict • includes **some** transition words and phrases that connect events in a **somewhat well-structured** sequence • ending of narrative **clearly describes** the resolution or attempts at resolution, and **explains** the character's insights	• **adequately establishes** and maintains a point of view • develops the conflict and its resolution by **describing** events and the actions of key characters • events and characters **reflect** factual evidence from the texts • **adequately** uses narrative strategies such as dialogue, description, and reflection to describe events and develop characters	• **demonstrates a near command** of the conventions of standard English grammar and usage, as well as of standard English capitalization, punctuation, and spelling with some errors • vocabulary is **appropriate** to the development of the narrative (vocabulary about the civil rights movement; vocabulary to narrate events, including effective transitions; sensory language)

PERFORMANCE TASK RUBRIC

Score Point	Organization and Clarity	Evidence and Reasoning	Language and Conventions
Needs Work ②	• beginning of narrative **introduces** the main character(s) and setting • includes a conflict • includes **few** transition words and phrases; events are connected in a **somewhat illogically structured** sequence • ending **attempts to** describe the resolution to the conflict and/or **attempts to** explain the character's insight	• **fails to** establish a consistent point of view • **attempts to** develop the conflict and its resolution by **describing** events and/or the actions of key characters • **some** events and characters reflect factual evidence from the texts • uses **some narrative strategies** such as dialogue, description, and reflection to describe events and develop characters	• demonstrates a **marginal command** of the conventions of English grammar and usage, as well as of standard English capitalization, punctuation, and spelling • there **are many errors; however, the text is still understandable** • includes only **one or two examples** of vocabulary that is appropriate to the narrative (vocabulary about the civil rights movement; vocabulary to narrate events, including effective transitions; sensory language)
Does Not Meet Standards ①	• beginning of narrative **does not establish** the main character(s) and setting • does **not** include a conflict • includes **limited or no** transition words and phrases; events are **not** connected in a logical sequence • ending is **unclear and/or does not explain** how the conflict is resolved or the character's insights	• **partial narrative development** without a clear presentation of the conflict, its resolution, description of events, or character development • events and characters **do not** reflect factual evidence from the texts	• demonstrates **almost no command** of the conventions of standard English grammar and usage, as well as of standard English capitalization, punctuation, and spelling • there **are many errors that disrupt** the reader's understanding of the text • **does not** include vocabulary that is appropriate to the narrative (vocabulary about the civil rights movement; vocabulary to narrate events, including effective transitions; sensory language)

from **Warriors Don't Cry**

by Melba Pattillo Beals

¶1 Reporters hung from trees, perched on cars, and darted about with their usual urgency. Cameras were flashing on all sides. There was an eerie hush over the crowd, not unlike the way I'd seen folks behave outside the home of the deceased just before a funeral.

¶2 From time to time, as we walked about, we nine students acknowledged each other with nods and smiles. Like the others, I felt compelled to stare at the uniformed men. Walking up close to them, I saw that some weren't much older than I was. I had been told that only white soldiers would be allowed at Central, because the presence of nonwhites would inflame segregationists. Nonwhites were sent to the Armory, where they would be used as support teams or to guard our homes in case of a dire emergency.

¶3 There were tears in Mother's eyes as she whispered goodbye. "Make this day the best you can," she said.

¶4 "Let's bow our heads for a word of prayer." One of our ministers stepped from among the others and began to say comforting words. I noticed tears were streaming down the faces of many of the adults. I wondered why they were crying just at that moment when I had more hope of staying alive and keeping safe than I had since the integration began.

¶5 "Protect these youngsters and bring them home. Flood the Holy Spirit into the hearts and minds of those who would attack our children."

¶6 "Yes, Lord," several voices echoed.

Words to Know

deceased: *(n.)* a dead person

Armory: *(n.)* a place where guns and other military equipment is kept

Questions

Text Structure

1. What word in **paragraph 1** signals that the text is a memoir? How does the title help you understand the author's perspective toward the people and events she discusses in her memoir?

Key Ideas and Details

2. What details in **paragraphs 1–3** help you understand when the event the author describes takes place? When does it take place?

¶7 One of the soldiers stepped forward and beckoned the driver of a station wagon to move it closer to the driveway. Two jeeps moved forward, one in front of the station wagon, one behind. Guns were mounted on the hoods of the jeeps.

¶8 We were already a half hour late for school when we heard the order "Move out," and the leader motioned us to get into the station wagon. As we collected ourselves and walked toward the caravan, many of the adults were crying openly. When I turned to wave to Mother Lois, I saw tears in her eyes. I couldn't go back to comfort her.

¶9 Suddenly, all the soldiers went into action, moving about with <u>precise</u> steps. I hoped I would be allowed to ride in the jeep, although it occurred to me that it didn't have a top so it wouldn't be as safe. Sure enough, all nine of us were directed to sit in the station wagon.

¶10 Sarge, our driver, was friendly and pleasant. He had a Southern accent, different from ours, different even from the one Arkansas whites had. We rolled away from the curb lined with people waving to us. Mama looked even more distraught. I remembered I hadn't kissed her goodbye.

¶11 The driver explained that we were not riding in a <u>caravan</u> but a jeep convoy. I could hear helicopters roaring in the distance. Sarge said they were following us to keep watch. We nine said very little to each other, we were too busy asking Sarge about the soldiers. At times the car was so silent I could hear my stomach growl. It was particularly loud because nervousness had caused me to get rid of my breakfast only moments after I'd eaten it.

¶12 Our convoy moved through streets lined with people on both sides, who stood as though they were waiting for a parade. A few friendly folks from our community waved as we passed by. Some of the white people looked totally horrified, while others raised their fists to us. Others shouted ugly words.

Words to Know

<u>precise</u>: (adj.) exact; following the rules or form

<u>caravan</u>: (n.) a single line of vehicles traveling together

Questions

Key Ideas and Details

3. What details in **paragraphs 7–9** allow the reader to infer the great level of danger the author and her fellow students faced?

Words and Phrases in Context

4. What does the author mean by *rid* when she writes "caused me to get rid of my breakfast"? What details in **paragraph 11** helped you understand its meaning? What does this moment help you understand about the author?

¶13 As we neared the school, I could hear the roar of a helicopter directly overhead. Our convoy was joined by more jeeps. I could see that armed soldiers and jeeps had already blocked off certain intersections approaching the school. Closer to the school, we saw more soldiers and many more hostile white people with scowls on their faces, lining the sidewalk and shaking their fists. But for the first time I wasn't afraid of them.

¶14 We pulled up to the front of the school. Groups of soldiers on guard were lined at <u>intervals</u> several feet apart. A group of twenty or more was running at breakneck speed up and down the street in front of Central High School, their rifles with bayonets pointed straight ahead. Sarge said they were doing crowd control—keeping the mob away from us.

¶15 Sarge said we should wait in the station wagon because the soldiers would come for us. As I looked around, I saw a group of uniformed men walking toward us, their bayonets pointed straight up. Their leader beckoned to us as one of them held open the car door. As I stepped outside the car, I heard a noise behind me. In the distance, there was that chillingly familiar but now muffled chant, "Two, four, six, eight. We ain't gonna integrate." I turned to see reporters swarming about across the street from the school. I looked up to see the helicopters hovering overhead, hanging in midair with their blades whirring. The military leader motioned us to stand still.

¶16 About twenty soldiers moved toward us, forming an olive-drab square with one end open. I glanced at the faces of my friends. Like me, they appeared to be impressed by the <u>imposing</u> sight of military power. There was so much to see, and everything was happening so quickly. We walked through the open end of the square. Erect, rifles at their sides, their faces stern, the soldiers did not make eye contact as they surrounded us in a protective cocoon. After a long moment, the leader motioned us to move forward.

Words to Know

<u>intervals</u>: *(n.)* spaces

<u>imposing</u>: *(adj.)* impressive, due to size or power

Questions

Key Ideas and Details

5. Based on details in **paragraphs 13–16**, how is the morning that Beals describes in this text different from the morning described in the excerpt from *The Little Rock Nine*?

Words and Phrases in Context

6. What does the use of the word *muffled* in **paragraph 15** allow you to infer about the crowd?

¶17 Hundreds of Central High students milled about. I could see their astonishment. Some were peering out of windows high above us, some were watching from the yard, others were on the landing. Some were tearful, others angry.

¶18 I felt proud and sad at the same time. Proud that I lived in a country that would go this far to bring justice to a Little Rock girl like me, but sad that they had to go to such great lengths. Yes, this is the United States, I thought to myself. There is a reason that I <u>salute</u> the flag. If these guys just go with us this first time, everything's going to be okay.

¶19 We began moving forward. The eerie silence of that moment would forever be etched in my memory. All I could hear was my own heartbeat and the sound of boots clicking on the stone.

¶20 Everyone seemed to be moving in slow motion as I <u>peered</u> past the raised bayonets of the 101st soldiers. I walked on the concrete path toward the front door of the school, the same path the Arkansas National Guard had blocked us from days before. We approached the stairs, our feet moving in unison to the rhythm of the marching click-clack sound of the Screaming Eagles. Step by step we climbed upward—where none of my people had ever before walked as a student. We stepped up to the front door of Central High School and crossed the threshold into that place where angry segregationist mobs had forbidden us to go.

Words to Know

salute: (v.) greet formally, often by a gesture of the hand

peered: (v.) looked carefully or intently, with some difficulty

Questions

Words and Phrases in Context

7. What words does the author use to create mood in **paragraph 20**? What is the mood? What does this tell you about the author's feelings about the moment she describes?

from "Minnijean Brown Trickey Looks Back"

interview conducted by Veronica Majerol

Upfront: What was your life like before you became part of the Little Rock Nine? Can you tell me a little bit about your community, your school, and your friends?

1   **Minnijean Brown Trickey:** I've never been asked that question before. Little Rock was a kind of quiet, sleepy Southern town and very segregated, which was the way it was and so it didn't seem to matter particularly. In terms of what segregation looked like was [we] couldn't try on clothes at stores, eat at drugstores.

Upfront: How, exactly, did you come to be part of the Little Rock Nine? What was the process?

2   **MBT:** Everybody says they remember the *Brown v. Board* decision. Maybe I do and maybe I don't, I can't remember, but there must have been some talk about desegregation. But in the spring of 1957, on the intercom and in my homeroom, it was said, "If you live in the Central district and you're interested in going to sign up [to desegregate Central High] . . ." and I did. So that was the beginning of it.

Words to Know

process: (n.) a set of steps or actions; a way of doing something

intercom: (n.) a device that allows people in separate rooms to communicate; common in schools for use by the principal and others to make announcements

Questions

Text Structure

1. Identify elements on this page that signal this text is an interview. Based on the title, what can you infer about the content of the interview?

Key Ideas and Details

2. Explain the significance of the *"Brown v. Board"* decision." What details in **Answer 2** help you determine its significance?

3 Upfront: And did you know how important it was at the time?

MBT: I think if you live in a segregated society, and I think if you live in the United States as a black person, you know really quickly that there are things that need to be changed. And how that is going to happen, you don't know, but you want to be a part of trying to make change. You know, I had a safe community, but it's no fun not being able to try on clothes, it's not fun to sit on the wooden bench at the shoe store while the white people sit on a soft bench in the front, and it's no fun seeing a really nice door on a restroom that says "White Ladies" and then down in the basement there's a restroom that says "Colored Women." So, although I lived in a safe community and felt a great deal of safety, I also felt denied and I thought on the day that I put my name on that list, sort of loosely I thought, "This may be something that can shift some of that, so why not? I'm beautiful, I'm smart, I'm talented, I've got a smile to die for. How hard can this be?"

Upfront: Did you have any reservations about doing it?

4 MBT: No. Not that day. The reservations came later when they said, "Oh well, if you go, you can't participate in any activity. You can't be in the choir, you can't be in athletics, you can't be in any clubs, you can only go to school." So there I'm thinking, I'd like to be in the choir too. That was the main thing.

Words to Know

denied: (*v.*) rejected; unacknowledged

reservations: (*n.*) concerns; fears that something bad will happen

---

Questions

Words and Phrases in Context

3. What does Brown Trickey mean in **Answer 3** when she says "This may be something that can shift some of that"? What is the "this" and the "that" she refers to and what is the meaning of *shift*?

Key Ideas and Details

4. What do the details in **Answers 3 and 4** suggest about Brown Trickey's perspective, when she was a teenager, toward desegregating Central High School?

Questions

Words and Phrases in Context

5. What was Brown Trickey really asking when she questioned, "What is he talking about?" in **Answer 5**?

Key Ideas and Details

6. What was the school board's attitude toward the students who would be desegregating the school? What details in **Answer 6** help you understand this?

Upfront: Do you remember what you were feeling on that morning of September 4, 1957?

5 MBT: The night before—Labor Day—[Arkansas Governor] Orval Faubus announced that he was bringing units of the Arkansas National Guard to keep the peace. And in our house we were saying, "What is he talking about?" And my mother drove as close as she could to the school and she came back and she said, "There are just soldiers everywhere and they wouldn't let me—they have it all blocked off for a couple of blocks around the school."

Upfront: That was the morning of?

6 MBT: That was the night before. My best friend, Melba Pattillo, who lived half a block away from me—our preparations were, "What are we going to wear? We're really excited. This is gonna be interesting." Though we had a hint of what was to come because when the school board selected the students, they published our names and addresses in the newspaper. So the calls—hate calls—kind of started immediately. So that was a little unsettling, and people would drive by and screech the brakes and have very loud mufflers. So there was some sense of, "Hmm, this is gonna be interesting." So on the first day it was just really excitement of going to a new school.

Words to Know

preparations: *(n.)* steps taken to prepare for something

school board: *(n.)* a group of people from the same community as the school who make decisions about how the school should handle certain issues

Upfront: Were you prepared for what actually happened?

7 **MBT:** How would you prepare? Prepare? I'm asking, What do you say? "Oh, you're gonna run into this wall of hatred?" You're a kid, so there is no preparation. Nobody knew what was gonna happen, to my knowledge. It was among the first [instances of integration], so it hadn't happened before as a <u>model</u>. We were scared, we were shaking because people were screaming obscenities and carrying stupid signs. It was a big shock because hatred is always a shock, I think. There was no preparation for that. I mean, I thought, "How could anyone hate *me*, personally?" No, there was no preparation. There can't be. There's no preparation for hate.

Upfront: And after those first three weeks, can you describe what it was like for you to be a student at Little Rock Central High School?

8 **MBT:** Well, we were out for three weeks. The first day we left, we had to go home, we had to go to federal court because there were injunctions filed . . . to delay integration. And then [there were] the negotiations between President Eisenhower and Orval Faubus for him to remove the National Guard. So it took [Faubus] three weeks to do that. And there was the Little Rock police, and the mob had grown quite bigger, and we got in [the school building], and it sounded like some kind of sports event. The roar of the crowd. And then we were told we had to leave, and we did. We went into the basement and got into these police cars and they told us to put our heads down and somebody told the drivers, "Once you start, don't stop." Then, of course, the mob beat up the reporters, which was [shown] on television. I want to just say what made it fun. What made it fun was after the first day, we got letters from all over the world, and I still have an envelope that says "Minnijean USA."

Words to Know

<u>model</u>: (*n.*) an example

Questions

Text Structure

7. Why does the author of the interview italicize "me" in **Answer 7**?

Key Ideas and Details

8. What details does Brown Trickey include to indicate that the desegregation of Central High School had become a major event?

estions

eas and Details

9. What inferences can you make about people's attitudes in the 1950s toward desegregation, based on details in **Answer 9**?

Words and Phrases in Context

10. What is the meaning of *strident*? What context clues in **Answer 10** helped you determine its meaning? What does the use of this word reveal about Brown Trickey?

Upfront: What did the letters say?

9   **MBT:** The letters all said we admire you. They were from outside the country, they were from outside the state, they were admiring. I mean that was the most certain thing about it, "Oh my god, this is cool. People are paying attention to this." Some hate [mail], usually unsigned from Arkansas. But most letters were from different parts of the world, saying people admired us and thought it was wonderful.

Upfront: In what ways did being one of the Little Rock Nine shape your life— either positively or negatively?

10   **MBT:** It made me really <u>compassionate</u> and made me kind, thoughtful, but also strident in speaking the truth. And saying things as I see them. Someone showed me our first press conference about 10 years ago. And the question was, "Why did you want to go to Central?" And I said, "When we're working hard and giving our lives in the war, it's all right, but when it comes time for equalization, we're turned down?" And when somebody showed me that, I said, "Oh my god, I'm that girl. I have been her all the time. This is who I am."

Words to Know

<u>compassionate:</u> *(adj.)* able to understand and feel sympathy for others

Upfront: Have you kept in touch with the other Little Rock Nine over the years?

11 **MBT:** Oh yeah, absolutely.

Upfront: Good friends?

12 **MBT:** Yeah, and we have raised money and we give scholarships every two years to nine students. Jefferson Thomas died two years ago. He was our wit, our cutting-edge social critic. We value each other much more. We went in different directions for a long time, and then as the country admitted that it happened in Little Rock and we could speak, we did, and we became really good mature friends.

Upfront: Have you had a chance to talk with any of the white students you went to school with at Little Rock?

13 **MBT:** No.

Questions

Words and Phrases in Context

11. What does Brown Trickey mean when she says "we could speak" in **Answer 12?**

Key Ideas and Details

12. How is Brown Trickey's answer to **Question 13** different from all her other responses? What can you infer about her from this?

Words to Know

scholarships: (n.) set amounts of money given to students to help them pay for school; often for college

Upfront: Is that something that you've ever had the urge to do?

14 MBT: I don't need to talk to them; they need to talk to me. I had an apology for one chili incident on [The] Oprah [Winfrey Show from David Sontag]. Before David died, he became friends with my daughter, which is kind of interesting because my daughter has been a park ranger at the Little Rock Central High School National Historic Site for 10 years. But then he would bring his family to see the visitor center, talk to her. David is the person who was really serious about his part in the situation and kind of understood it. So that is good.

Upfront: Have you forgiven David?

15 MBT: Well, people ask me, "Would you accept his apology?" And I say, well, you know, it was almost 40 years later, and I hadn't been apologized to, and it was unbelievable that that happened. It was wonderful. And we wait for apologies. So when I'm talking to kids about bullying, which I do, I can use that and say, "I waited almost 40 years for that apology," and that it's really important to apologize because you liberate people and you say, "Hey, this actually happened. Something happened." Because for a real long time, Little Rock was saying, "It didn't really happen, it wasn't violent." There was a lot of denial.

Questions

Key Ideas and Details

13. What inferences can you make about David Sontag based on details in **Answer 14?**

Words and Phrases in Context

14. What does Brown Trickey mean when she states in **Answer 15** that an apology can "liberate people"?

Words to Know

<u>urge:</u> (n.) a strong feeling or impulse to do something

Upfront: What advice do you have for students today who care strongly about a cause and want to make a difference?

16 **MBT:** I'd like for young people not to think of the people who were in the civil rights movement and [other] movements as special or somehow have something they don't have. Because we all started off with great <u>innocence</u>. We were ordinary teenagers, and we were interested in changing something. And [we believed] that we can and that we must.

Key Ideas and Details

15. What details does Brown Trickey provide in her responses that support her viewpoint that the members of the Little Rock Nine were "ordinary teenagers"? Why does she feel this is an important idea to communicate to students today?

Words to Know

<u>innocence:</u> *(n.)* a lack of exposure to or understanding of the negative side of the world

Literature Circle Leveled Novels

***Stuck in Neutral** by Terry Trueman*
Shawn, who has cerebral palsy, is unable to communicate or control his muscles but still enjoys the world around him. How can he make his father understand that he is happy to be alive? **Lexile**® measure: 820L

***The Giver** by Lois Lowry*
Jonas lives in a controlled society where life is peaceful, but personal choice has been eliminated. After he is selected to receive the memories of the past, Jonas struggles with the idea that his perfect society is flawed after all. **Lexile**® measure: 760L

***The Book Thief** by Markus Zusak*
Liesel Meminger steals her first book to cope with the death of her little brother, but as she lives through dark times in Nazi Germany, Liesel's stolen books bring her comfort, friends, and may even save her life. **Lexile**® measure: 730L

Fiction, Nonfiction, and Novels

***Hush** by Jacqueline Woodson.* Toswiah and her family are forced into hiding, which shatters their relationships, identities, and lives. Follow Toswiah's struggle to reinvent herself. **Lexile**® measure: 640L

***Behind the Bedroom Wall** by Laura E. Williams.* What will Korinna, a loyal member of the Hitler Youth, do when she finds out that her parents are hiding a Jewish family behind their bedroom wall? **Lexile**® measure: 660L

***Hoot** by Carl Hiaasen.* Find out what happens when three middle-school kids try to save a group of endangered miniature owls. **Lexile**® measure: 760L

***Trino's Choice** by Diane Gonzales Bertrand.* As Trino contemplates how he will live his life, he must choose between a group of thugs and the "school types" he loathes. **Lexile**® measure: 780L

***No Easy Answers: Short Stories About Teens Making Tough Choices** edited by Donald R. Gallo.* Read about teens who make tough moral choices. **Lexile**® measure: 790L

***Kids with Courage: True Stories About Young People Making a Difference** by Barbara A. Lewis.* Read about kids who help others, such as friends, young children, and homeless people. **Lexile**® measure: 820L

***Born Confused** by Tanuja Hidier.* Dimple Lala's parents want her to fit in with Indian culture, but she is too American. Dimple wants to fit in with Americans, but she is too Indian. Will she make both herself and her parents happy? **Lexile**® measure: 890L

***Shiloh** by Phyllis Reynolds Naylor.* Marty Preston finds a mistreated beagle pup. Should he return it to its owner, help it, tell his parents, or tell the police? **Lexile**® measure: 890L

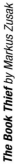

Films and TV

Dead Man Walking (MGM, 2000; R) Follow Sister Helen Prejean as she gets to know an inmate on death row and follows him to the end. (122 min.)

Erin Brockovich (Universal Studios, 2000; R) Brockovich exposes the corporate neglect and greed that resulted in illness and death for the residents of a small town. (130 min.)

E.T.: The Extra-Terrestrial (Universal Studios, 1982; PG) Eliot makes a friend from space and is willing to sacrifice everything to help him find his way home. (115 min.)

Freedom Writers (Paramount, 2007; PG-13) A teacher gives students in a racially divided school what they have always needed: a voice. (122 min.)

Patch Adams (Universal Studios, 2002; PG-13) For a depressed medical student, humor is the best medicine—even if it means risking his job. (116 min.)

Pay It Forward (Warner Home Video, 2000; PG-13) A boy decides to do good deeds for other people and asks them to "pay it forward," hoping that good deeds can change the world. (123 min.)

The Color of Friendship (Disney, 2000; G) An African-American politician and his daughter are given the task of reshaping the beliefs of a white South African girl. (88 min.)

The Pursuit of Happyness (Sony Pictures, 2007; PG-13) A single father overcomes homelessness and hopelessness to get a job that will allow him to support his son. (117 min.)

Websites

Free the Children Help other kids around the world by giving money toward building schools and providing education.

CNN: Be the Change Follow teens who travel around the world to help others—working on environmental issues in India; helping children in Cambodia, Tanzania, South Africa, and Thailand; and other efforts.

DoSomething.Org: What's Your Thing? This site lists nonprofits that work on many issues, including animal welfare, bullying, human rights, discrimination, and education.

The Matthew Henson Foundation Explore and view photographs and written information about the life and times of this dedicated explorer.

Magazines

Scholastic Choices Read about other teens who have made tough choices, and learn things that will help you in real-world decision-making.

The New York Times Upfront Dig through articles, polls, charts, and photos that can help you learn and do more about current issues.

Wildlife Conservation Magazine Find out about endangered animals and the people who are fighting to protect them.

Need: The Humanitarian Magazine Read about people who are working to help other people around the world.

COURSE III | Table of Contents

p. 4t: © 20th Century Fox Licensing/Merchandising/Everett Collection, b: © Sara Krulwich/The New York Times via Redux; p. 5tl: © Stephen Krow/iStockphoto, tcl: © Kevin Nixon/Future Publishing via Getty Images, tc: © Rustem Gurler/iStockphoto, © Jordan Siemens/Getty Images, tr: © Jean-Sebastien Evrard/AFP/Getty Images;

UNIT 1 | College 101

pp. 8–9c: © Barbara Penoyar/Getty Images; p. 11b: © Scholastic Inc.; p. 13b: © Scholastic Inc.; p. 15b: © Scholastic Inc.; p. 17b: © Scholastic Inc.; p. 25bl: © James Woodson/Thinkstock; p. 31bl: © Matt Slocum/AP Images

UNIT 2 | Survivor

pp. 58–59: © 20th Century Fox Licensing/Merchandising/Everett Collection; p. 61tc: © John Lau/Dreamstime; p. 64br: © Martin French; p. 69b: © Martin French; p. 79t: © Dennis Crow/Dreamstime; p. 82br: © 20th Century Fox Licensing/Merchandising/Everett Collection; p. 85bl: © 20th Century Fox Licensing/Merchandising/Everett Collection

UNIT 3 | The Power of Art

pp. 120–121: © Sara Krulwich/The New York Times via Redux; p. 129br: © Janette Beckman; p. 135b: © Heather Gatley; p. 138br: © Heather Gatley; p. 142br: © Heather Gatley; p. 148br: © Heather Gatley; p. 181c: © Everett Collection Inc./Alamy

UNIT 4 | Designing the Future

p. 184bl: © Stephen Krow/iStockphoto, r: © Justin Sullivan/Getty Images, tc inset: © Kevin Nixon/Future Publishing via Getty Images, tr inset: © Jean-Sebastien EvrardAFP/Getty Images, br inset: © Kevin Nixon/Future Publishing via Getty Images; p. 185l: © Rustem Gurler/iStockphoto, cl: © Jordan Siemens/Getty Images, cr: © SeongJoon Cho/Bloomberg via Getty Images; p. 187t: © June M Sobrito/Dreamstime; p. 189b: © Livia Corona; p. 195br: © Livia Corona; p. 203l: © Albert Watson, t: © Arturaliev/Dreamstime; p. 207bl: © Anthony Behar/Sipa USA via AP Images; p. 215bl: © Science & Society Picture Library via Getty Images

UNIT 5 | Space Invaders

pp. 242–243: © Jim DiBartolo; pp. 246–261: © Jim DiBartolo; p. 266t: NASA; p. 269bc: © Mary Evans Picture Library/Everett Collection; p. 272br: © Bettmann/Corbis; p. 275bl: © Mary Evans Picture Library/Everett Collection

UNIT 6 | Children of War

pp. 298–294: © Ahmad Gharabli/AFP/Getty Images; p. 305c: © Stephen Lovekin/Getty Images for Worldwide Documentaries; p. 314br: © Alain Nogues/Sygma/Corbis

UNIT 7 | Do the Right Thing

p. 348bl: © Bettmann/Corbis, t: © Bettmann/Corbis, br: © Bettmann/Corbis; p. 349tl: © Bettmann/Corbis; p. 352br: © Will Counts/The Indiana University Archives; p. 363bl: © Will Counts/AP Images

Grateful acknowledgment is made to the following sources for permission to reprint from previously published material. The publisher has made diligent efforts to trace the ownership of all copyrighted material in this volume and believes that all necessary permissions have been secured. If any errors or omissions have inadvertently been made, proper corrections will gladly be made in future editions.

UNIT 1 | College 101

"I Couldn't Imagine Wanting to Dye My Hair Blonde" by Christina Mendoza from *Real College Essays That Work* by Edward B. Fiske and Bruce G. Hammond. Copyright © 2006 by Christina Mendoza. Published by Sourcebooks, Inc. All rights reserved.

"Chunky Peanut Butter" from "Essay" by James Gregory from *College Essays That Made a Difference: Second Edition* edited by Erica Magrey. Copyright © 2006 by Princeton Review Publishing, LLC. Published by Random House, Inc. Reprinted by permission of Princeton Review Publishing, LLC.

Adapted from "Essay 3A" by Hugh Gallagher. Copyright © 1990 by Hugh Gallagher. All rights reserved.

"The Year of the MOOC" by Laura Pappano from *The New York Times*, November 4, 2012. Copyright © 2012 by The New York Times. Reprinted by permission of The New York Times.

From "A Homeless Girl's Dream" by Jeannine Amber from *Essence* magazine, August 2010. Copyright © 2010 by Essence Communications Inc. Reprinted by permission of Essence Communications Inc. All rights reserved.

UNIT 2 | Survivor

"The Story of Keesh" by Jack London.

From *Life of Pi* by Yann Martel. Copyright © 2001 by Yann Martel. Reprinted by permission of Houghton Mifflin Harcourt Publishing Company.

From *The Lost Island of Tamarind* by Nadia Aguiar. Copyright © 2008 by Nadia Aguiar. LLC. Reprinted by permission of Feiwell & Friends, an imprint of Macmillan Children's Publishing Group. All rights reserved.

UNIT 3 | The Power of Art

From *Letters to a Young Artist* by Anna Deavere Smith. Copyright © 2006 by Anna Deavere Smith. Reprinted by permission of Anchor Books, a division of Random House, Inc. All rights reserved.

"Zebra" from *Zebra and Other Stories* by Chaim Potok. Copyright © 1998 by Chaim Potok. Published by Alfred A. Knopf, a division of Random House, Inc. Reprinted by permission of The William Morris Agency, LLC. All rights reserved.

"I Want to Write" from *This Is My Century: New and Collected Poems* by Margaret Walker. Copyright © 1989 by Margaret Walker Alexander. Reprinted by permission of the University of Georgia Press.

UNIT 4 | Designing the Future

"La Vida Robot" by Joshua Davis from *Wired* magazine, April 2005. Copyright © 2005 by Joshua Davis. Reprinted by permission of the author.

From *Steve Jobs* by Walter Isaacson. Copyright © 2011 by Walter Isaacson. Reprinted by permission of Simon & Schuster, Inc.

"Building the Future Spacesuit" by Dava Newman from the NASA website.

UNIT 5 | Space Invaders

Graphic adaptation of "Zero Hour" by Ray Bradbury. Copyright © 1947 by Love Romances, Inc. Adapted and published by permission of Don Congdon Associates Inc.

From *The War of the Worlds* by H. G. Wells.

"The Invasion from Outer Space" by Steven Millhauser from *The New Yorker*, February 9, 2009. Copyright © 2009 by Steven Millhauser. Reprinted by permission of International Creative Management.

From *A Long Way Gone: Memoirs of a Boy Soldier* by Ishmael Beah. Copyright © 2007 by Ishmael Beah. Reprinted by permission of Farrar, Straus and Giroux, LLC. All rights reserved.

UNIT 6 | Children of War

Excerpts from "Babes in Arms" by William Boyd from *The New York Times Book Review*, February 25, 2007. Copyright © 2007 by The New York Times. Reprinted by permission of The New York Times.

From *First They Killed My Father: A Daughter of Cambodia Remembers* by Loung Ung. Copyright © 2000 by Loung Ung. Reprinted by permission of HarperCollins Publishers.

UNIT 7 | Do the Right Thing

"Alone in the Crowd" from *The Little Rock Nine: Struggle for Integration* by Stephanie Fitzgerald. Copyright © 2007 by Compass Point Books, an imprint of Capstone Press. Reprinted by permission of Capstone Press.

From *Elizabeth and Hazel: Two Women of Little Rock* by David Margolick as excerpted in *The Telegraph*, October 9, 2011. Copyright © 2011 by Telegraph Media Group Limited. Reprinted by permission of Telegraph Media Group Limited.

From *Warriors Don't Cry: A Searing Memoir of the Battle to Integrate Little Rock's Central High* by Melba Pattillo Beals. Copyright © 1994, 1995 by Melba Pattillo Beals. Reprinted by permission of Atria Publishing Group, a division of Simon & Schuster, Inc.

From "Minnijean Brown Trickey Looks Back" by Veronica Majerol from *The New York Times Upfront* magazine, September 3, 2012. All rights reserved.